THE
DIRTY
SOUTH

Exploring a Fantasized Region, 1970–2020

JAMES A. CRANK

LOUISIANA STATE UNIVERSITY PRESS

BATON ROUGE

Published by Louisiana State University Press
lsupress.org

DESIGNER: Mandy McDonald Scallan
TYPEFACE: Callua, text; Microbrew & Cabrito Sans, display

COVER IMAGE: Courtesy Shutterstock, Domen Colja.

Library of Congress Cataloging-in-Publication Data
Names: Crank, James A., author.
Title: The dirty south : exploring a fantasized region, 1970–2020 / James A. Crank.
Description: Baton Rouge : Louisiana State University Press, [2023] | Series: Southern
    literary studies | Includes bibliographical references and index.
Identifiers: LCCN 2023007781 (print) | LCCN 2023007782 (ebook) | ISBN
    978-0-8071-8013-6 (cloth) | ISBN 978-0-8071-8080-8 (pdf) | ISBN
    978-0-8071-8079-2 (epub)
Subjects: LCSH: Southern States—In popular culture. | Southern States—Public
    opinion. | Southern States—Race relations.
Classification: LCC F209 .C686 2024 (print) | LCC F209 (ebook) | DDC 975/.043—
    dc23/eng/20230524
LC record available at https://lccn.loc.gov/2023007781
LC ebook record available at https://lccn.loc.gov/2023007782

for Fred Hobson and Patricia Yaeger—mentors, architects
and for Linda Wagner-Martin, who taught me to *SMILE*

CONTENTS

ACKNOWLEDGMENTS

The work of this book is indebted to the financial support of multiple entities: the University of Alabama, especially the Research Grants Circle (RGC); the College Academy of Research, Scholarship, and Creative Activity (CARSCA); Deans Bob Olin, Joseph P. Messina, and Tricia McElroy; my department, especially Professors Joel Brouwer and Steven Trout; the National Humanities Center (Summer Fellowship 2018); the Bogliasco Foundation (fall of 2019 Fellowship), especially Laura Harrison, Page Ashley, Gerald "GIGI" Casel, and the cohort of homies.

Special thanks to those who worked as readers for early versions of this book, especially John McGowan (and his Herculean efforts to polish this manuscript in the end stages), Merinda Simmons, Linda Wagner-Martin, and several others who were kind enough to slog through my prose. I should also like to thank the staff of the Harry Ransom Center, especially Michael Gilmore in the Visual Materials Department and the larger staff of the library at the University of Texas, Austin; major thanks go to Eric Dienstfrey and Katie Quanz for their digging, scanning work, and general love of tea; I have some of the best colleagues ever, and they have been there for me every step of this process, so thank you: Wendy Rawlings, Trudier Harris, David Deutsch, Lauren Cardon, and all my colleagues in Team English.

I have wonderful friends and family (biological and chosen) who have helped me in more ways than I can say: Jeff (every book is yours); Phyllis and Bill Agnew; Linda "Gramma" Angell; Dad, Shelly, Steve, Don, Daniel Crank; Abbie and Renee; Merinda, Nathan, Arlo; Memorie, Joe, Sam, Tucker; Samantha Hansen; my English family Paul and Al Cooper Cook; Erich Nunn and Amy Clukey (the band); Michael Bibler and the whole Society for the Study of Southern Literature crew; Kate, Layton, and Joshua Whitman; Brett Odom,

Mike McGraw and Brother Ikey; and my amazing students, especially Marie Burns, who helped to prep the final manuscript for me.

This book is dedicated to the memory of Mik Mukherjee and my sweet girl Maddie, forever and ever, amen.

THE DIRTY SOUTH

A DIRTY BOOK

I've been doing this for half my years. I've been mouthing off in bars, trading shame for self-respect. My trajectory is crystal clear. I can see it in the stars that frame the shame above my neck. That frame the shame above my neck.

—"Pash Rash," Jeff Rosenstock

I'm writing a dirty book.

For almost two decades, that has been my silly answer to the question, "What is your next project?" When you're a professor, you are asked that question by a lot of people: family, friends, committees, colleagues. As a profession, we don't quite know how to celebrate accomplishment beyond anticipating our next one. Ever since I entered graduate school, I had this idea for a book about southern culture and dirt; in my head, I devised a deceptively simple guiding principle I could spout easily between floors in an elevator or while passing potatoes at Thanksgiving: My next project claims that we can best understand what a culture values by sorting through its trash. I don't mean here the kind of detective or paparazzi sleuthing—uncovering another's secrets by examining private objects—instead, I imagined a methodology operating under the assumption that, in order to understand what a culture privileges, one must first examine what it throws away.

Even though such a claim sounds simple, implications of "cultural trash" are profound, especially in relation to the American South. Trash and dirt seem like obvious ways to classify southern imaginaries; many southern cultural and literary texts purposefully engage with dirt or trash, either in aesthetic or subject. But, in examining southern conceptions of dirt, we are presented with more questions than answers: Why do claims of southern authenticity and exceptionalism hinge on rhetorics of dirt, waste, disposability, and garbage? Why are cultural and literary texts of or about the South during the last fifty years so drawn to smudges in the margins? What are some of the ways those shameful rhetorics get owned as an identity worthy of pride, and what are the consequences of that ownership—for example, white southerners' ownership of the phrase "white trash" through shifting, paradoxical historical moments. Even today, the number of literary and cultural texts offering the poor white-trash man as an authentic version of southern identity is dizzying: how did such a figure become so conspicuously tagged as a marker of crucial authenticity for the South, and why does his importance continue to persist during an era of globalization in which regional identification is declining?

When I first engaged with southern studies scholarship, I found myself puzzled by the state of the field as it emerged into the twenty-first century. Many of the books of the early 2000s could have been written in 1953; it was always the same Neo-Agrarian concerns, always the same teasing out of exceptionalism and backward glances. I wanted to know more about southern studies' fascination with whiteness even as "New Southern Studies" was beginning to denude fantasies of nativism and essentialism.[1] I wanted to know what kind of complexity any field might claim with a cohort of scholars satisfied to read white-trash stereotypes (hillbillies, rednecks, and so forth) as authentic approximations of a vast and dynamic region?

STANDING GROUND

In March of 2012, I attended my first conference of the Society for the Study of Southern Literature (SSSL) in Nashville. There, I found scholars actively clapping back to the reactionary southern studies scholars I was reading. Opening myself up to that community profoundly changed my understanding of southern culture and literature. Essays and papers at the conference touched on all aspects of southern identity, many pointedly challenging the centrality of whiteness in the field. It's difficult to place an origin story on one's understanding of their scholarly position, but that March, I forged friendships with other young scholars who engaged in the kind of work I found meaningful. Those friendships remain crucial to me as a scholar, and my colleagues continue to challenge me to be self-reflexive of my investments in the South and southern culture.

That year and month—February 2012—also marked another plot in the long, tragic history of vigilante executions of African Americans in the South. Only a few weeks before the conference on southern literature, on the night of 26 February 2012, George Zimmerman murdered a young, unarmed Trayvon Martin for no reason other than his unfounded suspicion that Martin was a criminal. As the head of his neighborhood watch in Sanford, Florida, Zimmerman felt authorized to trail the boy. He first saw the youth walking back from a convenience store and followed the boy as he crossed over into his neighborhood. As soon as Trayvon Martin entered his subdivision, George Zimmerman called in his suspicions to a nonemergency police dispatcher and described the seventeen-year-old Black boy to her: "This guy looks like he is up to no good or he is on drugs or something." Later in the call, Zimmerman angrily spits out his opinion of those who look like Trayvon Martin and how they walked around with impunity in his neighborhood, "these assholes, they always get away."[2] The call ended with the police advising Zimmerman to stop following the young man and to wait for them to arrive. Less than fifteen minutes later, Zimmerman had fatally shot Trayvon Martin.

Despite his confession that he had murdered Trayvon Martin, George Zimmerman was ultimately acquitted in the ensuing trial. Though Martin was unarmed and Zimmerman had a gun, Zimmerman's defense team claimed the man acted in self-defense, and the murder of the Black teenager went unpunished. The clear injustice of the case shocked the world. Those sickened by the acquittal marched in the streets, and their resulting anger over the verdict eventually inspired three activists, Alicia Garza, Patrisse Cullors, and Opal Tometi, to found the "Black Lives Matter" movement.[3] For these organizers as well as countless others, the murder of the boy was a clear manifestation of the ultimate disposability of Black bodies in twenty-first-century America.

Much of Zimmerman's defense hinged on Florida's "stand your ground" law which empowered citizens of the state to use lethal force when they felt threatened, even if they had the possibility of safe retreat. The underlying (stated) explanation for the law's existence references citizens' need to protect themselves with lethal force if (they feel) threatened. It reads, in part, "A person who is not engaged in an unlawful activity and who is attacked in any other place where he or she has a right to be has no duty to retreat and has the right to stand his or her ground and meet force with force, including deadly force if he or she reasonably believes it is necessary to do so to prevent death or great bodily harm to himself or herself or another or to prevent the commission of a forcible felony."[4]

In both formation and enforcement, "Stand Your Ground" laws like the one in Florida do not recognize the inequitable parsing out of deadly power. In *Stand Your Ground: A History of America's Love Affair with Lethal Self-Defense*, Caroline E. White notes that Florida's version of the law flatly ignores how "legal structures conspire with classist and racist exclusionary principles to ensure armed citizens remain predominantly white, male, and economically privileged" (164). Furthermore, giving power to certain citizens, especially as Zimmerman got his through a program like the "National Neighborhood Watch," assumed those in command were able "to differentiate between dangerous criminals and the law-abiding citizens they are tasked to protect" (165). Such differentiation also assumes those in power (mostly white, male, and upper-middle class) won't "make this distinction through the prism of widespread social biases."

Ultimately, a jury of his peers decided George Zimmerman had stood his own ground, even though where he shot the young man was not his home and the land they were on did not belong to him. Astonishingly, the jury believed that Zimmerman had acted to protect his own life, even though Trayvon Martin had no weapon. The disconnect between the verdict and the facts of the case was vast. Zimmerman was not responding to a threat to his life but to his way of living; the threat was existential: "Martin's mere presence as a young Black man in the predominantly white middle-class gated community" (White 166). Zimmerman believed Trayvon Martin's existence in his neighborhood was a crime of enough magnitude to justify execution, even if his presence only constituted a "threat to the sanctity of Zimmerman's expansive castle." It was clear enough to the nation that the murder of Trayvon Martin was not about a threat to safety but about protecting "white property" from the "menace" of Blackness, and Zimmerman's acquittal further exposed "the unholy alliance between lethal self-defense and white supremacist power" (White 166). The meaning of "stand your ground" was clear—though the law might naively profess to be blind to the inequities of power it was enforcing, the verdict gave license to violently excise any "dirty people" threatening white power. Zimmerman may have pretended to be a policeman, but his actions suggested he felt he was acting as a garbage man: to Zimmerman, tailing and ultimately murdering Trayvon Martin wasn't about enacting justice; it was about taking out the trash.

To say Trayvon Martin's murder transformed my thinking on this book about dirt is a profound understatement. The verdict infuriated me; inside my brain, the language of the law percolated. As a literary scholar, I believe words matter, and the seeming simplicity of the language only proved its messy contradictions. *Stand. Your. Ground.* Each word pushed me back to what I was writing and to the field of southern studies. First, the word, "stand": I couldn't help thinking, of course, of the twelve southerners who, in the words of Michael Kreyling, "invented" southern literature in the early decades of the twentieth century.[5] Their text had been a reference to the lyrics of "Dixie," an anthem of southern exceptionalism and regional pride. *I'll Take My Stand* was a call to arms, to fight against the progressivism they saw infiltrating their culture and, in the words of Allen Tate, "to take hold of . . . [southern] traditions" through "violence" (176). Surely their influence and inventing/invoking the South's literary tradition was part of the architecture that led to the whitewashing of conceptions of southern power, pride, and revolution. To "take a stand," one must first have something to stand up *to,* a real or perceived threat compelling one to fight. The "stand your ground" law in Florida quite clearly decoded and exposed the threat to be Blackness.

The word "your" in the phrase was even more insidious. I thought through the thorny history of ownership throughout the South, especially in relation to colonial settlers and Blackness. In a plantation system, white colonists worked land that belonged to indigenous people; that work was done by enslaved Africans who had no potential for meaningful possession. Since the Emancipation Proclamation, Jim Crow southern machinations helped to ensure that southern African Americans would, even under the best circumstances, be unable to own anything without permissions and authorizations of white power structures. Likewise, colonialist visions of ownership virtually guaranteed that indigenous and immigrant communities would have no stake in white landowner profits. In short, the notion of a nonwhite "your" was a chimera, a discursive waving of hands; its meaning denuded into vacuity.[6]

The final word, "ground," completes the triptych—southern landscapes have defined the mythos of its exceptionalism. From early settlers of the territory to national speculation in agriculture and cash crops, the South has long been defined by an abiding obsession with land. One can think of Gerald O'Hara's lilting advice to Katie Scarlett in *Gone with the Wind:* "land is the only thing in the world that amounts to anything" (49), or, in the most iconic vision of Scarlett in Selznick's bloated movie: she bends down in the ruins of Tara to pull a rotten turnip from the ground, her determined face smudged with mud; in a Technicolor silhouette, she vows to never go hungry again, to fight with everything she has to save *her* beloved plantation. White fantasies of southern essentialism and exceptionalism are inexorably connected to ownership of dirt.

Value assigned to southern land represents a border that can be policed. Once you own ground, you are authorized to protect it. You stand on it, but you stand *up* for it, too. In just those three words—*stand your ground*—I felt the brutal truth of white authority's power to define identity and the absolute abdication of responsibility of those in power to imagine alternate definitions for regional identity. I saw the long, bloody trail of Black and indigenous bodies left in the wake of national, even global, fears and anxieties. And I felt it as a part of the region, of course, but also as a part of the field in which I found kinship, southern studies; the history of violence was implicated in framing the South as a region worthy of study. There was no escaping it: if you were a white scholar working in southern studies in 2012 and had any kind of self-reflexivity about your work, you felt dirty. The true dirt the region and the field of southern studies refused to own was a history of executing Black men and indigenous people with no repercussions, no justice.

After the murder of Trayvon Martin, I realized my project needed to juxtapose southern investments in class and whiteness with the margins they create. As I explored the shadows of those margins and came to terms with my place in southern studies, one word came back to me over and over: *dirty*. It's how I felt, of course, but it also suggested possibilities for unlocking critical questions that my monograph would attempt to answer. *Dirty* offered myriad possibilities for thinking through how the South operated for almost half a century. And it was useful in describing the terror and tragedy of the murder of a seventeen-year-old Trayvon Martin. *Dirty.* That was in George Zimmerman's mind when he trailed the young boy through his neighborhood. His perspective on Trayvon Martin wasn't unique; it was endemic to a whole history of white thought on Blackness. *Dirty.*

After careful thought, I realized Zimmerman didn't see Martin as trash; trash is something that can be expelled and forgotten. It's a trick we pull on ourselves, but we do it daily. We pretend it's invisible; we disengage our ownership of it. But not dirt. Something dirty is visible, and that visibility threatens us. Something dirty requires us to continually evaluate our relationship to it, our ownership of it. *Dirty.* Zimmerman's anger at Martin's presence in his neighborhood was, ultimately, white fury over African American visibility. "These assholes," Zimmerman said to the police; "they always get away." Maybe Zimmerman didn't think of himself as a garbage man, after all. Maybe he saw himself as a cleaner. To Zimmerman, Martin wasn't trash, he was dirt; scum. Dirty was a far more accurate description of the mostly static relationship white southerners have had with African Americans over the course of a century. *Dirty.* It was the way I felt about the region, the nation, the field of southern studies; it described the history of lynching, of Jim Crow, of the forced enslavement of Africans, the erasure and murder of indigenous people, the disenfranchisement of immigrant communities and people of color, of white failure to empathize with outsiders or to own the darkness of southern history. It was all dirty.

In the wake of Zimmerman's verdict, I studied theories of dirt. I turned to three female scholars who had written extensively about the word: Mary Douglas, Julia Kristeva, Patricia Yaeger. I found inspiration in many authors, but especially those three: Douglas writes about dirt as "a matter out of place,"[7] and connects an anxiety over our constant need for purification to the critical stability of cultural/personal identity formation; Kristeva suggests the dirtiness of the abject as what we turn from and, yet, inevitably turn back to, an idea that compels and repels us simultaneously; and Yaeger offers dirt as one of the crucial frames through which we might reimagine not just southern women writers but a corrective to reconsider the region. On the scaffolding of their ideas, I tried to imagine a project that looked at the word *dirty* as a critical apparatus to explore the region.

This book is profoundly curious about southern imaginaries and their connections to dirt, such as white trash's association with being of or from the land, clay-eaters, farmers, men and women of the soil. There are many ways that dirt works as a rhetorical marker defining different communities in the region across multiple axes of identities—race, gender, sexuality, class, and region. Our conception of what is impure or disposable speaks to our value and belief structures in profound ways, and dirt made sense as a rubric for understanding not just the texts I had chosen for my study but the events taking place around me as I wrote about them. I am convinced that identities on the margins of the American South often are defined through connection to dirt—a discourse contesting value, a way of speaking about the fundamentally polluted, impure—and that these dirty identities (which threaten conceptions of southern whiteness, purity, and cleanness) must be discarded, erased, or hidden in order for discourses of southern exceptionalism to remain unchallenged.

LIVING IN SHITTOWN

In 2012—the same year that Trayvon Martin was murdered—there was another significant event connected to dirty southern imaginaries. That year, Alabamian John B. McLemore sent an email to the producers of the National Public Radio show and podcast *This American Life* asking for help in exposing what he thought was the cover-up of a murder in his town of Woodstock, Alabama. When producer Brian Reed traveled to investigate McLemore's claims a year later, he found them specious. However, Reed continued talking with Mc-Lemore, and the resulting podcast exploring their odd friendship premiered five years later, in March 2017. It was an instant success. In the first few days, *S-Town* was downloaded ten million times, breaking all previous records for podcast consumption.[8] Part exploration of Reed's investment in McLemore, part excavation of the mystery of Woodstock (referred to by McLemore as "shittown," from whence the podcast derives its name), and part an unraveling of the reasons behind McLemore's eventual suicide, *S-Town* and its immense popularity again fundamentally affected my composition of the monograph.

During the first few episodes of *S-Town,* Brian Reed tries to understand the kind of pressures that McLemore might face as a sensitive intellectual living in rural Alabama, including anxieties over sexuality. "Since everyone 'round here thinks I'm a queer anyway," McLemore offhandedly confesses to Reed on the phone about how he might answer questions of why someone has traveled all the way from New York to visit him in Alabama, "I could just tell them I'm sucking your damn dick."[9] As he learns more about McLemore, Reed finds the man is not out in his community, that he struggles with his sexuality in relation to his stature in the town. McLemore doesn't even feel comfortable being completely candid with Reed about how he identifies; throughout the podcast, he only hints at it: "Let's just say I might be a fan of David Sedaris," he says at one point; later, acknowledging the danger of being gay in a rural Alabama community: "in other words, I might know who Audre Lorde and Ann Bannon is, if you get the idea. Of course, that could get you killed around here."

For Brian Reed (grieving the suicide of a friend), John McLemore's sexual identity represents nothing less than a grave hamartia. After McLemore's suicide, Reed decides to seek out one of McLemore's former lovers, Olin Long, to see if the man might offer any information to help him understand why McLemore decided to take his own life. Though touching, the man's remembrance of his relationship with McLemore doesn't initially offer Reed a satisfactory answer. Unable to fully understand what Olin and McLemore saw in each other, Reed settles on their intimacy, which Olin describes in asexual terms:

> We got on well. He was somebody that I could—there was intimacy there. And I'm going to tell you the definition of intimacy that was given to me by a counselor. Intimacy is the feeling that I can tell another person my thoughts and my behaviors without fear of judgment. If I can tell them the things that I've

done, even things that I'm not proud of, and they're still going to answer the phone and say hey, Olin, how are you getting along. That's how John would do—say, how are you getting along? So we did have a close friendship there.

Reed lingers a bit on Olin's "close friendship" with McLemore, and imagines his friend frustrated by a desire for a "conventional" relationship. But there is something unsettling—distasteful even—as Reed moves through episodes in *S-Town* and meets with McLemore's former secret lovers to parse out their potential for meaningful relationships. It is especially troubling that Reed is a straight man from another region mediating and defining what constitutes meaningful queer relationships in Alabama; being a gay southerner is an identity for which Reed has no legitimate expertise or understanding beyond broad caricature.

By the end of the podcast, Reed ceases to narrate McLemore's life and instead turns to narrating his own panicked motives for the man's suicide. He frantically throws out guesses, many disconnected to the facts of McLemore's life. Reed's first hypothesis over the root of McLemore's depression connects back to the title of the podcast, the shittown of Woodstock. He speculates that it was how much McLemore hated the town that drove him to kill himself, but Reed clearly indicts, by association, the entire region of the American South. Ultimately, Reed concludes that McLemore's tragedy rests at the crux of his being a southerner: a gay man tethered by a need to take care of his mother and thus remain locked in an unforgiving small southern town. For Reed, the town's inability to validate McLemore's dirty little secret is what finally was too much to bear. The supposed tragedy for Brian Reed is twofold and reminded me very much of white anxieties over the figure of the tragic mulatto during the nineteenth and twentieth centuries:[10] Reed's version of McLemore bifurcates him into two identities seemingly in conflict, of being queer and a southerner. Having to hide one's sexuality is a move Reed doesn't fully appreciate as an urban East Coaster descending into the *shit* of the Deep South, to tell a tale of trashed life. Everything is dirty in *S-Town*, and the tragedy of McLemore, Reed offers, is that he cannot own his own dirt openly in a town and region so disgustingly shitty as Woodstock, Alabama.

Not only does Reed investigate McLemore's romantic life, he also explores John McLemore's sadomasochistic relationships. When the podcast enters the territory of dominance and submission and describes McLemore's desire for the release that pain offers, it truly exploits McLemore and the "dirty" details of his private life. For example, one of the first things McLemore confesses to Reed is an open disgust for individuals with tattoos, and yet Reed later learns that McLemore has been tattooed throughout his life. When Tyler shows Reed a photo of McLemore's back tattoo long after the man's suicide, it's as though a crucial piece of the puzzle has fallen into place: for Reed, the tattoo represents a symptom of McLemore's melancholy over his inability to find validation within his community and his abject self-hatred. Talking about the photo, Reed finds himself sick:

> This picture is really disturbing. It's John's back, which when I visited John was not tattooed. Like Tyler said, there's a whip that looks as if it's laying across his shoulders and neck, apparently attached to the handle on the other side of him. And that all across his back, top to bottom, are dozens of red lash marks, like in a famous historic photo that John included in a collage in the 53-page manifesto he sent me documenting society's moral decline. A photo of a slave named Gordon who was believed to have escaped from a plantation in Louisiana, and whose back was photographed and distributed by abolitionists as visual proof of the terrors of slavery.

For Reed, this obsession with darkness is the key to unlocking McLemore's dirty secrets; because he could not leave the town that tormented him, Reed imagines him turning his rage inward, hoping to punish himself the same way southerners punished runaway enslaved Africans. Unlike "Gordon," who was tormented by real people with real whips, Reed's conception of the tattoo suggests McLemore is flagellating himself. His wounds are self-inflicted. Reed cannot understand that McLemore's expression of his loss of power could also be celebratory. For Reed, this kind of pain is darkness, but for McLemore, it is clearly redemptive: he calls his sessions with Tyler going to "church."

I was initially captivated by the first chapters of the podcast, but, by the end of the series, I found myself repulsed. Very quickly, I realized the podcast was not interested in the real man but rather, in exploring, in the words of Michael Bibler, "the McLemore that Reed has edited for us." Reed's investments in McLemore are bizarre and gross. At best, his reading of the man's life is naive; at worst, it is exploitative. Hearing Reed's ponderous thoughts on what queerness might have meant to McLemore reminded me of the consequences of narrativizing what is "dirty." Reed's musing are bad interpretations of a life for which he has no context. But, no matter the stakes, Reed robs McLemore of agency, even in ownership of the power exchanges he engages in with other men. For Reed, such actions mark McLemore as a damaged individual whose masochism is directly tied to self-loathing and an inability to find a meaningful monogamous relationship with another man. Reed is more than a bad reader; he infects his conclusion over the tragedy of McLemore with a heterofuturity that refuses alternate identities as valid or meaningful. As Daniel Schroeder argues, Reed "tries to translate McLemore into a framework he understands—shaping the story into a total tragedy with country songs and gay movies to lead the way—rather than allow his complex love life, like so much else about him, to speak for itself."

The instant and sustained popularity of the podcast made it clear that Reed's obsession with the character of the tragically queer McLemore was not isolated to Brian Reed; the podcast's exploitation of McLemore and his private world was largely responsible for its success. It's obvious to even a casual listener that Reed cared little for the consequences of exposing the dirty secrets of McLemore's life to the public; in fact, the podcast advertised itself as confessional storytelling. With no impunity whatsoever, the producers of *S-Town* invited multiple publics to gaze at McLemore's dirty secrets and peruse them as casually as one might scroll through a thread on Reddit. As a queer man in Alabama in 2017, one whose circumstances permitted him to be out in his community, I was disgusted by the dirt-loving publics of *S-Town*. McLemore's sexuality and his history with men was a narrative that belonged to him alone; a decision over how and when to tell that story was an authority that should have been reserved only for him. The robbing of McLemore's agency even after his death as well as the popular exploitation and narrativization of his tortured relationship to his region and his sexuality was more than reprehensible; it was criminal.[11] How does one reconcile robbing a dead man of his voice, of speaking for or about a life for which he has no context, of inventing motives and investigating the secrets of a body literally buried in dirt?

What Reed seems painfully ignorant of in *S-Town* is the complexity of being queer and southern. For him, gay men in the South are a dirty little secret whose stories are tragic enough to be made into films like *Brokeback Mountain*. Reed is a fine storyteller but an awful historian. As John Howard explains in his book *Men Like That,* there are two identities within southern culture that offer us a chance to find a queer genealogy for gay men in the South: "men like *that*—which is to say . . . self-identified gay males—as well as men *who like that*, men who like queer sex . . . but do not necessarily identity as gay" (xviii).

The schism between the two identities has a wide gulf of consequences for men who identity with them, and some of those consequences can be lethal. And yet, Reed's presentation of McLemore as one of the "men like that" felt little more than a marketing decision. The daily experiences I had as a gay man in my protected bubble of Tuscaloosa had blinded me to the truth about the lived lives of gay men in the rural South: here were men whose dirt could be exploited for profit. Writing for *Vox,* Aja Romano articulated a portion of my frustration over the show, saying in part "I'm not so sure, however, that making the choice to undermine the autonomy of a dead man, even if it yields greater understanding of him, isn't hurtful to others—particularly to those who grew up queer in the South, unable or unwilling to fully explore their identities due to fear of societal repercussions." *S-Town* does a profound disservice to John McLemore, of course, but Brian Reed also fundamentally and (seemingly) purposefully does damage to the emerging queer communities throughout the South that struggle daily for visibility and validity. In refusing to take responsibility for the potential repercussions of violating the consent of a dead man, *S-Town* wants to have it both ways; it wants, on the one hand, to be a serious investigation of region and identity, but it wants to offer a story, a narrative, as its ultimate diagnosis of McLemore's soul-sickness.

VERY FINE PEOPLE

By releasing the podcast early in 2017, producers surely were attempting to be timely, especially in the wake of the surprise Electoral College victory of Donald Trump in November of 2016. Romano asserts as much, describing the podcast as a part of an ongoing process to explain Trump's victory and respond to what progressives did wrong in 2016. Losing white working-class voters to Trump sent progressives on an endless search that would eventually culminate in an appeal to the left to empathize with the poor, white male, whose votes in the Rust Belt sealed Trump's electoral victory: "the media has been awash in attempts to empathize with the downtrodden white working class of regions like John's, and *S-Town* initially proceeds as though it will ask us for a similar level of progressive empathy for the heartland." Shows like *S-Town* want its audience to buy into the concept that progressives should be more empathetic about rural, white (largely male) Americans, but, I'd offer the problem is not (dis)investment with the white working white class. We hear their stories all the time. What we don't listen for are the silences—silences, for example, created in the spaces between the tragedies of Trayvon Martin,

Eric Gardner, John McLemore, Rekia Boyd, and Miriam Carey; often, we don't hear them because another story gets layered on top of theirs. Even in death, these figures are not allowed to contest their dirtiness, reclaim their identity, and stand *their* ground; they are forced instead to be connected to other dirts grievously disconnected from their identities.

If we could just understand the poor, white southerner, the impoverished hillbilly, or the redneck from the heartland—political rhetoric from 2017 suggests—we would be able to explain to them why progressive ideology or liberal economic reform is in their best interest. But the "shittown" is not just in Alabama. As Christina Belcher notes, "Many of us are being poisoned in this shit world, in shit towns across America. Lead seepage into drinking water has caused a state of emergency in Flint, Michigan. High levels of lead in the blood, particularly of pregnant women and children, causes learning disabilities and behavioral problems." The election of Donald Trump also made it clear that, whatever fantasy we had about a dirty South being bordered was a lie: the importance of naming something dirty had become nationalized. Trump's presidential legacy was nothing if not dirty: vulgar, racist, corrupt, and portending ecological ruination. Belcher notes, "In March 2017, the Trump administration announced a sweeping executive order that effectively demolished Obama-era policies on climate change. Repealing climate regulations, such as emissions restrictions for coal-fired power plants, Trump has supposedly 'unshackled' fossil fuels industries. Coal industry jobs can return to the country." As coal continues to poison and infect rural communities, "Rural America, we are told, is ecstatic. Surrounded by coal industry workers, Mr. Trump signed the executive order he promised his rural voters during his campaign, the group of smiling men ready to get back to work, to 'make America great again.'"

Trump's presidency from 2016 to 2020 repositioned "white trash," especially white, lower- and middle-class males, as the center of an American, if not uniquely southern, ontology. In his inauguration address, Trump vowed to remember "the forgotten men and women of our country,"[12] clearly coded references for poor, white (largely) men who turned out to support him. Trump's inauguration and presidency only confirmed America's obsession with white authority and the discursive dirtying of those on the periphery of that authority. If we ever finally saw these truths as a nation, it was during the four years of Trump's presidency, for that's the time we understood that dirt was not just a southern problem but intimately tied into our national spirit. The more Trump raged, the more garbage piled up: immigrants, transgendered soldiers, welfare recipients, thugs—whatever his invective, it reminded me daily of how we define dirt by first calling it out. Donald Trump's rhetoric defined for his followers what was, ultimately valuable, and, by contrast, disposable. He dirt-ied everything from "bad hombres," to "shithole" countries, to the notion of truth itself, which, in what is perhaps the most impressive accomplishment of his presidency, he managed to muddy. If a truth was unappealing to him, he simply called it "fake news," a term he successfully "deployed as a weapon against everything from errors in good faith and promptly corrected . . . to the most meticulously documented truths" (Frum 116).

Just as Reed's dirtying of McLemore's life has the potential for lethal conse-quences, so, too, did Trump's dirtying of truth and history. In August of 2017, a rally was held in Charlottesville, Virginia. Emboldened by Trump's recent election and his open vitriol, white supremacists ceased doing their work in private and came out to show the public what their hatred looked like. Osten-sibly labeled a "Unite the Right" rally, those assembled came to protest the re-moval of Confederate monuments throughout the country. They picked the town of Charlottesville and the grounds of the University of Virginia because of its connection to the Confederacy. On 12 August, a white supremacist de-liberately slammed his car into a group of counterprotestors; the force of the impact killed Heather Heyer. Speaking to reporters after the murder, Trump refused to denounce the white supremacist who murdered Heyer, saying, "you had some very bad people in that group [the white supremacists], but you also had people that were very fine people, on both sides." And the reason they were "very fine"? They were fighting for southern pride: "You had people in that group that were there to protest the taking down of, to them, a very, very important statue and the renaming of a park from Robert E. Lee to another name."[13] Even in Trump's condemnation of the death of a young woman, there is this sick rhetoric demanding a return (or to maintain) our national focus on white men, if only because, in Trump's mind, the left's appeal to diversity and inclusion undermined their standing, dirtied their reputation. In August 2017, Trump showed us where he would take his stand, and it was the same dirty ground of the Agrarians and their neo-Confederate progeny.

I'm writing a dirty book.

A group of southern studies scholars were in Amsterdam for the Modern-ist Studies Association that day in August of 2017. We were presenting papers on Plantation Modernism when we got the news of the murder, and in our sadness, we found community. Weeks later, someone joined the Facebook group of the Society for the Study of Southern Literature to congratulate us on the work we were doing on behalf of white authorship and history. Everything that had been problematic about our collective investment in studying the culture and literature of the South crystalized for us that fall. More than ever, I was convinced: southern studies needed to assert its value by owning some dirt if its own.

As a white southern scholar, writing a dirty book felt more important to me than ever, and the concept of dirt had never felt more fully significant than in the spring of 2018 when I first began to imagine the book you're reading. Regardless of where white southern-studies scholars position themselves, the discursive space I claim is the same bedrock bullshit where those twelve southerners first took their stand. That ground is still muddied with blood and slime; I want to name it, call it out, so I can come to terms with its consequences. It's personal. I have to own up to that history. But I am not naive—I know it is not enough to make it visible. This kind of sludge is dynamic: just like the trash we send out to landfills, this southern shit doesn't disappear; it simply migrates to other spaces, other discourses. It is my hope that this book might be, in some ways, a way of calling out dirt and its attendant complications for region, race, and shame. But, to begin to name southern studies' dirt, white scholars must, like Prospero does with Caliban, locate our complicity and confess where we stand: "this thing of darkness I acknowledge mine."

It is hard to take a stand in a field of study when the ground seems ever shifting—I'd like to suggest a new way of imagining our scholarship—let's call it dirty southern studies—which might steady some of the tremors. I first conceived of "dirty southern studies" in an essay for *south*, where I offered a way to mediate the garbage of southern studies and openly and publicly adjudicate its value with candid assessments of the bodies and communities it presumed to represent. A dirty southern studies could "re-focus our critical lens on what has become invisible through its dogged visibility. In short, our work should be obsessed with trash: It should be garbage-gazing, litter-loving. It should investigate invisibilities, speak through silences, make public stories that are silenced through fear or shame, and recuperate the 'throwaway bodies' that the culture refuses to validate" ("Down N' Dirty" 167). Perhaps a "dirty southern studies" would offer scholars a chance to form their own communities by redefining "what it means to live 'down' here amongst the trash and the filth; to own our desire for regional identification; to resist rhetorics of shame; to make our home here; to make the region better; to shape our discourse and create a new vernacular that contests hierarchies of value and whiteness and heteronormativity that have largely been unchallenged" (166).

The goal of dirty southern studies is not simply to reproduce usual strategies characterizing our relationship to trash and dirt but rather to reposition dirty imaginaries as critical tropes that animate discourses of exceptionalism about the American South. If this book is a beginning, it is necessarily fumbling and infantile, but even so, I do hope it stands on its own, begins to break a new ground, and claps back at the history we inherited.

Throughout the difficulties of this book's composition, I found myself asking the same question: what good is scholarship if it cannot excavate and uncover value in things that have been labeled dirty? If scholarship does not galvanize the scholar and the reader to resist and refuse entrenched power dynamics and dominant histories that elide and bury communities of color, what is it worth? Feminist indigenous scholars like Cheryl Suzack, Shari M. Huhndorf, and Mishuana Goeman have long reclaimed "lost" voices and cultures, and that work is very much the future of southern studies, too. I suppose I feel the need for reclamation more acutely in southern studies because the presentation of the history of "southern" culture and literature as "exceptional" stories often obfuscates the enduring presence of whiteness. Why does southern studies exist at all if not to resist dominant discourses of or about the region in which odes to a vanishing white exceptionalism find safe harbor or hidden avenues for valuation? Why talk about dirt at all if you don't first take up the dirtiness of southern studies? In working through the iterations of dirt in the book I wrote, I realized the useful work of southern studies—the *only* work of southern studies as far as I am concerned—is being done, has been done, will be done by those who have long been tossed aside by the field, marginalized, devalued, buried. The true southern studies folk of 2023 and beyond all at one point in time have been labeled dirty.

Where I find myself now as I begin to compose *The Dirty South* is in a precarious place: precarious in space, in state, in region, in historical moment. Books are living things, and this one is especially dynamic. I am sure much of what I started with will change, but I know some things will not: let me tell you what kind of book this *isn't* going to be: this isn't a book about where a real South exists, nor about what states belong in the U.S. South and which do not; it's not a book about southern exceptionalism of any kind; it's not about what "authentic" cornbread tastes like or any other *Garden and Gun* nonsense; I'm not going to engage in conversations and dialogue about the Agrarian influence over the conception of tradition; I am not doing a deep dive into the literary mind of the South or fetishizing the southern novel. I hope we are done with that; I know I am.

Let me tell you what I hope this book will be: a project not just of academic but of social importance that might illuminate the margins of southern culture by speaking to the ways in which peripherality signaled contestations of value in the region; a study that examines high and low culture to make useful connections about how things, people, communities, and regions are labeled as dirty; a fifty-year history of the region and its representation in both literary and popular culture that, like a kaleidoscope, uses a singular instrument to spin and refract multiple images of the American South that have a profound relationship to what is dirty. That's my goal.

I hope I can write a book that can be heard by those who need to hear it, who might find in it solace and comfort. And I recognize that audience as a community constantly pushing against conceptions of value that devalue them. Because dirty imaginaries don't just do cultural work, they animate narratives difficult to contest—in strictest fact, lethal to contest for many, especially African Americans. *The Dirty South* asks us to come to terms with where and how those narratives mark certain people, certain practices, and certain beliefs as "dirty" and to work out possible productive relationships in the contemporary South to their historical and still active weight, and to figure out ways to productively contest them *now.* That productive contestation involves an honest and thorough engagement with the dominant narrative in its historical, literary, and legal manifestations, but it also invites engagement with the voices who have worked to contest that dominant narrative and who, in that contestation, have indicated alternative narratives and alternative paths forward. And to do so by looking beyond the fetishization of the novel and literary exceptionalism to cultural texts mostly ignored by most academic books. So, I want to be clear, and as a general warning to any and all readers that have made it this far and still don't know:

I'm writing a dirty book.

THE DIRTY SOUTH

One peculiar feature of exceptionalist narratives about the American South is a preoccupation with the region's dirtiness. The South has long been relegated to the trash heap of American cultural imaginaries since it first began to be colonially settled in the eighteenth century: representations of the region have been littered with the language of waste, pollution, and garbage. In our contemporary moment, such representations remain familiar: the South is disposable, unnecessary; its people poor, illiterate "trash"; its customs and traditions worthless and backward; its "toxic" food consisting of processed garbage; its cultural achievements middling at best. These constellations of images describing a fundamentally "dirty South" have connections to economic and cultural realities about the region that are easy to locate. But to work through the conception of a contemporary notion of "dirty South" and its connections to discourses about southern exceptionalism is to search for a history whose origins are less clear.

The Dirty South examines the shifting significances of the South as a constructed, fantasized region in the American psyche. I argue that the South has been portrayed in a range of genres—from novels to films to comic books to popular music—quite differently since the end of the civil rights era. The phrase "dirty South" captures these portrayals starting in the year 1970 when the simultaneous pressure of the urban riots of the 1960s and the nonviolence movement had faded from the scene in the years of the rightist backlash. This study traces a dirty South into our contemporary moment (arguably still an era of rightist backlash) to examine the sustained fascination of southern dirtiness, while simultaneously probing that fascination's causes and its consequences; I pay particular attention to the ways different artists and audiences put the dirt of the South to use. This book mobilizes the concept of a "dirty South" to examine the role the South plays in the national imaginary and the ways that southerners have used "dirt" to create and police boundaries *and* to contest those boundaries, with a focus on the period from 1970 to the present, when the South, emerging from the civil rights era, began to represent a number of new possible identities for the nation as a whole and for itself.

I am engaged in this work because the South's hold on the imaginations of southerners and non-southerners alike needs some unpacking; the study takes its cue from scholarship interrogating southern essentialism and nativism by unpacking investments in southern culture and rhetorics of exceptionalism. It likewise engages with those scholars by denying conceptions of a monolithic notion of southern identity or region: My book situates itself among the generative work of new southern studies to reimagine the study of the U.S. South as a nexus of interconnected, but manufactured, identities—a study based around causal associations that often manifest in wildly ideological ways, a kind of "heuristic southern studies." I explore how a "dirty South" is different from, as well as dialogues with, other iterations of the region that have also been a part of national, if not global, discourses.[1] *The Dirty South* sets out a historical argument about changing images of the South and the role those images play in the national imaginary; I offer the image of "the dirty South" to explore that shift, its multiple manifestations and meanings, and its social, political, and psychological (personal) consequences.

The book frames narratives of or about a dirty South as a multifaceted nexus producing conflicting, occasionally contradictory, claims, primarily by juxtaposing the region with tropes of dirt: soil, garbage, trash, grit, litter, mud, swamp water, slime, and pollution. The source material for these explorations are prominent or popular literary and cultural texts of or about the U.S. South over the last half-century. Moreover, the book works through conceptions of dirt and waste by studying how southern identity gets articulated and contested primarily through mediums we consider to be debased, dirty, or "trashy": comic books, country music or hip-hop lyrics, horror movies, and cookbooks. In each chapter, I focus on a prominent literary or cultural text from the 1970s and examine how the authors emphasize some aspect of a dirty southern imaginary in their composition. I place that text into a historical moment connecting with other texts of its time, but I also show the continuation of the specific iteration of a dirty South by tracing the trope all the way through our contemporary moment. Each chapter ends by highlighting another popular or prominent literary or cultural text of the first decades of the twenty-first century that narrates a similar investment in the dirty southern iteration in which the chapter opens or, critically, contests the inherent whiteness of the earlier dirty imaginary. Thus, the monograph argues both for a recognition of this unique kind of representative trope and affirmation of its endurance over the course of the last fifty years.

The study begins with the chapter "The South's Got Something to Play: Of Glitter and Gangsters," which connects the emergence of two wildly popular musical genres of the 1970s—the outlaw backlash against Nashville's corporatized country music and New York's hip-hop—with regional fantasies of difference. I look at the lyrics and lifestyles of prominent "outlaw country" music stars of the 1970s and compare them to the lyrics and culture of the Atlanta "dirty South" hip-hop world of the late twentieth and early twenty-first centuries, as both musical genres position themselves as correctives emphasizing value in marginalized figures and practices. Drawing from my essay in *south: a scholarly journal*, "Down N' Dirty," I argue that both 1970s country music and early 2000s dirty South hip-hop work to assert the artistic merit of "trash" as, ultimately, the authentic iteration of racial or regional identity in a genre that values artifice and aesthetics.

Next, I examine the central figure of terror for the civil rights workers and disenfranchised African Americans of the South throughout the 1960s: southern white "vigilantes," who came together in force to attack and intimidate them. In "Let Us Now Praise Hillbilly Justice: *Deliverance* and Dirty Elegies," I suggest James Dickey's 1970 novel presents an elegy for what he argues is a slowly vanishing culture of "white trash" southerners, especially their exceptional capacity for violence. I connect *Deliverance* with other texts that attempt to argue for value in white-trash culture and claim them as a genre that I call "dirty elegy." I end the chapter by looking at a contemporary dirty elegy from after the 2016 presidential election—J. D. Vance's *Hillbilly Elegy* (2016)—marking an extension of Dickey's lamentation about a fading form of authentic American ontology. I claim that, by memorializing the "dirty" white "trash" of the South, authors create a driving narrative repositioning the "forgotten" white southerner as a misrepresented figure, one deserving understanding, not condemnation. Further, by celebrating the immediacy of white vigilantism, these dirty elegies argue for systemic oppression of Black and brown bodies through formal and informal white policing, which I connect to the murder of immigrants in El Paso in 2019.

Extending my argument on the horror of vigilantism, I start my third chapter, "GTFO: The Violation of Sunken Places," by offering John Boorman's campy 1972 filmic adaptation of *Deliverance* as a primary example of "hixploitation horror." Drawing on archival work from the Harry Ransom Center in

Austin, Texas, and its materials relating to the filming, production, and imagining of Tobe Hooper's 1974 film *The Texas Chain Saw Massacre,* the chapter plots a history of representations of the freakish, white redneck-monster in American films, from *Massacre* to the 2017 film *Get Out,* directed by Jordan Peele. I offer these films as American nightmares anxious over transgressive border crossings, excavations, and uncoverings of things, places, or people not meant to be seen—figures and spaces long repressed by national consciousness. In uncovering places and people meant to remain hidden, the victims of these films are subject to brutal revenge perpetrated by the repressed underclass through a ritualized, disfiguring touch. Exploring the popularity of films like *Chain Saw* and *Deliverance,* I argue that horror films from 1970 to the 2020s present the American South as a sunken space ready to ensnare and violently avenge itself by torturing the unimaginative or naive national consciousness that represses it. I end by offering Peele's *Get Out* as a profound meditation on the consequences of these revenge narratives, especially in his critique of the broken system of American mass incarceration routinely imprisoning African Americans.

I transition from the unforgiving sunken places of *Get Out* to the fetid, Louisiana swampland. "Dirty Ethics and Swampy Ecology" examines the phenomenon of comic-book creator Len Wein's "Swamp Thing," which first appeared in 1971's *House of Secrets* and became an instant success. I connect the "dirty" birth of the monster—created from a powerful mixture of manufactured chemicals and swamp water—to the 1969 oil spill in Santa Barbara, California, that sparked the birth of "Earth Day" as well as the beginning of the first meaningful environmental laws passed in America. I move from the swamps of the 1970s to the bayous of the 2000s and the film *Beasts of the Southern Wild,* where the movie's characters, in the words of Patricia Yaeger, "recycle a few things while leaking and expending everything else. In other words . . . the science of halfway practices." Using "halfway practices" and bricolaged trash—"making do with what [is] salvaged from other waste-making classes"—as crucial points of inquiry, I investigate eco-critical, literary, and graphic-novel narratives of and about Hurricane Katrina, where the representation of the South as a "dumping ground" creates real environmental conditions that continue to exacerbate apocalyptic natural disasters.

In my coda, "Recycling the South," I use the image of the recycling bin as an icon that might help to think through the work (both artistic and scholarly), done on behalf of the American South, to find useful ways to spin southern culture, to re-signify it, to create something worthwhile out of the history and narratives produced about it. I position the work of Michael B. Twitty and his concept of "Afroculinaria" as an example of the kind of work that can be achieved through dirty southern studies. Thinking through southern food-ways, I use Twitty's critique of white celebrity southern chefs as a model to contest the work of organizations like the Southern Foodways Alliance within southern studies scholarship. My coda ends back where I began, with a final call for dirty southern artists and scholars to explore other cultural, literary, filmic, and comic texts that complicate or contest claims made in the book, and I offer that such projects do not have be in prestige genres but can also exist—must exist—in "dirtied" spaces, too: social media, websites, performances, as well as our classrooms.

My approach to southern literary and cultural texts also seeks to speak to and about those marginalized from "prestige" communities and argues for a reclamation of their "dirtied" value. As part of this conversation, I want to make a broader argument for the importance of the humanities, whose value always feels contested, secreted, hidden, and dirty. One major goal is to present a book in a vernacular that addresses a more general and perhaps not solely scholarly audience, to present a case for how work in the humanities might have cultural and political consequences beyond the narrow focus of the academy. While *The Dirty South* is clearly about fantasies—fantasies of region, of nation, of consumption—it engages with them postmortem as a coroner might. This study explores why dirty southern fantasies endure not because they locate a vein of authenticity or project an image of relevancy for the American South but because they aid so conspicuously in the zombified work of tethering investors (real and imagined) to a graveyard of ideas. But I'm not interested in picking apart the bones of the dead; I want to know why dirty southern imaginaries persist and what cultural work they do: *The Dirty South*'s principles are teleological, not eschatological.

The Dirty South also explores my fantasies and investments. I examine subjects and genres that have long fascinated me—horror movies, comic books, country music, hip-hop—and, in some sense, fascinations central to my understanding who I am as a person. I am aware that, in reading this book, you will find me tending my own gardens. But that is true of any monograph: a good work of scholarship invites you to its dirt, not divides you from it. It should make clear its borders as well as acknowledge its limits, but it should also be an open space of play. In the prologue, I have clarified why this work is important to me, but I hope I've also sufficiently signaled an invitation to collaboration, a call to kneel down in the garden and work together. But, before we begin our work, I'd like to be clear about what I mean by "dirt," and how my concept of it has been informed by scholars. I'd also like to situate the book in its historical moment of the 1970s and explain why the decade is critical to understanding the persistence of dirty southern imaginaries into our contemporary moment.

DIRT! DANGER! DESIRE!

Rubbish is something people look at all the time without onus or shame or desire, whereas waste is something that must be secreted away, hidden, a matter of attraction and shame.
—Patricia Yaeger, *Dirt and Desire* (2000)

In *Waste and Want: A Social History of Trash,* social historian Susan Strasser asserts that what we think of as "trash" is not a collection of things but rather an epistemology, a narrative, subject to reading and interpretation: "Nothing is inherently trash" (5). What we consider to be dirty can, likewise, be contextual, but the conversations surrounding trash hinge on contestations of value that come from an object's usefulness, while discourses on dirt tend to enact claims about purity, pollution, and order. Unlike trash, dirt's relationship to value remains locked in a fixed binary: a trashed object is expunged of value, but a dirty object retains its potential value despite its soiling. Trash is ejected; dirty objects can be cleaned. Even so, how we conceive of trash and dirt describe less an essential identity and more a narrative of "human behavior." We behave in similar ways to trash and dirt largely because they represent fundamental threats to systems of order. Strasser suggests the central connection between our relationship to garbage and dirt is the act of sorting itself: "Trash is created by sorting. Everything that comes into the end-of-the-millennium home—every toaster, pair of trousers, and ounce of soda pop, and every box and bag and bottle they arrive in—eventually requires a decision: keep it or toss it. We use it up, we save it to use later, we give it away, or at some point we define it as rubbish, to be taken back out, removed beyond the borders of the household" (5). As good poststructuralists, we recognize a word like trash does not describe the existence of the inherently valueless as much as it signals a rhetorical marker describing an object or thing that has shifting and contextual value: consequently, much like sexuality, we can appreciate, then, that trash does not have a singular essence but a history.[2] Strasser offers as much when she says, "As everyday life and ordinary housework have changed over time, so has this process of defining what is rubbish, as well as the rubbish itself, the contents of the trash" (5).

In the act of sorting, Strasser finds connections to how trash and dirt help us establish a relationship to structure. Like sorting trash into bins, "sorting the dirty from the clean," she writes, also "involves systematic ordering and classifying" (5). Beyond that nominal linkage, Strasser finds garbage and dirt share a commonality in their "special dimensions": "Nontrash belongs in the house; trash goes outside" (6). Likewise, dirt must be removed from spaces that are clean to spaces that are unclean (or spaces that, at the very least, are made to contain the unclean). Borders are obviously vital to these classifications because they protect from both philosophical and psychological threats to how we order and manage our lives: not just in the line between house and outside but between "marginal places" and the household, between "locations for purifying activities" and the larger word, "the intersection between the private and the public, the borderland where the household meets the city, the threshold between the male and female 'spheres' of the nineteenth century" (6). More significantly, Strasser claims that much of the process of sorting the dirty from the clean and trash from nontrash critically connects with perspectives of power and subjugation. "Discussions of marginal places and marginal behaviors often merge with discussions about marginal people," she writes, and "above all, sorting is an issue of class" (8–9). Sorting the trash from the nontrash and the dirty from the clean is intimately connected to conceptions of order.

In her groundbreaking *Purity and Danger: An Analysis of Concepts of Pollution and Taboo,* sociologist Mary Douglas defines dirt primarily in relationship to systems of order: "dirt is essentially disorder," she writes. "Dirt offends against order. Eliminating it is not a negative movement, but a positive effort to organise the environment" (2). Douglas would agree with Strasser's contention that dirt is often contextual; understanding dirt's relationship to a specific culture and historical moment is critical to understanding how such a culture affirms order and structure. "There is no such thing as absolute dirt," she asserts, "it exists in the eye of the beholder" (2). And yet, in recognizing what is dirty, Douglas finds that we forge unity. The lines between clean and unclean don't just separate concepts of what is hygienic from what is polluted or corrupt but from what is forbidden and what is allowed. For Ben Campkin and Rosie Cox, editors of *Dirt: New Geographies of Cleanliness and Contamination,*

Douglas's importance in understanding the power of dirt lies fundamentally in her connection between dirt and acts "that transgress established borders, confound order, and disrupt dominant belief systems" (4).

Douglas notes, "I believe that ideas about separating, purifying, demarcating and punishing transgressions have as their main function to impose system on an inherently untidy experience." We order systems, she suggests, not primarily through a conception of what is fundamentally pure or sacred, but in reverse: by first defining what is transgressive and, therefore, dangerous. We know what is clean only first by understanding what is polluted. Moreover, for order to prevail, we require a system constantly policed; the work of defining dirt for Douglas is work on behalf of a recognition and valorization of what a culture prioritizes as something worthy of continuance: "Dirt is that which must not be included if a pattern is to be maintained," she concludes. "To recognize this is the first step towards insight into pollution" (40). By the conclusion of *Purity and Danger*, however, Douglas makes a startling connection between dirt's potential for danger and a damaging disruptor of order—a connection that is at the heart of this study's claim about why dirty southern imaginaries remain statically compelling for over a half-century.

Douglas examines closely the very moment when an object is thrown away into the bin. For her, the act itself has no violence, no risk, but also no compulsion; trash is "recognizably out of place, a threat to good order, and so . . . vigorously brushed away" (160). So, when does trash become dangerous? Douglas finds potential danger bound in trash's breakdown, its gradual hybridity: in the moment we identify something as valueless, there is the potential for danger. And the danger comes from looking inside the trash can after we have thrown the object away, when the visibility of former value haunts us, threatens us even; in that state, trash still retains some of its identity, but it is hopelessly dirtied: "they can be seen to be unwanted bits of whatever it was they came from, hair or food or wrappings. This is the stage at which they are dangerous," she claims:

> Their half-identity still clings to them and the clarity of the scene in which they obtrude is impaired by their presence. But a long process of pulverizing, dissolving and rotting awaits any physical things that can be recognized as a dirt. . . . it is unpleasant to poke about in the refuse to try to recover anything, for this revives identity. So long as identity is absent, rubbish is not dangerous. . . . The danger which is risked by boundary transgression is power. Those vul-

nerable margins and those attacking forces which threaten to destroy good order represent the powers inhering in the cosmos. (160–61).

Douglas's understanding of danger here is precisely the kind of ontological threatening of disrupting systems of classification by which we recognize the familiar. Peter Stallybrass and Allon White summarize Douglas's conception of the threat as "transgression," which they find connected to the symbolic in that it collapses "the general processes of classification which bear most closely upon the identity of the collectivity . . . [and] the heterodox symbolic material of the Imaginary" (194). Douglas argues that dirty trash threatens the symbolic order classifying our understanding of lines that border not just our homes and communities but ourselves.

The inability to distinguish between collective identity and the symbolic order provides an easy transition to think about transgressive dirt, then, not simply in cultural but also psychoanalytical terms. Perhaps no post-Freudian scholar has written more specifically on the processes by which pollution and dirt threaten a symbolic order than Julia Kristeva in her concept of abjection. Kristeva situates the abject as an internal understanding. The abject is an in-tuitive reaction—meaning, essentially, one not necessarily connected to social or cultural understandings but to biological imperative—reactions to the ab-ject cause a "revolt of the person against an external menace from which one wants to keep oneself at a distance—it may menace *from inside*" (165). Kriste-va's practical examples—blood, shit, vomit—suggest things inside the body whose visibility outside of it create a disruption in classification: we see them and recognize their familiarity but are shocked by their crossing outside of borders. The threat of the exteriority, or we may say, the visibility of the abject is a menace both *from* inside and *of* the inside, the space where it is supposed, by classification, to reside.[3]

The consequences of the abject's relationship to visibility and invisibility—especially in relation to exteriority and interiority—are essential in under-standing the simultaneous draw and disgust one finds in the dirty. Just as Douglas remarks on the dangerous pull of dirt, Kristeva describes the abject's curious powers over its subject: "the jettisoned object . . . [the] radically ex-cluded . . . draws me toward the place where meaning collapses. A certain 'ego' that merged with its master, a superego, has flatly driven it away. It lies outside, beyond the set, and does not seem to agree to the latter's rules of the game. And yet, from its place of banishment, the abject does not cease challenging its master. Without a sign (for him), it beseeches a discharge, a convulsion, a crying out" (2). The "crying out" that Kristeva mentions reminds me of Douglas's compelling danger, or, at the very least, a symptom of desire: an ache on behalf of the subject to make whole the connection between the self and the abject, to refix classifications.[4] In a complicated way, Kristeva seems to suggest that the abject does double work in disrupting classifications while reaffirming them; we find the same kind of paradox in Douglas's conception of dirt. Like dirt, then, the abject works through contradictory impulses to immediately repel us, but also ceaselessly to compel us. Kristeva recognizes the abject's relationship to desire: The abject stays "close, but it cannot be assimilated. It beseeches, worries, and fascinates desire, which, nevertheless, does not let itself be seduced. Apprehensive, desire turns aside; sickened, it rejects. A certainty protects it from the shameful—a certainty of which it is proud holds on to it. But simultaneously, just the same, that impetus, that spasm, that leap is drawn toward an elsewhere as tempting as it is condemned" (1). All of the words we've been working with to locate a methodology of dirt are present in Kristeva's conclusion—but the one word that sticks out most is, of course: *desire.*

Kristeva's dangerous desire for the dirty abject calls to mind the work of feminist and southern studies scholar Patricia Yaeger's *Dirt and Desire: Reconstructing Southern Women's Writing, 1930–1990* (2000). In it, Yaeger argues for a reworking of the unimaginative investment in the celebration of a cohort of domestic southern women writers in the twentieth century, but the crux of her book rests in an exploration of the "blasted remains . . . [the] throwaway" (xi) bodies ignored by southern studies and the connection trash has to ambivalent desires and repulsions to dirt. Yaeger offers a critical distinction between rubbish and waste, the former of which she finds banally visible, able to be viewed "without onus or shame or desire," while the latter has a more complicated relationship to visibility because of its paradoxical connections to "attraction and shame" (87), desire and repulsion.

Douglas's and Kristeva's highlighting of the transgressive nature of dirt creates symbolic potential for Yaeger; there is a pull and fascination—Yaeger calls it desire—for what dirt might offer to community formation.[5] While Yaeger finds dirt a salient means of rhetorically mapping the borders of what constitutes purity/pollution and order/excess, she also finds dirt to be "the stuff of rebellion, the foundation for play, the ground of racial protest and gender unrest" (*Dirt and Desire* 265). It is precisely this notion of dirt as a simultaneous critical line between order and disorder and a heuristic for revolutionary play that informs my book's conception of why dirt works as a marker for southern cultural and literary texts for a half-century. To imagine a "dirty South" is to imagine a series of "dirty communities," defined by their relationship to arbitrary lines policed by white (largely masculine) systems of authority. Yaeger pushes us from the question "How do such authoritative cultural borders create communities through narrative?" to "How do such communities narrate themselves?" Yaeger's assertion that "dirt is a community creator, the main source of exchange in stories," reminds us how (dirty) narratives do real cultural work. Certainly "dirt" has a pejorative power to mark disorder, but it also suggests a power to unite and to enfranchise. Yaeger marks this twofold power of dirt as ontological: it is both "a producer of systems" and also "a disrupter of systems" (264–65).

In our longing for alternatives to systems of power, we locate the second part of Yaeger's title, desire—insomuch as we recognize our investment in the creative potential for ways to disrupt systems by which we find ourselves bound.[6] The creative potential of dirt offers contradictory relationships, of both disavowal and claim, abdication and ownership; the paradoxical possibilities for our relationship to dirt mark, for example, white southerners' valuation of guilt over the region's dark history. I want to explore the ways in which images of a dirty South offer a similar kind of potential, both for the region and for a nation that increasingly looked to eject notions of racial, intellectual, moral, and economic poverty from aspirational national discourses after the 1960s.

Using Yaeger's, Douglas's, and Kristeva's conceptions of dirt, pollution, and the abject, *The Dirty South* examines how sociological, philosophical, and psychoanalytic conceptions of dirtiness help us to understand the American South's relationship to systems of order, classification, and representation.[7] Building on these three scholars' meditations on dirt (and dirt's reflection in both literary and cultural texts), I want to examine iterations of a "dirty South" in our contemporary moment, inarguably a markedly changed national scene since the most recent of these scholars published their monograph just twenty years ago; in addition to the rise of rightist authoritarianism, there is, of course, a profoundly changed media scene (cable, Internet, and so forth), a proliferation and dissemination of images and their exploitation by a new breed of politicians and capitalist snake-oil salesmen (shock jocks, Fox News, Breitbart, Facebook, Twitter, and so on)—all of which offer a fundamentally different national scene than any of these scholars could have predicted. When it comes to stereotypes (white trash, threatening Blackness, dirty Souths), it's their resistance to revision that I find remarkable—zombie tropes, ones you can never kill—as everlasting as the racism that undergirds them. I want to take the South's current temperature, with a story about where the nodal points, the hot spots, are in the "post–civil rights era," but I am also keen to locate some kind of origin story for when the South—long associated with trash, decay, disease, and filth—crystallized in the national imaginary as fundamentally and irredeemably "dirty." *The Dirty South* works through these issues by focusing primarily (though not exclusively) on the nonliterary object, favoring cultural over literary texts, and widening the frame of the three scholars beyond fetishization with the novel or short story.

THE TRAGEDY OF THE JIM BONDS

As I begin my examination of why and how dirt is so powerful in understanding contemporary imaginaries about the American South, I'd like to offer an example of how such a reading proves useful. Circling back to Douglas's danger of hybridity, we find a startling connection to the racism of the American South, where an anxiety over purity creates a fear of threatening Blackness. Race is the ultimate discourse to locate anxieties about a dirty South: for white discourses describe a Blackness that is not utterly worthless, but flawed, needs to be worked on. It is a specific form of racism that does not propose or enact genocide but recognizes creatures it acknowledges as human (however grudgingly) in some respects (to be made Christian, to be acknowledged as sexually of the whites' species, to be clothed—as animals are not—and so forth) but deemed "dirty." The dirty thing is a disturbing hybrid that threatens clear distinctions and categories: its mixed ontology is a dangerous threat. In short, an ontology that distinguished between the clean and the dirty was (is) central to racism, segregation, and to a white supremacy upholding racial inequities. But abjection of the other redounds to some kind of abjection of the self: no racial guilt without racism—and racism operates on a very straightforward binary of dirty/clean: there is nothing hidden about it.

I'd like to claim the American South as an example of "spaces of abjection," which translates Kristeva's concept of the abject into spatialized structures, what Campkin and Cox define as "the interactions between material, corporeal, environmental, psychological and social realism and systems through which the subject or society attempt [*sic*] to impose or maintain a state of purity" (5). Such an examination of the region in context with classification and purity is a tricky enterprise, for, to speak candidly, the American South has a complicated history of representation throughout the twentieth century, especially in matters of hygiene, disease, and pollution, not to mention connections to symbolic concepts of dirt, such as morality, racial purity, primitivity, and poverty.[8] Teasing out each iteration of a dirty South's relationship to matters of practical and symbolic dirt will be the nominal subject of each chapter in this book, but suffice it to say, connections between the region and species of dirtiness manifest not a singular conception but a series of narratives, sometimes with conflicting, if not contradictory, voices. For example: abjection also can describe the South in the national imaginary: part of the morality play that sees the South as dirty, racist, and illiterate—a way for the rest of the nation to experience its rectitude through abjecting the South while also feasting on its voyeuristic glimpses of the southern grotesque. But we must also consider the processes of abjection internal to southern racism.

Thinking through a history of white southerners' dirt, we might start such an untangling of these complicated narratives' voices by examining the South's dizzying connection to a national (even global) anxiety over racial identity and purity. It seems oversimplified to make the claim that "Distinctions between dirt and cleanliness are . . . used in racist constructions of others" (Campkin and Cox 6). In conceiving of a Black other that was, fundamentally, polluted, we can locate both the kind of racist categorization necessary to manufacture narratives of dominance but also the kind of nationalist discourse of the American colonial project. At the basest level, an anxiety over hygiene signals larger fears of contamination. Fear of infection from diseases has long been a basis for American narratives justifying forced subjugations of marginalized peoples as well as a means to justify interference and domination over non-European cultures.[9]

When we disentangle discourses of hygiene from anxieties over "ritual pollution" or disease, "we are left with the old definition of dirt as matter out of place" (Douglas 35). A conception of the unclean in relation to the African Americans of the South, for example, says nothing about actual fears of contamination but rather reveals fundamental anxieties over classification: "Where there is dirt, there is system," Douglas concludes, "Dirt is the by-product of a systemic ordering and classification" (35). Armed with this kind of understanding of dirt, narratives about hygiene clearly articulate a "part of the 'civilizing' mission of empire" (Campkin and Cox 6). Empire retains control over its symbolic power through narratives of cleanliness and hygiene. Moreover, nationalistic discourses, especially aspirational nationalistic discourses, use narratives about hygiene to control systems of classification that order power and authority in ways that conform to their entrenched standards. Dirt can be a way to define what is potentially polluted about a part of a nation or culture, but it is also a way to reassert the fundamental purity of that culture or nation.

As an example of one of the nodal points I mentioned above, consider the fixation on racial purity through the southern anxiety over miscegenation that exploded after the Civil War.[10] The fear of race mixing connects to Douglas's model for pollution and purity. We might consider fears over miscegenation, especially in the South, as a concept of the transgressive that Stallybrass and White find a model of "the grotesque," that is "formed through a process of hybridization or inmixing of binary opposites, particularly of high and low, such that there is a heterodox merging of elements usually perceived as incompatible, and this latter version of the grotesque unsettles any fixed binaryism" (44). The unsettling of a fixed binary reminds us of Douglas's insistence that dirt can be dangerous at precisely the moment when trash breaks down inside the bin, when "their half-identity still clings to them." Even if we use the classic rock of old southern studies and its fixation on the literary, we needn't look to the margins of the southern canon to find how such dangerous anxiety is visible; in fact, we could turn to *the* central southern literary text of the twentieth century to find how anxiety over racial mixing drives the central conflict of the narrative: Faulkner's *Absalom, Absalom!*

Consider, then, Shreve McCannon in his Harvard dorm room blandly predicting the end of Western civilization as the Black branch of the Sutpen tree, in the figure of Jim Bond, slowly infects the South, eventually climbs north and corrupts everything: "I think that in time the Jim Bonds are going to conquer the western hemisphere. Of course it won't be quite in our time and of course as they spread toward the poles they will bleach out again like the rabbits and the birds do, so they won't show up so sharp against the snow. But it will still be Jim Bond; and so in a few thousand years, I who regard you will also have sprung from the loins of African kings" (Faulkner 378). The potential danger of a mixed-race's "half-identity" in the trope of the tragic mulatto was not, of course, an anxiety Faulkner planted in Shreve by happenstance; as Shreve is the character most geographically removed from the South in *Absalom, Absalom!* his voice suggests all white anxieties over racial purity and their inherent threat originate from "down there." It has to be the dirty South where such an impurity begins, for intermixing and hybridity must inevitably come from a space of dangerous abjection. In the world of the abject, such intermixing begins a process that, for Shreve, will literally pollute the world, spreading "toward the poles": anxiety over a dirtying of white identity by its connection to Blackness isn't necessarily a threat to the power dynamics of white authority; for Shreve, it is a threat to processes of classification and systems of order that define (white or Western) civilization itself. It's supremely dangerous, and, because of its danger, eminently compelling—compelling enough that Shreve and Quentin spend countless days hashing out the story despite Shreve's lack of connection to the region or its people.

TELL ABOUT THE SHAME: THE NATION'S DIRTY LAUNDRY

Not until the mid-twentieth century would the literature of shame and guilt gain preeminence. Still another intriguing quality in the self-conscious Southerner arose in the years after Appomattox and is seen to this day. . . . the Southerner, apologist or critic, began to perceive a certain value in his defeat, his poverty even (if he acknowledged it) his guilt and his shame.
  —Fred Hobson, *Tell About the South: The Southern Rage to Explain* (1983)

Shreve's directive to Quentin—"Tell about the South"—reverberates inside the latter's head through Faulkner's novel; to tell about the South, Quentin finds he must tell of his own crippling ambivalences and emotional paradoxes surrounding racial guilt. Southern white guilt over segregation and racism offered a kind of value. While it seems, on the surface, contradictory to claim that dirty things can be valuable—shame and guilt connected to an object or a series of practices feels like an odd kind of value—when shame or guilt predicates another kind of identity, perhaps attractive and compelling, it invites the purely opposite feelings of pride and exceptionalism. In echoing the complications of Shreve's directive, *Tell About the South: The Southern Rage to Explain,* Fred Hobson shows how attraction and shame (even attraction *to* shame) is one of the litanies of paradoxes "to add to the scores already detected in the Southern character" (11). Hobson finds that what unites even paradoxical kinds of white southern expression (throughout his study, he uses the term "apologist" and "critic" of southern culture as his stark binaries) is an ability "to perceive a certain value in . . . guilt and . . . shame." The value Hobson means here also has a bifurcated relationship to visibility. For Hobson, the southern writer or critic found shame "a more social and public and less deeply held commodity than guilt" (344). Shame and guilt were a kind of capital for the southern apologist or critic; shame was a trashy investment one could own publicly, sometimes arbitrarily connected to the territory of the guilty secret and hidden recesses of the interior.

Like Hobson, Yaeger locates a similar value in the "South's economies of racial guilt" (*Dirt and Desire* 63). In fact, she argues, we often prove our commitment to systems of order by subscribing to communal conceptions of practices—ideas, thoughts, and actions—worthy of pride and shame. A communal shame over a shared history—regional, national, and so forth—gets vastly more complicated when the connection is to the American South during a historical moment unconnected (chronologically) to specific, dramatic events. For Hobson, the twentieth-century southern apologist's shame over the "Lost Cause" of the Confederacy became a kind of economy for which he might gain capital—especially during a historical moment defined by antagonism to the values of the plantation South.[11] Because both Hobson and Yaeger are, by and large, talking about white southerners' shame and guilt over racial violence, segregation, and regional history, we can locate an even starker connection between southern dirt and shame.

Yaeger seems to suggest racial guilt works as a dirtied value by recognizing its endurance in the project of southern expression: "Dirt comes into play in southern literature," she offers, "because of its metaphoric power in day-to-day life; it offers a category of alienation that has peculiar powers of abjection" (*Dirt and Desire* 65). She connects the conception of dirt as a matter of order and purity to Molly Ivins's reading of white children born in the South in the decades before the 1960s who were warned not to interact with African Americans for fear of being polluted by their inherent "dirtiness." Borrowing extensively from Mary Douglas along with Peter Stallybrass and Allon White, Yaeger eventually connects anxiety over purity and pollution with not just racial but class anxieties, especially in the way "people in power consolidate their sense of power by obsessing over the distasteful lives of those with less power" (67). Beyond being a trope of southern literary texts, Yaeger finds dirty guilt consistently "evokes the tragic history of dirty in the South, the way that dirt as property, as money-making machine, is mingled not only with desire but with blood" (166).

In *The Dirty South*, I extend Hobson's goal in *Tell About the South*—of analyzing southerners' self-understandings, their ways of telling their own stories—and (even more crucially) how those stories "get told" to national audiences hungry to consume narratives of dirty guilt and shamefulness. In offering contemporary versions of these dirty imaginaries, I hope to reveal how non-white and non-hetero southerners (and, often non-southerners) negotiate their own relationship to, or resignify the image of, a dirty South (perhaps to contest dominant narratives). For much of the South's history after the Civil War, the stories told to the nation—indeed, the world—articulated a crucial truth Douglas doesn't necessarily spend a great deal of her book investigating: To maintain a sense of order (even through narratives), one must be prepared to police the systems of classification with violence. The South's racial violence throughout the twentieth century—often connected to fears of miscegenation—had specific ties to how the South operated in discourses surrounding American nation-building. Many scholars and historians have marked the characterization of the South in the prevailing national story about America as a region saddled with the worst excesses of racial oppression, violence, and injustice.[12] Such emphases on southern abuses are not unfounded; indeed, the region offers countless narratives of horrifying and brutal atrocities committed by white southerners, who ostensibly claimed to protect white virtue, but in actuality, worked on behalf of segregation to entrench borders between whiteness and Blackness. By narrativizing the depravity and brutality of violent enforcements of segregation, national discourses in the mid-century disavowed the South as a site of extremism counter to the definition of fundamental notions of democracy.

The project of abjection in response to a national crisis of racial violence and enforced subjugation of Blackness by white Americans became one of the defining identities of the American South.[13] It was in the South—down there— that problems of racial segregation became violent. The dirty South of racial violence was, in and of itself, a process of classification, an affirmation of the symbolic order of a nation, but the association was not without its own danger, for violence in cities like Chicago and Detroit threatened the cleanness of the narrative. In practice, offering the dirty South as a space of the unclean in a project of nation-building discourses of the civil rights movement worked to enforce what Houston Baker and Dana Nelson termed "a putative and decidedly Manichean geography": "In order for there to exist a good union, there must be a recalcitrant and secessionist 'splitter.' To have a nation of 'good,' liberal, and innocent white Americans, there must be an outland where 'we' know where they live: all the guilty, white yahoos who just don't like people of color" (231, 235). When we examine how the dirty South might have been narrativized in response to an anxiety over national ownership of racism, one can see how categorization and order frame and reproduce borders, communities, and regions whose danger stems from a profound connection to the subject who disavows them. The connection between a dirty southern imaginary and a national abjection of the region is dangerous precisely because racial violence is, of course, a national (if not global) problem whose visibility in other non-southern places threatens the separations of order and classification of American democratic paradigms.

Leigh Ann Duck's *The Nation's Region: Southern Modernism, Segregation and U.S. Nationalism* (2006) chronicles the consequences of a project of nation building that begins by (r)ejecting the South: she argues that "discussions of an anomalous South regularly displace fundamental questions about political affiliation from discourse surrounding the nation-state" (3). Duck shows how this discourse purposefully misrepresents its stake in disavowing the problems the South represents: "While associating the nation with democracy and change and the region with racism and tradition," Duck concludes, "U.S. nationalism repeatedly celebrated the latter paradigm, failing either to address its incongruity with liberalism or to analyze the desires that rendered this restrictive model of collectivity attractive to so many national audiences" (3). Duck focuses on the way in which a discursive divide creates favorable conditions for the entrenchment of national segregation. She explains the rhetoric of segregation as "a necessary concession to a backward culture," as fundamentally masking "the presence of apartheid in other areas of the country" while also refusing "the contemporaneity of the South with the larger nation" (3).

Duck chronicles how southern modernist authors imagined and complicated dialogues surrounding tradition and modernity; her book is useful for working through the dirty South primarily because it plots a history for a national investment in a southern identity "simultaneously courted and disavowed in U.S. nationalism" (4). Here, I find useful connections with Yaeger: a project of claiming any dirty thing, especially a region, invites a freedom for the one initiating the project of dirtying. There is an obvious and overt disavowal in marking something dirty; it is not too much to say that, in the rhetorical act of claiming a thing dirty, one makes an immediate claim about value—of both the thing being described and ejected (dirty) and of the thing doing the describing and ejecting (clean). Following Yaeger's claim about the double-work of dirt as a producer and disrupter of systems and Duck's articulating of the discourse of U.S. nationalism's investment and disavowal of the region, we find ourselves moving toward a more holistic understanding of just what a project of dirtying the South might offer to a larger, national investment.

However, a discourse about southern racism isn't necessarily a disavowal; it can also be part of a reform agenda, a way of acknowledging racism and trying to overcome it, a classic ploy to insist that the liberal do-gooder is a hypocrite, calling out the sins of others that the liberal really doesn't want to overcome.

Certainly one effect of a dirty southern imaginary is a process of abjection that Duck finds useful in "contain[ing] contradictions between divergent models of U.S. citizenship" (19). But beyond masking the paradoxes inherent in an always-problematic singular progressive American voice, the marker of a dirty South also creates a profoundly static model whose elasticity in containing contradictions and describing multiple kinds of shifting identities makes it particularly enduring. Duck notes that such a vision "has been remarkable for its prominence and virulence" (21). I believe that a dirty southern imaginary endures precisely because of its malleability, its ability to persist over a half-century and through multiple iterations and generations. Indeed, if there is a difficulty in exploring how "dirt" and the "South" are related, it is in attempting to locate the myriad relationships between the two: trying to enumerate something so diffuse is a bit like trying to steady a handful of sand—it's likely to sprinkle *everywhere*. I am not so much interested in a holistic accounting of all the ways in which dirt can—however tenuously—describe southern culture, customs, or texts as I am in why the dirty southern imaginary itself remains so resilient.

And perhaps the key to the survival of representations of a dirty South lies in a simpler explanation, one we find in Yaeger's conclusion: The dirty South is a fertile territory for play and experimentation. The very ethos of a dirty South suggests multiple competing images and tropes, each of which might work in harmony with a national project of tradition and exceptionalism. (Duck notes that several imaginaries of southern ontology created by U.S. nationalist discourse present it as "a privileged site of a coherent and binding white culture" for example [20].) Within a framework that allows for simultaneous claims of exceptionalism (of tradition, of profit, of economy) and dirtiness, one can find virtually limitless connective possibilities.

A DIRTY DECADE

While this is a book exploring *what* the dirty South is—a rhetorical marker describing a system of order used in national and global imaginaries to contain and border the South as unclean, trashy, polluted, tainted, immoral—it must first answer the question: *When* is the dirty South? In the following chapters,

I'll investigate cultural and literary texts that explore multiple kinds of dirty southern identities that both enforce and disrupt systems, that at once police boundaries and promote revolutionary play intended to make those boundaries fluid. But I first want to situate the book in its historical moment—a time in which southern stories began to coalesce around a singular conception of the South as a site of waste, the trash heap where abject culture and dirty history combined. Hobson explored the mid-century, a time he argued was the rise of the school of shame and guilt, and Yaeger took her cue from the roughly half-century after the Great Depression. This book picks up an overlap by starting in the middle of Yaeger's decades of focus—1970—but moves far beyond her end point into our contemporary moment. My choice to begin in another decade, one in which an imaginative shift takes place wherein the South moves from being a repository, a trash bin—crucially necessary during the civil rights era as an outland to bolster narratives of American exceptionalism—is because that period is when the South became a potential symbol of dirty, dangerous pride.

In proposing a history of the dirty South, I want to think first about the implications of what such an identity might mean to a broader national, and, indeed, global, perspective on the American South. I focus on representations of the southern half of the United States not simply as a place of ignorance and poverty (as Mencken did with his "Sahara of the Bozart")[14] or the backwards-glancing Neo Confederates of Tate and the other eleven southerners,[15] but instead as a site of spatial abjection, a place of terror, depravity, and immorality, at the crossroads of a paradox involving the fascination with the exotic and the ambivalence of the familiar. This version of South, a painfully horrific region peopled with monsters—violent rednecks and vigilante mobs—makes it is impossible not to conjure images of the civil rights movement of the 1960s, for it was in that decade that the southerner and the region itself became inextricably linked with violent responses to federally enforced integration.

But more concretely, not since the end of the Civil War did the American South come to inhabit a specific place in American consciousness as a true national problem than in the decades during and following the civil rights movement. Frequently, consequences of any single movement's importance are most saliently experienced in the literary and cultural texts that mark the ending of the historical moment they describe. So, while much of the tumult of the brutality of the civil rights era takes place in the thirteen years between the murder of Emmett Till in 1955 and the assassination of Martin Luther King Jr. in 1968 (in Mississippi and Tennessee respectively), one finds a proliferation of dirty southern imaginaries mostly in the cultural texts of the 1970s. A focus on southern injustices was a critical way for the nation to disavow its ownership over violence inflicted on behalf of systemic racism in other parts of the country, but the project of defining a dirty South in the 1970s was, in large part, a reaction to and an attempt to contain the racial animus that was exploding across America during the decades of the 1960s.[16]

The Dirty South examines closely the figure of ultimate terror of the dirty South of the civil rights era: the white rural outlaw or vigilante. Obviously, the poor, white folk as a trope of the region was not born in the 1970s or even the 1960s.[17] The emphasis on the poor white southerner—as opposed to his aristocratic plantation-owner brother—became one of the major symbols of a South that, in the years following Reconstruction, was increasingly besieged by economic woes because of the inheritance of a ruined infrastructure. However, beyond his dogged isolation and poverty, the redneck monster of the 1970s has little in common with the Jeter Lesters of the 1930s. If representations of the post–Civil War South emphasized the intellectual and economic (and, one might argue, aesthetic) poverty of the region from 1865 to 1925, representations of the region in the 1970s shifted into a new kind of symbolism, one in which the American South transformed into a scary, horrific, violent, dirty space in which were grafted all iterations of abjection and impurity.[18] Moreover, that image of the South is still with us today, as zombified and compelling as ever: we witness it in literary and cultural texts, but we also can see how it operates in expressly political ways, too.

ONLY IN THE PANHANDLE: A DIRTY HISTORY

At a campaign event in Panama City Beach, Florida, on 8 May 2019, then-president Donald Trump attempted to rally support for a wall that would stretch across the border shared between the United States and Mexico; the president argued that the wall was necessary because (according to him) there were hordes of immigrants illegally attempting to enter the country. "You have 15,000 [migrants] marching up, and you have hundreds and hundreds of people, and you have two or three border security," he told the crowd.[19] Trump insisted that a wall would prevent immigrants from entering, and he promised that it would protect citizens. For Trump, migrants from Mexico were mostly criminals; he had already passed judgment on them during the press conference where he announced his candidacy—"They're bringing drugs, they're bringing crime, they're rapists," he casually intoned. In Panama City, Trump turned to his supporters and asked what appeared to be a rhetorical question: "How do you stop these people?" From the front of the crowd, someone shouted an answer: "Shoot them!" The audience roared with applause. Trump took a moment, and lightly chuckled. "That's only in the Panhandle you can get away with that statement," he laughed. "Only in the Panhandle."

Less than three months later, on Saturday, 3 August 2019, in El Paso, Texas—a city not in the Florida Panhandle—a gunman entered a crowded Walmart and opened fire on the largely Latino/a shoppers. The individual was a twenty-one-year-old white man who had worked briefly in the tech industry; he posted a manifesto to the website 8chan titled "The Inconvenient Truth" echoing many anti-immigrant fears and anxieties Trump promoted at his rallies. "This attack is a response to the Hispanic invasion of Texas," he writes; "I am simply defending my country." In the essay, he argues murder was the only effective way to scare Mexicans and other Latinos from immigrating to "his country." For him, violence was an "incentive" to help men like him take back America: "Hispanic population is willing to return to their home countries if given the right incentive. An incentive that myself and many other patriotic Americans will provide."[20]

The man believed that his attack would result in political gains—"This will remove the threat of the Hispanic voting bloc"—and also terrify white Americans from intermarrying into what he saw as an impure culture—"I am against race mixing because it destroys genetic diversity and creates identity problems." Perhaps aware that his crimes would, inevitably, be connected to the nativist discourse of Trump, he ended by declaring, "My opinions on automation, immigration, and the rest predate Trump and his campaign for president." A fervent belief in violence as patriotism, an emphasis on violent retribution from those who cross borders and threaten the purity of whiteness, and fears over what might happen if minorities are enfranchised did indeed predate Trump. Though it had been decades, the nation had heard that rhetoric before, had listened to voices of other white vigilante murders who claimed lynching as an act of patriotism designed to protect their communities from outside threats; they had witnessed just how those threats were dismissed by politicians and presidents as an exaggerated species of expression that easily disavowed national ownership over racial prejudices. The El Paso murderer was right: his dirty and infectious ideology predated Trump and existed well beyond the borders of the Florida Panhandle.

Sixty-three years before that manifesto, on 24 January 1956, *Look* magazine published its own bombshell, an article by William Bradford Huie titled "The Shocking Story of Approved Killing in Mississippi," an exposé of the murder of Emmett Till, an African American teenager from Chicago visiting family in Money, Mississippi, in August of 1955.[21] The boy's murder at the hands of local white men was one of the first publicized atrocities signaling a new species of violent retribution targeted at outsiders from the region who dared to violate heavily bordered and segregated rules governing the Jim Crow South; the significant attention the case received in the American press exposed both Mississippi and the South as a land of dangerous, vicious racial violence. It was not just Till's murder at the hands of southern white men that captivated the nation, it was the graphic details: the sadistic and brutal attack by two local white men, Roy Bryant and J. W. Milam, was horrific. They abducted, beat, disfigured, shot, and finally dumped the young boy in the nearby Tallahatchie River.

Equally repugnant to readers outside the South was the pettiness of the boy's supposed "crime": according to the testimony of Carolyn Bryant—though she later recanted much of her accusations—Till's only transgression was that he had attempted (humorously) to flirt with her. When the boy's mangled body was delivered back to his mother in Chicago, she insisted that reporters be present at an open-casket funeral. Images of Till's disfigured and mutilated corpse made its way to the front pages of newspapers and magazines; readers were horrified by what they saw. Mamie Till Bradley's decision to publicize her son's open-casket funeral did more than just show the world her son's disfigured corpse; it "focused attention not only on U.S. racism and the barbarism of lynching but also on the limitations and vulnerabilities of American democracy" (White, Bay, and Martin 637).

Though the murderers were clearly guilty, they were acquitted of their crimes at trial in September of 1955; later that year, a grand jury failed to indict them even for kidnapping the boy. In the pages of the 24 January 1956, issue of *Look,* Milam and Bryant—who could not be tried again for the same crime, and thus were free to tell their story with impunity—offered their own manifesto. According to the men, their initial intention was just to terrify Till; like the El Paso gunman, they thought they might "scare some sense into him." They brought him to what Milam called "the scariest place in the Delta," but Till was not frightened. Milam was at a loss: "We were never able to scare him. They had just filled him so full of that poison that he was hopeless." The more Till talked back to the men—including, according to the confessions, assertions by the boy that he had slept with many white women—the more Milam found himself determined to murder him, not simply as a punishment for his "crime" of flirting with Carolyn Bryant but as a message to the nation that African American enfranchisement in the South would not be tolerated. Milam saw a greater existential threat than just one boy who dared to violate southern customs; he saw in Emmett Till a harbinger of a potentially explosive movement, one that threatened to disrupt an increasingly delicate balance that held Black southerners in check:

> I never hurt a n-- in my life. I like n--s—in their place—I know how to work 'em. But I just decided it was time a few people got put on notice. As long as I live and can do anything about it, n--s are gonna stay in their place. N--s ain't gonna vote where I live. If they did, they'd control the government. They ain't gonna go to school with my kids. And when a n-- gets close to mentioning sex with a white woman, he's tired o' livin'. I'm likely to kill him. . . . I stood there in that shed and listened to that n-- throw that poison at me, and I just made up my mind. "Chicago boy," I said, "I'm tired of 'em sending your kind down here to stir up trouble. Goddam you, I'm going to make an example of you—just so everybody can know how me and my folks stand.

Like the murderer from El Paso in 2019, J. W. Milam in 1956 saw violence as his fundamental duty to protect his way of life from an external threat: the savage beating and murder of Till was meant to intimidate outsiders to stay away from the South altogether; the threat of violence would remain, in the words of the El Paso gunman, "an incentive" to other agitators.

The exoneration of Milam and Bryant could mean only two things to the editors of *Look:* "The majority—by no means all, but the majority—of the white people in Mississippi 1) either approve Big Milam's action or else 2) they don't disapprove enough to risk giving their 'enemies' the satisfaction of a conviction." The "enemies" of the white people in Mississippi were progressive integrationists pushing to enfranchise African Americans throughout the nation, and white Mississippians' tacit approval of acts of violent repercussions for these activists represented nothing less than a profound and enduring reaction to the threat of a progressive agenda. White southerners, "by no means all, but the majority," as the editors of *Look* claimed, believed in the power of fear to terrify those outside the region—to "scare some sense" into them, to borrow Milam's words, or, failing that, "to make an example of" those who refused to be cowed by their tactics. Till's murder, funeral, as well as his murderers' acquittal and magazine confession actually had the opposite effect from what Milam anticipated: rather than arresting the momentum of enfranchisement for African Americans, it emboldened activists and civil rights leaders, who were quick to point to Emmett Till's murder as an example of why systemic change needed to take place throughout the region. Just a few months after a grand jury refused to indict Milam and Bryant, the Montgomery Bus Boycott began, and northern activists began to turn their attention to desegregating mass transit throughout the American South.

Five years after the *Look* article, on the afternoon of 14 May 1961—Mother's Day—a bus consisting of "Freedom Riders," civil rights activists and protestors traveling South from Washington, DC, to promote the desegregation of bus travel in the southern states, arrived in Anniston, Alabama, not far from the city of Birmingham. The Freedom Ride of 1961 was an activist attempt to test southern enforcement of *Boynton v. Virginia,* a Supreme Court case that had declared segregated interstate travel unconstitutional. Though the activists had experienced some pushback during the first leg of their trip (most notably in South Carolina), in Alabama the group was attacked three times: first at the Anniston bus station, where they were met by a prominent leader of the Ku Klux Klan, William Chapel, who organized a mob of over fifty men armed with makeshift weapons: rocks, pipes, baseball bats, knives, and chains. After enduring the initial attack by remaining inside their bus, the activists were escorted by state police (and then quickly abandoned) to a spot just outside the outskirts of town. This time, another, more violent, crowd assembled and again attacked the vehicle; one of the men in the mob threw a firebomb through the bus's window while another held the door closed to prevent escape. When the mob retreated over fears that the fuel tank might explode, the Freedom Riders finally pushed through the bus door and fled outside, where they were viciously beaten.

Like the murder of Till, the attacks on Mother's Day of 1961 reverberated across America; stories of mob violence in the Deep South captivated the public. In his book—aimed at young readers with no context for the 1960s and 1970s—Larry Dane Brimner makes it clear that, at the time of the attacks, the nation was surprised by the savage news coming out of Alabama: "No one outside the South can understand the violence. . . . People worldwide were shocked and dismayed" (77). But what happened in Anniston was only one of countless acts of violence committed by white southerners on nonviolent protesters throughout the 1960s; groups of men formed quickly and effectively under such organizations as the Ku Klux Klan and the White Citizens' Councils to combat what they saw as the infiltration of agitating outsiders who meant to threaten entrenched power dynamics, customs, and traditions venerated throughout the South, including Jim Crow laws that worked to disenfranchise and segregate African Americans. Though violent clashes with activists and protesters were nominally illegal, law enforcement agencies throughout the region did little to prosecute mobs attacking the interracial group of Freedom Riders; indeed, Alabama police officers arrested some of the victims of the Anniston attack for disturbing the peace, and local law enforcement refused medical help for them, many of whom lay bloody and beaten on the side of the road. It took intervention by the Reverend Frederick Lee Shuttlesworth to gather the wounded and bring them to a nearby hospital.[22]

The Freedom Riders were attacked less than a week later in Montgomery; finally, federal officials intervened to order a police escort for the final leg of their trip. But safe passage had little meaning for the riders after their experience in Alabama: white southern mobs were galvanized; furious at the uninvited presence of the protestors, the men of these mobs were determined to send a message both to the activists and to the larger nation: they were angered by a quickly evolving social dynamic, enraged that outsiders were coming to their towns to challenge their traditions, and prepared to exercise their vengeance through violent acts of aggression virtually impervious to persecution by local or state police. The men of these mobs were figures to be feared; their very presence at protests was enough to dissuade other activists outside the region to not come south. In his memoir, comedian and actor Robert Guillaume admits that, despite his fervent desire to be politically active, he could not bring himself to travel to any southern state: "I didn't go [to Mississippi]," he writes, "because I was afraid of being killed. . . . [My] fear was that some redneck would strangle me" (Ritz and Guillaume 80). Though Guillaume felt a sense of shame not participating in a movement he held dear, he recognized the reality of the situation: "I wanted to survive" (81). Guillaume's fears were well founded: many outside protestors did not make it back home.

Three years after the Anniston attack, James Chaney, Andrew Goodman, and Michael Schwerner, members of the Congress of Racial Equality (CORE), which had been instrumental in registering Black voters in Mississippi, were abducted by men of the local chapter of the Ku Klux Klan, as well as several members of the nearby Neshoba County and Philadelphia, Mississippi, police departments. The three activists were shot and buried in a nearby swampy

Freedom Riders on the outskirts of Anniston, Alabama, 14 May 1961.

area; their bodies were not discovered until months later. Local law enforcement refused to investigate the case; the federal government was forced to intervene. It took three years for any indictments to come down, but when they did, eighteen individuals received light sentences for their involvement in the murder and coverup. If the attacks on Till in 1955 and the freedom riders in 1961 were intended to sound a warning to outsider agitators who planned on protesting in the South, by 1964 the murders of the three men in Mississippi and the gruesome discovery of their remains were confirmation that the consequences of coming to the South could be lethal. The message to activists, protestors, and any individual not from the region who came to the southern states to agitate for social change or challenge segregation was clear: Enter the borders of the South at your own risk; you might not make it out alive.

Vigilante attacks from 1955 to 1964 represented a sustained tactic of violent southern intimidation against outsiders; the violence would come to define the region during the civil rights era. Even as the nation began its nascent movements to enfranchise African Americans, those efforts were met in the South with brutality from white mobs desperate to fight back against a changing social landscape. After newspapers and television reported the multiple attacks on freedom riders and activists in the first years of the 1960s, for the rest of the decade, the American South came to represent nothing less than a savage land of vigilante justice intended to threaten, intimidate, and terrify white and Black activists, progressives, and liberals throughout the nation. Violence became a defining feature of the South as a site of terror: any town in which brutal attacks occurred, no matter how big or small, came to represent the region. Though many of the sites of violence in the 1960s took place near major cities, stories filtering out of the region described towns that most of the nation did not know: Anniston, Greensboro, Montgomery, Money, Selma.[23] These southern cities were by no means backwoods swamp towns or under-populated country hamlets, but, to an American public that had little previous knowledge of them, they became synonymous with a vast expanse of rural nothing below the Mason-Dixon Line.

The creatures who inhabited the darkly foreboding terrain of the rural South gradually became the stuff of the nation's nightmares. Though individuals' faces were often hidden behind masks, photos and news reports from the decade proved these men were largely working-class southerners. Some, of course, were firmly middle-class, even affluent, but the central terrifying figure, the monster of the American civil rights story, emerged as the poor, rural white southerner, a figure who was desperately isolated, locked away from history and progress, inhabiting a code and a community that was incompatible with the progressive sweep of the decade; he was determined to police the borders of his community with a brutality and a fierceness that was above (and, in many instances, indistinguishable from) the rule of law.[24]

They were a mob even as an individual—bestial, unforgiving, anonymous. Their identities may have been hidden safely behind streaking white gowns or coned hats that swept across the southern landscape, but, as Erskine Caldwell suggested in the title of his book thirty years before the freedom rides, the nation had "Seen Their Faces": they were the undershirted boys spitting on Black protestors sitting-in at lunch counters in Greensboro, North Carolina; they were a mask of rage, frozen in mid-scream, that flanked Ruby Nell Bridges Hall and Autherine Lucy as they walked to their first day of school; they were the half-tucked greasers holding down James Zwerg while others kicked and pummeled his unconscious body.[25] They were, in short, violent monsters whose viciousness could barely be contained in the frame of the photo in which they appeared, conjured, it would seem, by the darkest of America's dirty nightmares.

They screamed on the cover of every newspaper and haunted the flickering screens of televisions.[26] Against the progressive agenda the nation was beginning to embrace—school integration, political enfranchisement for poor and African Americans, the protection of voting rights for all men and women, and the fight for economic equality—the poor, white southerner stood as a bold and reactionary roadblock, a golem breathed to life out of the fatal marriage of recalcitrance and fury; little matter if the southerner was George Wallace or Byron De La Beckwith: their exact name and economic circumstances didn't matter. To an American public consuming stories of their anger and violence in magazines, newspapers, and even on the national news, they were all the same: monstrous hillbillies.[27]

The hillbilly outlaw offered a fitting image on which much of the nation's anxiety remained fixated; the figure was a symbol of a clinging desire to remain set—if not paralyzed—in a contested tradition and troubled history; defined against the figure of progressive white liberals and civil rights allies throughout the nation, the southern hillbilly remained determined by, even proud of, southern heritage and community. However, the hillbilly's rough and relentless attacks to perceived threats against tradition or home offered the most terrifying and lasting anxiety of all. By situating any perceived threat to the progressive ideals of democracy in the 1960s as an economic, rural, intellectual, and racial problem endemic to only one region of America, it is easy to understand how the hillbilly haunted national consciousness for more than half a century. The fact that the hillbilly stereotype was a figure of little to no empathy and one who possessed a comic disregard for intelligence of any kind only made its terror more insidious.

The violent murders, vicious beatings, furious counterprotests, and extensive, corrupt coverup of vigilante crimes of the early 1960s shook the foundations of American exceptionalism.[28] The South was firmly on the radar of the American public as a space where vengeful mob law[29] and angry hillbilly justice meant that even those who stood for the greatest of what America could be were liable to be brutally murdered by a defiant southern culture determined to uphold its power.[30] Moreover, the kind of vigilantism that the hillbilly practiced operated in concert with local police. State and local law enforcement either refused to prosecute white southerners who committed criminal acts against activists or used systematic and entrenched power dynamics to ensure that the criminals who committed violent acts never faced punishment. Jury trials throughout the South—such as Bryant and Milam's in Till's murder—

nearly always exonerated white defendants. The horror of the hillbilly vigilante's lawlessness was not solely about race: that the hillbilly was white was only one modality of his potential to terrorize; of equal importance was his poverty.[31] By identifying white-trash southern poor first through a connection to whiteness, the figure's poverty became obscured by white supremacists and white nationalists eager to fight back against progressive views of white liberals and African American protestors.[32] Similarly, the emphasis on the hillbilly outlaw's poverty was central to the stereotype; to read all southern white men as some form of hillbilly meant to engage uncomplicatedly with a heuristic of poverty: whether that poverty was economic, emotional, or intellectual mattered less than regional connotations.[33]

Almost sixty years after the attack in Anniston, and not too far away in my current home of Tuscaloosa, Alabama, I find myself coming back to the literary and cultural consequences of bifurcating America's discursive commitment to racial progress and civil rights in the figure of the heroic (usually white, male, and nonviolent) activist with the villainy of the (always white, male, and violent) southern backwoods hillbilly.[34] I am, of course, bothered by the erasure of Black voices and agency in the story of American civil rights and the proliferation of whiteness on both sides. But I am also troubled by how the hillbilly outlaw functioned for America during the decade of the 1960s; I am specifically disturbed by the dirty value a hillbilly vigilante imaginary offered to the nation, both as a figure of ejection, as a national refusal of ownership of racial violence, but also, in the words of cultural historian Anthony Harkins, a marker "of an uncorrupted culture and value system who challenged modern urbanity and pointed out the spiritual and ethical costs of materialistic 'progress'" (174). This ambivalent value suggests that the hillbilly outlaw's importance is inextricably tied to his dirty identity—at once a figure of monstrosity and aggrieved racial animus but also of a gradually fading cultural ideal whose belief structures and systems of order remain resonant with white Americans, well into the twenty-first century.

Thinking about the draw of the hillbilly outlaw pushes me back to Patricia Yaeger, especially her essay on "dirty ecology." In it, she recalls how compelling trash can be when "debris and light vie for screen time." Yaeger finds herself drawn not to either isolated trope but their juxtaposition in the symbol of "luminous trash," "glowing debris, garbage that lights up." In the sudden brightness of what was meant to be expelled, that has been darkened by its connection to dirt, Yaeger locates a shifting value. The trash she examines "investigates a culture of racial neglect, [and] creates a zone of history-making for Katrina's disposable bodies," but Yaeger suggests there is more cultural work that "luminous trash" might do, including providing "a steady critique of white capital" or interrogating the "Southland's (and our nation's) commitment to toxic inequality."

A conception of luminous trash also critically connects to another major cultural obsession in the 1970s: the popularization and corporatization of country music as well as its response in the genre of "Outlaw Country" in which artists sought to reframe the focus of country music into a more gritty and dirty aesthetic. By celebrating the displaced and marginal figures of country music, outlaw country sought to be both transformative and transportive as it suggested other sites and spaces for authenticity in a genre bothered by questions of whiteness and class. That conception of luminous trash to critique capital and the toxic (economic and ecological) inequalities of the nation likewise continue into the contemporary moment in a genre of music from which I take the name of this study: the dirty South. In order to understand what value an outlaw sensibility might have offered what was—and arguably still is—the whitest genre of music, I'd like to begin *The Dirty South* by examining the rise of hillbilly outlaw country throughout the 1970s.

CHAPTER 1

THE SOUTH'S GOT SOMETHING TO PLAY

Of Glitter and Gangsters

Lord it's the same old tune, fiddle and guitar
Where do we take it from here?
Rhinestone suits and new shiny cars
It's been the same way for years
We need a change.
>   —"Are You Sure Hank Done It This Way?" Waylon Jennings, 1975

The South got something to say.
>   —André 3000, acceptance speech for "Best New Rap Group," 1995 Source Awards

Let's go to Luckenbach, Texas
Willie and Waylon and the boys
This successful life we're livin' got us feudin'
Like the Hatfield and McCoys.
>   —"Luckenbach Texas," Bobby Emmons / Chips Moman, 1977

Well it's the M-I crooked letter coming around the South
Rolling straight Hammers and Vogues in that old Southern slouch . . .
Deep, the slang is in effect because it's Georgia . . .
Like collard greens and Hoecakes, I got soul
That's something that you ain't got.
>   —"Southernplayalisticadillacmuzik," OutKast, 1994

NASHVILLE, NUDIE, NIXON

In the summer of 1969, the television broadcasting company CBS decided to replace its wildly successful but increasingly controversial comedy variety show *The Smothers Brothers Comedy Hour* with a much more conventional—albeit hokey—program based around the burgeoning popularity of country music.[1] Created by Frank Peppiatt and John Aylesworth—writers that had worked on television shows like Perry Como's *Kraft Music*

Hall, *The Judy Garland Show*, *Frank Sinatra: A Man and his Music*, *The ABC Comedy Hour*, and *The Julie Andrews Hour*—*Hee Haw* premiered on 15 June. The program paired comedic scripted sketches with live performances by some of the most iconic superstars of country music; Peppiatt and Aylesworth imagined the show "as a country-flavored version of *Rowan & Martin's Laugh-In*" (Braxton). However, by the end of the week of 15 June, *Hee Haw* had already "matched 'Laugh-In' at the top of the ratings chart . . . and its popularity continued for the remainder of the summer. It was added to the CBS prime time schedule in December" (Braxton). Though the show remained successful during its next two seasons, CBS pulled it from its prime-time lineup in the summer of 1971 as "part of its purge of shows such as 'The Beverly Hillbillies,' 'Mayberry R.F.D.' and other rural-oriented programs that the network felt were not hip enough to attract a desired younger viewership" (Braxton).[2]

The success of *Hee Haw* left no question, however, that the television show could work at any time slot or on any network. Peppiatt and Aylesworth inked a lucrative syndication deal for their variety show. A few months later, on 18 September 1971, the third season of the show premiered with a brand-new episode in what would become the beginning of its first-run syndication. Just as popular—if not more so—*Hee Haw* continued to produce original content for over twenty years, one of the longest-running shows in the history of television syndication.[3] *Hee Haw*'s popularity did not just stem from its aping of the gags from "Laugh-In" or borrowing the structure of other popular variety shows of the time: its success mostly came from a connection to the growing appeal of the genre of country music and the traditions associated with it. Many of the music numbers that appeared between sketches in the show harkened back to regional "barn dances" and folk humor whose traditions dated back far before the 1970s.

The show also blended two different types of musical traditions from two different locations on a continuum that defined the genre: country and western music.[4] The connections between the world of western and country music were obvious in the casting of the hosts of the show: Buck Owens and Roy Clark shared hosting duties for a good portion of the television program's run, and their conflicting backgrounds invited audiences and enthusiasts of both genres of music to come together.

Associated with a new kind of country sound—dubbed "Bakersfield" after his adopted hometown in California—Buck Owens's popularity was already firmly established by 1971.[5] Known for *Billboard* hits such as "Act Naturally,"

A still from the first-run syndicated episode (in the third official season) of *Hee Haw* on 18 September 1971. Hosts Buck Owens, *left,* and Roy Clark, *right,* introduced humorous and corny comedy sketches interspersed with performances by major performers in the world of Nashville country music.

"Tiger by the Tail," and "Tall Dark Stranger," Owens's celebrity paired well with the comparatively little-known multi-instrumentalist Roy Clark. Their chemistry proved immediately compelling, and their humor felt unforced and intuitive. They were able to play off one another, both vocally and musically: as part of a recurring segment of the show, Owens and Clark would perform "fragments of a hoedown tune," then would stop and seamlessly engage in scripted comedic dialogue before continuing with their song. The segment would become one of the defining motifs of the popular variety show.

Hee Haw's immense popularity hinged on its presentation of country music as a soundtrack to backwoods silliness. The regressive nature of the show was startling; while *Hee Haw* played up the trope of the dumb hillbilly or the dim-witted redneck picking and grinning on a banjo, the show itself was masterfully shot and edited. Producers of *Hee Haw* decided to go against conventional wisdom that prioritized filming a variety show in front of a live audience; instead, the producers decided to shoot the series in a studio, which "allowed for more nuanced approaches to television lighting than a stage show could achieve" (Laird, "Country Music" 255). In fact, the entire production of the show was "on television's vanguard," as it presented a nonstop series of wholesome gags and sketches that were only interrupted by songs and commercials, "a quality some television commentators now characterize as 'post-modern.'" Whatever the aesthetic, *Hee Haw* was far from a dirty show; in fact, its appeal was its squeaky-clean family-friendly humor.

Hee Haw eschewed linear progression and interconnected sectioning that were hallmarks of other variety shows; the show favored purposeful lack of connection between the various pieces that constituted the main action of the program: indeed, "fragmentation was both its aesthetic and its practical reality" (Laird, "Country Music" 255). Instead of focusing on complicated premises or long, drawn-out scenes, the writers offered mostly one-liners and quick sketches that relied on sight gags. The combination of the show's frenetic pace coupled with a manufactured down-home sincerity made for a popular phenomenon that charmed American audiences with its purity and wholesomeness. The editing of the show also attempted to promote a kind of unrehearsed sincerity: "When performers flubbed the lines on the cue cards, those mistakes became 'bloopers' that wove their way into the collage of any given episode." The connection made between audience and performer was profound for the newly evolving medium of television, and the show adapted to a changing country aesthetic, even going so far as replacing the farmland haybales of their set for "city street and shopping mall sets" in 1992 in a bid to appeal "to both the urban and suburban milieus" (Jeremy Hill 113).

The enduring success of *Hee Haw* also stemmed from its translation of the hugely popular genre of "radio barn dance" into a new decade and a new medium, television. Most effectively exemplified by the popularity of *The Grand Ole Opry,* the radio barn dance had a long history. *The Opry* began running as *The WSM Barn Dance* on 28 November 1925; a weekly series presenting live recordings of country, western, swing, and rockabilly, the program was wildly successful, moving from a regional radio station to a national network, NBC. *The Grand Ole Opry* was one of the catalysts for the popularization of country music, and it launched many of the stars of the genre from the 1930s through the 1960s.[6] The creators and producers of *Hee Haw* saw their show as an extension of the *Opry*'s mission of promoting country music stars; only the show was able to rely on techniques and resources vastly superior to radio. Laird notes that much of *Hee Haw's* popularity can be attributed to the production team's long-term vision of translating the *Opry*'s success:

> *Hee Haw* got what a lot of producers missed in the medium's earliest days when television sprang forth from its radio parent. In many ways, the show

maintained the feel of the radio barn dance but executed it with a high degree
of media savvy. It bucked against the bid for glamour or, at any rate, middle-
class respectability. . . . But it also moved quickly and communicated a sense of
spontaneity, fun, and sincerity that resonated with millions of viewers. It fully
embraced its television potential . . . yet structurally, it echoed the radio barn
dances with a balance of music and humor—both from big name guests and
regular cast members—executed to an updated tempo. (, "Country Music" 256)

Hee Haw's aesthetic may have been "a throwback of country music from a by-
gone era [of] radio barn dances of the 1940s . . . and a heavy emphasis on rube
comedy and hayseed image" (Cusic, *Discovering* 113), but the "'country' music
performed on the show was considerably more removed from its rural roots
than was the 'country' humor" (Malone 199).

The disconnect between the musical numbers and the slapstick hayseed
comedy routines might have felt inconsequential to American audiences who
had little familiarity with the origins of country music, but "many of the show's
critics, particularly those from the ranks of country music, learned to toler-
ate the hillbilly clichés" and fooled themselves into believing the program
was "a self-parody, or a burlesque of outsider's conceptions of rural society"
(Malone 199). One critic found the "commercial success" of *Hee Haw* "strange.
It presented an image of country music, and of rural life, that most musicians
had been resisting for years: that of the hayseed buffoon. Nevertheless, the
backwoodsy-silly skits were produced and merchandized through the most so-
phisticated and urbane of techniques" (273). For many viewers, the "grotesque
parody" (273) of hillbillies proved more compelling than any connection to music, and "suggested that the humor of country music was more traditional than
its music" (274). Moreover, *Hee Haw* did not concern itself with manufacturing
any kind of credibility or gritty authenticity for the region or music it sought
to present to American audiences. Indeed, much of the show's clean humor
invites audiences to not take the characters—and, by extension, the music of
the performers—too seriously. As a result, the show produced a complicated,
conflicting response from many of those "country music industry performers
[that] strove to achieve [respectability] during the same era" (Laird, "Country
Music" 256) even as they were forced to perform on a cartoon variety show that
disparaged their aesthetic.

The initial backlash against *Hee Haw*'s popularity came from within the
country music scene. Country singers and songwriters began to question the

integrity of a figure like Buck Owens and his gradual de-evolution from serious musician to television comic. For many, the transition was a "cynical decision" that transformed someone the country music world admired into "a hillbilly clown" (Dawidoff 232). It did not help that the show's popularity made Owens much wealthier than he ever was as a musician, leading him to brag that he'd tape the program in week-long sessions, and, at the end, "leave and they'd hand me $200,000" (qtd. in Ching 102). Though the program attempted to blend stereotypical redneck humor with serious country music stars—some well-established in the Nashville scene during the radio days—the Technicolor buffoonery of the comedy sequences embarrassed musicians who recognized *Hee Haw* as one of the few televised venues that welcomed them. Major country singers from the decade—Merle Haggard, George Jones, Loretta Lynn, and Conway Twitty—showed up to sing their latest songs and gamely tried to muddle through the stereotypical hillbilly comedy, but they largely acted with disdain for the antiseptic aesthetic of the show. Famously, "Merle Haggard refused to perform against bales of hay" (Laird, "Country Music" 255) and forced the producers to create a new set for him. *Hee Haw*'s complicated popularity makes it clear that, while the show did more to help promote country music than any other television show of its kind, it had to leverage a large chunk of country music's integrity to do so. Consequently, the legacy of the show as one of the longest-running syndicated programs in the country also must contend with its legacy of shame, for the show "has received the most criticism for stigmatizing country music with stereotypes it has yet to shake" (Cusic, *Discovering* 113).[7]

At the same time that *Hee Haw* was attempting to reconcile increasing popularity with American viewers and savage criticism from old-school country acts, country music was itself grappling with something of an existential crisis. As country songwriters sought more airtime on radio stations, they began to experiment with techniques and aesthetics borrowed from other popular music of the time, especially rock 'n' roll and rhythm and blues. For much of the 1920s through the 1950s, country music had emphasized humility, sincerity, and a dirty aesthetic of poverty that became synonymous with its earliest stars, such as Jimmie Rodgers, Hank Williams, and Bill and Charlie Monroe.[8] And yet, by the 1960s, American popular music had begun to be infiltrated by new forms and personalities threatening country's dominance on the radio. Moreover, as radio gave way to new media such as film and television, the importance of *seeing* musicians and performers became essential to their success.

Music was no longer just about audial experience, but visual, and the rock 'n' roll and R&B stars of the late 1950s and 1960s begged to be viewed: their musical acts were sometimes second to their fashion, and they adopted personalities that were unique, brash, outlandish, and ostentatious. It had become clear to most popular musicians and singers by mid-century that, in order to become a celebrity in the world of television, one had to cultivate a popular persona that was singular and unforgettable.[9] If country music stars wanted to break through and make a name for themselves in these quickly evolving visual media, they could no longer rely on simple folksy music to be taken seriously: they needed to be conscious of the importance of image.

Though many country music stars of the late 1950s into the late 1960s resisted the move from radio to television, those who embraced the transition found that there was more money and fame to be had in the world of the small screen than they could have imagined. They also realized that, by combining the aesthetic of popular rock 'n' roll with traditional music, they could gain a much wider audience than shows like the *Opry* offered. At first, however, "the country industry didn't know whether to welcome the first wave of rockers as kindred spirits or run them out of town at gunpoint" (Doggett 238). Crossover rockabilly singers like Carl Perkins began being "thrown together on package tours and radio barn dances," but Perkins recognized early that, even though he shared a similar background to the country stars he performed alongside, he was viewed as a threat: "They knew I was a country boy just like them," he recalls, "I'd picked cotton, and I'd been raised on Hank Williams and the *Grand Ole Opry* just like they were. But when rock n' roll started to eat into their sales, then the mood seemed to change" (Doggett 238).

As an example of a country star who initially resisted the influence of rock 'n' roll in the late 1950s, Porter Wagoner founded the early part of his career "on fidelity to 'real' country" (Doggett 239). A singer who emphasized the real-world difficulties growing up poor and hungry in Missouri—his music was dubbed "hard country" by critics—Wagoner had minor hits with RCA Studios during the 1950s, such as his "A Satisfied Mind."[10] However, Wagoner recognized that "country music wasn't making it. . . . All we could work was the little clubs, the skull orchards, the dives. . . . RCA was having problems selling country records, and they wanted everybody to do more rock. Me included. . . . I told [them] I couldn't, that it didn't suit my personality" (Doggett 238). By the time Elvis Presley found success with his blend of rock 'n' roll, rockabilly, country, and gospel,[11] Wagoner was well on his way to bowing out of music altogether: "I was scared there would be a blast from another area of rock 'n' roll," he confesses, "Country music was dead, and rock was gigantic" (Doggett 240). Though Wagoner could not meld his dirty music style to compete with the brashness of rock 'n' roll, he did find that he could shape his image in a way that would make him unique.

Wagoner's country music may have been on its way out, but his "western" aesthetic was still "fixed in the public mind" (Malone 145). Based on wholesome "singing cowboy" types like Gene Autry and the "Hollywood exploitation" of that trope, "most hillbilly singers became fascinated with the western image and eventually came to believe their own symbols."[12] These singers would often arrive at performances dressed as if they had just come from a rodeo, with boots, spurs, and ten-gallon hats. But, as the decades went by, "the costuming became more elaborate and gaudier, with the brightly colored, bespangled and sequined uniforms" (Malone 145) dominating the scene. One of the main figures to be associated with these western costumes was Nudie Cohen, an ex-boxer from Brooklyn who moved to California in the late 1920s.[13] Cohen's aesthetic was wholesome enough for the big screen—he made a name for himself as a costume designer for the film company Warner Brothers—but also dirty: before he began his movie work, he "had also had some experience as a brassiere and G-string manufacturer for the strip-tease industry" in Manhattan (203). His outfits were sought after by some of the earliest western singers, who longed to mirror the costumed cowboys of their childhood. Though his early outfits were somewhat restrained, they "became progressively more outlandish with their bright colors, ornate decorations and fringe." By the middle of the 1960s, "success for country musicians became almost defined by the number of Nudie suits in their wardrobe" (203).

Perhaps the most famous example of a Nudie suit celebrity, Porter Wagoner found his enduring popularity profoundly connected to an ever-evolving outlandish aesthetic. His image was prominently advertised on his own television program, *The Porter Wagoner Show,* an early forerunner to the success of *Hee Haw* in the 1970s.[14] Beginning about a decade before *Hee Haw* in 1960, the thirty-minute show "was a showcase for . . . talented performers" (Malone 271), such as Norma Jean Beasler, Speck Rhodes, Mack Magaha, Buck Trent, and, of course, a young Dolly Parton. But the star of the show was Wagoner, and even though his television program relied on singers and musicians for entertainment, the enduring popularity of the show came largely from the popular fascination with Wagoner's bizarre aesthetic: "a striking figure . . . in one of the many brightly colored, rhinestone-studded cowboy suits which Nudie Cohen had begun providing for him in 1953" (271). Unlike most of the country music stars of the 1960s—many of whom, like Johnny Cash, also had their own television program—who were "adopting business suits or modish attire," Wagoner instead relied heavily on his ostentatious, rhinestone-freckled cowboy costuming to promote his music and his show. His exotic appearance brought in a new audience compelled less by the songs he sang or his instrumental prowess but by "the sequined wagon wheels sewn on [his] brightly colored western suits, and his hair which is of a color and style far different than that of their peers" (Jimmie Rogers 235). Wagoner had manufactured and perfected an image of gaudy, nonthreatening, and sequined cowboy that captivated American audiences.

Similarly, Wagoner's decision to pivot from Norma Jean to Dolly Parton as his primary duet partner in 1967 further manifests his emphasis on style over substance. Together, the two would perform on the show, singing songs and riffing off each other in comedic numbers. Sometimes the songs and the comedy would mix, but during the run of *The Porter Wagoner Show,* performers' images always took center stage. Parton was every bit as outlandish in her clothing as Wagoner. If Wagoner was a cartoon western cowboy in sequins and rhinestones, Parton was "a living country Barbie Doll" (Edwards 189). Indeed, her "enactment of excessive femininity is exaggerated to the point of parody and camp" throughout her seven-year run on the program, and she plays throughout the show with the antithesis of "the chaste mountain girl and the town tramp" (Edwards 194). Together, Wagoner and Parton became the President and First Lady of television country music for the establishment of an increasingly profitable time for producers and recording labels during the late 1960s and into the 1970s, and their partnership was as wholesome and no-threatening as the squeaky-clean sitcoms of the 1950s. But it was their marrying of a redneck/rural aesthetic with a rock 'n' roll couture-trashiness that became their enduring legacy. As Parton would famously quip about her appearance: "it takes a lot of money to look this cheap"[15] (qtd. in Edwards, "Backwoods" 189).

An emphasis on clean style over dirty sincerity was also at the heart of the formation of the so-called Nashville Sound of the late 1950s and 1960s when producers and labels began to experiment with techniques and instruments that had been far more common in popular music and crooner ballads.[16] More and more producers found that there was money to be made in the fusion of a country aesthetic with arrangements from wholesome popular music. Small changes began to appear on records in the mid-1950s: "the fiddle and steel guitar seemed on the way to banishment" in favor of "country pop" (Malone 256). Attracted by the "pool of talent and an expanding network of promoters, booking agents, [and] publishers" who had settled in Nashville to be involved in the *Grand Ole Opry* program, the city quickly became ground zero for labels that wanted to make money off country's popularity. Session musicians who "rarely toured or acted as members of professional bands" lived and worked in the city "on constant call to back up any singer who happened to need them for recording purposes," even though their familiarity with one another often "inspired a sameness of sound that inhibited creativity" (257). The Nashville Sound was profitable enough that producers were willing to sacrifice a little creativity for profit. Major old-school country stars signed by big recording companies—especially RCA, which had invested much in Nashville—underwent a transformation; artists like Jim Reeves, Skeeter Davis, and Marty Robbins all found success in their fusion of country aesthetic with popular styles.[17]

But, if country music tried to use its wholesome Nashville Sound to appeal to popular audiences—many of whom were younger listeners favoring a steady diet of British rock 'n' roll, rollicking rhythm and blues numbers, and slick rockabilly tunes—producers would find country audiences trended far older and more conservative. Moreover, though country pop and the Nashville Sound were successful investments for producers and labels, they were far from the most popular music of the time. Young listeners, many of them consumers of the "counterculture soundtrack," favored substance and songwriting over style and spectacle.[18] And country music's insistence on the clean, smoothed-out sounds of slow-moving ballads as well as a generation of rhinestone cowboys did not appeal to them. In fact, country music was, by and large, quick to distance itself from youth counterculture or the music of revolution.

Merle Haggard's initially tongue-in-cheek rejection of the counterculture's value system, "Okie from Muskogee," became a hit with "good, wholesome" anti-progressive country listeners who longed for a music that might express their "fear and disgust for" all the dirty counterculture, "hippies, peaceniks, and radicals" (Malone 319). Supposedly written "on the spur of the moment when [Haggard's] bus passed by the Muskogee city sign, and apparently intended as a joke,"[19] (319), the song nevertheless struck a chord with middle-class country audiences who connected to the narrator's pride in being a small-town yokel, unhip, square, one of the old generation, who, as Haggard sings, defines itself by its opposition to the youth culture typified by San Francisco hippies:

> We don't make a party out of lovin'
> We like holdin' hands and pitchin' woo
> We don't let our hair grow long and shaggy
> Like the hippies out in San Francisco do.
> I'm proud to be an Okie from Muskogee,
> A place where even squares can have a ball
> We still wave Old Glory down at the courthouse. . . .

Whether intended as a joke or not, the song became an anthem of unabashed patriotism and was celebrated as an unironic articulation of heartland values. The song's popularity caught the attention of conservative politicians, and eventually "gained for [Haggard] and for country music the endorsement of . . . Richard Nixon" (Malone 319).[20]

The popularity of both Nashville Sound country music and *Hee Haw*'s seemed tied expressly to a right-wing political backlash against the revolutions of the 1960s. The replacing of *The Smothers Brothers*—an acerbic, challenging, biting, and politically aware television show—by a conventional, clean, corny (and remarkably moral) program engaged in far more conventional humor aimed at pleasing white middle-class Americans was, for one critic, television's way of "adapting to the climate of the Nixon era . . . pursuing their own version—conscious or unconscious of a southern strategy. . . . one might call it the Spiro Agnew of the CBS line-up, the key to the heart of the 'silent majority'" (Harrington 97). Nixon's affinity for country music was not altogether surprising; the genre had quickly become a haven for those who resisted revolution and the social uprisings of the civil rights and feminist movements of the 1960s.[21] Writing in 1973, critic Richard Goldstein would articulate the concerns of many progressives who saw country music as an existential threat to the politics of reform and liberalism, not to mention to the growing diversity of the American population:

> Country music comes equipped with a very specific set of values . . . political conservatism, strongly differentiated male and female roles, a heavily punitive morality, racism, and the entire constellation of values around which is centered the phrase "rugged individualism." To me, it is, truly, the perfect

musical extension of the Nixon administration. . . . The President wishes to identify with the system of values which country music suggests, which is to say a strongly suburban, strongly conservative, strongly Protestant audience which damned well ought to frighten every long-haired progressive urbanite, and every black man who is not part of it. (114)

Goldstein was not just responding to country music's popularity with Nixonites: a year before his article appeared, the Country Music Association produced a compilation album entitled "Thank You, Mr. President," celebrating the accomplishments of Nixon and connecting his party's conservative values with country music's. On the album, Tex Ritter, one of the biggest country music stars of his generation, begins each song with a direct address to the president, trying to unite the message of country music with Nixon's political agenda; in one of his introductions, for example, he suggests that the genre is, in fact, a multivocal affirmation of Nixon's support across the nation: "Country music, which in reality is the voice of your silent majority, can sing about the troubles of the present with as much love of country as in the past." In country music, Nixon had found an ally, and the nation had taken notice.

On 17 March 1974, mired deep in the dirt of a national scandal that would lead to his eventual resignation, Nixon traveled to Nashville to help the *Grand Ole Opry* move from its old building, the Ryman Auditorium, to a new home in a sprawling series of buildings known as Opryland.[22] The president was simply out to seek "refuge in an institution that seemed solidly identified with Middle America" (Malone 373). In addition to presenting Roy Acuff with a yo-yo, Nixon spoke briefly about country music's appeal to the nation in primarily moral terms: For Nixon, country music was virtuous, not dirty. Sitting at the piano on the Opry stage, Nixon held forth. *The New York Times* reported, "Noting that country tunes talk about family, religion and patriotism, Mr. Nixon said that 'country music is America' and swung into 'God Bless America' at the piano, raising his voice loudly to lead the singing." As Nixon left the venue, Acuff, the so-called "King of Country Music," spoke to the audience: "That's what it takes to be a real President. . . . He's a real trooper as well as one of our best Presidents" ("Nixon Plays Piano").

The divide between country music and the nation could not have been more evident than that night at Opryland, almost five months before Nixon resigned. If it was not obvious before 17 March 1974, Nixon's piano debut at the Opry had made it clear: in the middle part of the 1970s, country music and

A beleaguered President Nixon attempts to revitalize his popularity mid–Watergate scandal by attempting to yo-yo with Roy Acuff at the opening of the Opry House in 1974; both attempts were, ultimately, unsuccessful.

its antiseptic "Nashville Sound" were in no way dirty, dangerous, or hip: they were the music of squares, the soundtrack of an increasingly out-of-touch president, and a generation content to confuse spectacle with authenticity: in short, Nashville country music in 1974 was a rhinestone-studded jumpsuit of a *Hee Haw* joke. It would take the lyrics of a tired RCA workhouse-songwriter Waylon Jennings to articulate the attitude of a new generation of country artists when he plainly declared, "We need a change."

BREAKING HEARTS AND BREAKING LAWS

The "change" that country music underwent during the mid-1970s emphasized a return to a dirty aesthetic, simultaneously a call to past traditions as well as a borrowing of new forms and styles; it rejected the wholesome patriotic, conservative (and right-wing "morality") establishment music epitomized by the Opry and Acuff and instead looked to the music of the counterculture, especially its embracing of the gritty underbelly of the American Dream. If what was missing from country music was a sense of danger, dirt—as Mary Douglas suggests—offered that in spades.[23] New figures began to emerge in the middle of the decade—musicians like Willie Nelson, Waylon Jennings, and Tompall Glaser—who embodied a conscious rejection of both the ethos and the aesthetic of the "virtuous," clean-cut, Nixon-approved, flag-waving, sequins-and-hay-bales country music on television screens across America. Together, this new cohort would embrace a collective identity, the dirty rebel outlaw, though, as Malone notes, their behavior was not so much lawless but a "rebellion . . . against the immobility and conservatism of the Nashville establishment" (398). Moreover, the group challenged the very structure of the Nashville Sound record labels' emphasis on profit over artistry and the corporatization of the music scene in that city.

As one of the main figures of outlaw country, Willie Nelson created a niche within Nashville country as a renowned songwriter. Originally from Abbott, Texas, Nelson moved to Nashville in 1960, already with a slew of songs to his credit, several of which had been recorded by major country artists of the time, such as Patsy Cline, Ray Price, and Roy Orbison. But his own career as a performer was less successful. Eventually signed to the behemoth of RCA—arguably the most influential label in all of country music—his first album, *Country Willie: His Own Songs* (1965), failed to chart any major singles.[24] Though he joined the Opry in that same year, by 1970, he had retired and moved back to Texas "to an audience that had always been with him, to a climate and ambience that were appealing, and to an already growing music scene" (Malone 396). Wanting to start over with a purer sound uncomplicated by associations with the Nashville corporatization of RCA, Nelson left the label and signed with Atlantic in 1973 and later with Columbia, who released his complicated concept album *The Red Headed Stranger* in 1975 to critical and popular acclaim. Though he certainly did not intend it, Nelson's revitalization of his career through his abandonment of the Nashville scene, his embracing of a new audience and a new state, his split from RCA, and subsequent signing with labels that favored artistry over profit and offered more creative control, would become a path that many other musicians followed.

One of the musicians that followed Nelson's lead was Waylon Jennings—who later became the artist most synonymous with the outlaw country movement. Jennings found in Nelson's professional trajectory a way to escape from what he saw as a banal and boring career fulfilling the wishes of his record label. Unlike Nelson, Jennings had found some sustained success with mainstream country music audiences throughout much of the 1960s. But his popularity seemed tied to his image as a gritty rebel. Starting in 1966, Jennings

The cover of Waylon Jennings's 1972 album *Ladies Love Outlaws*, which marked a dramatic shift both for Jennings's career and for country music.

would release several albums for RCA—*Folk-Country, Leavin' Town,* and *Nashville Rebel*—that crafted an identity for the musician as a lawless hood, the bad boy of country music. Malone notes that, when "he came to Nashville in 1965, his dress and grooming habits still reflected the fifties rockabilly culture from which he emerged. With his swept-back, unparted hair, high collars, and tight blue jeans, he looked like a hood hanging out on the corner or cruising around in his hotrod. . . . his dark good looks and experiments with drugs, drink, and high-living . . . did their part to evoke an aura of lawlessness" (400). Jennings solidified his aesthetic as a bad boy on his 1972 album *Ladies Love Outlaws,* the record that brought the term "outlaw" into the popular vernacular of country music. The album's embrace of the antihero persona as opposed to the Porter Wagoner–inspired shiny-cowboy heroes of the past matched Nelson's penchant for antiestablishment behavior off the stage as well.

On the cover of the album, Jennings appears in all black, looking more robber than revolutionary, with his hair grown long and his pistol on his hip; standing low beneath him, a little girl looks up in awe and reverence at the outlaw towering over her. It was an image shift for Jennings, but a signal shift for the genre. After the album landed on the charts, "the word 'outlaw' began to replace 'rebel' as a descriptive label for Jennings and his music, and he began to dress the part—beard, black hat, vest, black trousers" (Malone 400). Moreover, critics and publicists throughout Nashville began to use the term to refer not just to Jennings but to "other Nashville musicians who seemed at odds with the 'establishment,'" as well as to those outside of Nashville, including "the entire Austin community of musicians" (400).

Jennings's new aesthetic sharply rebuked the jokey, clean-cut conservatism of *Hee Haw* country music in the 1970s: "Who listens to the Opry nowadays," Jennings asked two years after the release of *Outlaws,* "Ain't nobody out there listening anymore." Of the ostentatious silliness of Buck Owens and his *Hee-Haw* persona, Jennings would add, "he does some of the most ridiculous damn things I ever heard" (qtd. in Ching 119). But Jennings saved his sharpest criticisms of the Nashville sound and RCA's tight control over his musical and personal aesthetic: "They wouldn't let you do anything. You had to dress a certain way: you had to do everything a certain way.... They kept trying to destroy me.... I just went about my business and did things my way.... You start messing with my music, I get mean" (qtd. in Corcoran 221). Jennings's "mean streak" would show up in the title of his very next album, 1973's *Lonesome, On'ry and Mean,* which saw Jennings trade in much of his RCA accompaniment for a telecaster and a dirtier, more visceral sound.

Though Nelson had begun the exodus from Nashville, Jennings became the poster child for backlash against the city and everything the corporatized country music establishment had come to represent. In 1975, on his wildly successful *Dreaming My Dreams,* he recorded what would become the defining song of the outlaw movement, "Are You Sure Hank Done It This Way?" in which Jennings attacks contemporary country music and its reliance on "the same old tune, fiddle and guitar," the silly caricatures on *Hee Haw,* and the ubiquitous "rhinestone suits and new shiny cars" of figures like Porter Wagoner. Challenging his fellow artists to imagine a new kind of ethos and sound, Jennings asks, "Where do we take it from here? / It's been the same way for years / We need a change."

"Are You Sure Hank Done It This Way" works both as an airing of Jennings's personal grievances with a studio that tried constantly to control his creativity and image as well as a mournful jeremiad for what he saw as country music's profound straying from its roots. Unlike Hank Williams, who—in Jennings's fantasy anyway—had made his name by crafting lyrics mined from the dirty parts of his life, especially his sorrow and guilt, Jennings sarcastically offered that the current way to become famous in Nashville was to work thanklessly for a label, "ten years on the road, makin' one-night stands / speedin' my young life away." With his lamenting repetition of the phrase "I don't think Hank done 'em this way," Jennings chastised the industry that turned the Opry into political theater and made stars out of Hollywood cowboys and wholesome but stupid overall-wearing hayseeds. Regardless of his feeling for RCA, Jennings's albums in the mid-1970s were nothing less than meta-genre attacks on contemporary country music, and they made him the lead figure of the outlaw artists, whose success in country became a matter of both pride and anxiety by stakeholders in the scene. Along with figures like Johnny Cash, Hank Williams Jr., David Allan Coe, Tompall Glaser, and Jessi Colter (Jennings's wife), the outlaw movement soon began to surpass the popularity of the saccharine rhinestone Opry artists that were holdovers from the decade before.[25]

Outlaw country artists became so incredibly popular in the 1970s that they began to steadily eclipse the sales of mainstream Nashville Sound artists by 1975. Big studios took note. In 1976, RCA decided to capitalize on Jennings's outlaw image by releasing the compilation album *Wanted! The Outlaws,* featuring songs by Jennings, Nelson, Glaser, and Colter. It became the biggest album of the decade, selling over a million copies, and was the very first platinum country record. Recalling the runaway success of the compilation, Jennings remarked on his pivot from the sparkly cowboy aesthetic of Wagoner to a dirtier image of a criminal on the run from the law:

> The cover was pure Old West—Dodge City and Tombstone. Now, we weren't just playing bad guys; we took our stand outside the country music rules, its set ways, locking the door on its own jail cell. We looked like tramps.... "Don't fuck with me," was what we were tryin' to say. . . . We loved the energy of rock and roll, but rock had self destructed. Country had gone syrupy. For us, "outlaw" meant standing up for your rights, your own way of doing things. It felt like a different music, and outlaw was as good a description as any. We mostly thought it was funny; Tompall immediately made up outlaw membership certificates. (Jennings and Kaye, *Waylon* 221)

"Don't fuck with me!": Waylon Jennings on the success of the compilation album *Wanted! The Outlaws,* featuring songs by Jennings, Willie Nelson, and Jessi Colter.

Proclaiming themselves "the rightful heirs to the Hank Williams legacy" (Metress 15), Jennings, Nelson, and Colter looked to Williams as the "original outlaw," who represented an authentic voice with creative control over his music.

Through their songs, "the outlaws were trying to tell Nashville that it no longer understood what country music was all about" (Metress 15). According to the outlaws, what country music was really "all about" was the dirty side of life: rambling, hard-drinking men who pined for the good-hearted women they had to leave behind. Most of their most famous hits—including the two hits from *Wanted! The Outlaws,* "Suspicious Minds" and "Good Hearted Woman"—emphasized the separation of the spheres of masculinity and femininity within the outlaw aesthetic: men were hell-raisers in love with the road, but despite their ramblings, dirty outlaw country men could always count on their woman to welcome them back once they tired of their travels. Nelson's "Good Hearted Woman" offers as much:

> He likes the bright lights and night life and good timin' friends
> And when the party's all over, she'll welcome him back home again
> Lord knows she don't understand him but she does the best that she can
> This good hearted woman lovin' a good timin' man.

The song would go on to become one of Nelson's most famous hits and a mainstay of the outlaw country movement. And it would highlight the outlaw country musician's attachment to one kind of convention: traditional roles for gender. For Jennings, the man gets to be dirty, to be an outlaw, but the woman must remain clean and pure, "the good-hearted woman" who cares for babies and stray dogs. Consequently, the relation to dirt is problematized by the fact of this "pure" refuge. Moreover, outlaw music's emphasis on, to borrow another songwriter's phrasing, standing by "your man" showed clear outlines of the culture war that was both central to and precipitated by Nixon's "southern strategy." Outlaw country artists may have wanted to reject everything that mainstream country music stood for, but they did not reject wholesale its conventions about men and women.

LUMINOUS HILLBILLIES
The emergence and popularity of the outlaw country artists of the mid-1970s is a useful example of how an ethos of dirt stands, ultimately, as a marker of authenticity and value celebrating disconnections from establishmentarian notions of respectability. For Jennings and Nelson, "outlaw" defined not just a "bad guy" aesthetic but an entire attitude about a genre of music actively contesting their artistic and musical value. Recalling his early career in Nashville to interviewer Terry Gross, Willie Nelson remembers that he was never able to be commercially viable to record producers:

> Nelson: There was no slot that I fit in. My chords—my songs had a few chords in them, and the country songs weren't supposed to have over three chords, according to executive decisions. And if it had more than three, then it wasn't country, and it shouldn't be recorded. And my voice wasn't exactly—I was nowhere near Eddy Arnold. My phrasing was sort of funny. I didn't sing on

the beat. I had too many chords, and I just didn't fit the slots, you know? And I wouldn't take orders. I just—I couldn't, you know? I didn't know how to take direction that well. So I wouldn't fit in any of these slots, and so I became one of those guys that, you know, they had to call something else.

Gross: What were you called?

Nelson: Well, troublemaker at first. And then they found the word outlaw, and they decided that smoothed it out a little bit. So they started calling us that. ("Willie Nelson: The 'Fresh Air' Interviews")

Nelson contesting his value as a singer-songwriter, resisting assimilation in the Nashville Sound, and embracing of his "outlaw" identity reminds me of Patricia Yaeger's interest in glowing debris asserting its identity as trash but critically resisting, refusing, and denying its lack of value. Yaeger's articulation of "luminous trash" offers a way for us to think about how the popularity of this dirty aesthetic of "outlaw country" renegotiates conceptions of "authenticity," "exceptionalism," and "place" both within and without the genre of country music.

In one of her last works of scholarship, Yaeger declared that her singular fascination had become "luminous trash, glowing debris, garbage that lights up—like the tossed-away sled at the end of *Citizen Kane* or the illuminated basketball hoops that David Hammons makes out of Harlem debris or the bright garbage that a dirty robot collects in *Wall-E.*" In the juxtaposition of what is trash and what is valuable, Yaeger asserts that luminous trash does cultural work by "animat[ing] [the] wasteland," and by doing so, reminds us of the value of light that might originate from what is seemingly dark and worthless as well as the potential value of shining light on "dark" things (Yaeger, "Beasts). Outlaw country musicians of the early to mid-1970s emphasized a similar kind of luminosity in their performative evocation of what seemed inherently valueless to the country establishment. For Nelson, as it was for Jennings, "outlaw" became a useful marker to illuminate displacement from establishment country into a proud ownership of their status as outsiders, all the while insisting that their music and aesthetic had an authenticity to it that refused to be ignored.

In fact, if one could label the aesthetic or ethos of the outlaw country musicians, "luminous trash" might be the most apt way to describe how they saw their identities within mainstream country. Turning away from squeaky-clean singing cowboys like Gene Autry or smoothed-out crooners like Eddy Arnold, outlaw country musicians embraced the role of villain. They were the men that mainstream country refused to acknowledge as valuable; they were not the protagonists of old songs: they were messy antiheroes who made mistakes, got into fights, had fuzzy moral compasses, and did not experience happy endings. In Jennings's 1972 eponymous song for his hit album *Ladies Love Outlaws,* he sings in a gruff baritone about the appeal of an identity that, on the surface, seems utterly worthless:

> 'Cause ladies love outlaws like babies love stray dogs
> Ladies touch babies like a banker touches gold
> And outlaws touch the ladies
> Somewhere deep down in their soul.

Like a stray dog, the outlaw man that Jennings envisions in his song has an intrinsic value intimately connected to contested identity: at once as something valueless and disconnected but also uniquely mysteriously compelling.

However, it should be noted that, if mainstream country music stood for ideals a more progressive nation inherently rejected, it also remained the site of a singular fascination for those same progressives. Whether that fascination was of ritual purification, a way of asserting one's own righteousness against the "dirty" other or a more redemptive ritual embedded in that fascination— not just repudiation, but a salvaging of something that puts ways forward, offering alternatives to a stale us/them dichotomy—is almost beside the point. What matters is that outlaw country allowed those progressive audiences a re-imaging of a national narrative, national possibilities. For me, the outlaws are a model in large part because they did make something new, they did break an old mold. However, though they changed things for the better, they still trafficked in the same sexual politics that made country music decidedly unhip to progressives during the decade.

Outlaw country men could be the villains who rejected the conventions of family and home and monogamy, but the women's worth was defined almost completely by adherence to the same values. Jennings offers himself as a stray dog—or, in the next line, like the baby—an object in need of constant care. In short, an outlaw man is luminous trash, deeply flawed, vulnerable in his alienation and outcast status, begging to be understood and cared for, looking for the unconditional love of a good woman, a hybrid between mother and lover. For Jennings, the outlaw man may be trash, but his separation from the strictures of established rules and his prioritizing of an individualized morality give him a shine, a glow, that is exceptional, that allows him, in fact, to connect with any woman, touching them in the most secret and intimate of places, "deep down in their soul"—because outlaw men's women are looking for someone to care for, in every sense of the word "care." Jennings did not glamorize the life of such a man—at least, not in a conventional way—but offered him as a figure of value not in spite of but because of the dirty details of his criminal life. The outlaw man's story refuses to be ignored, resists demands for its invisibility. He is luminous trash glowing to remind country music of the value of resistance to the establishment, and as a counterbalance to the artifice of external spectacles and glitter: Nixon and Acuff yo-yoing on the Technicolor stage of the new Opry, RCA's calculations about how to craft wholesome images of its stars, Porter Wagoner's rhinestones, *Hee-Haw*'s celebration of redneck clowns: the luminous outlaw glowed internally, required more than just a surface investment, and reframed an entire genre that was beginning to value style over substance.

And yet, while outlaw country artists certainly saw themselves leading a revolution that embraced the luminosity of the throwaway, their emphasis on bucking the system became its own kind of aesthetic. It was not the rhinestones of Nudie Cohen's suits that became emblematic of the outlaw country movement, but the all-black suits, cowboy boots, buckles, and spurs of the villain. Famously, Johnny Cash, a figure that was able to cross back and forth between the worlds of mainstream country music and the counterculture, would make an image for himself as "the Man in Black," and connect his aesthetic choice to a moral code.[26] Cash's exterior darkness was, paradoxically, what made him luminous to fans who saw in him an interior glow reflecting back those who felt alienated and marginalized from systems of power.

"We're doing mighty fine I do suppose," Cash offered in the eponymous song from his 1971 album *Man in Black,* "In our streakalightnin cars and fancy clothes / But, just so were reminded of the ones who are held back / Up front there ought to be a man in black." Cash's black outfits were not just a fashion statement, he explained in the song, but reclamation of the debris left on the side of the road after country music's rejection of the counterculture and their dirty associations authored by Nixon style conservativism: "I wear it for the sick and lonely old, / For the reckless ones whose bad trip left them cold / I wear the black in mourning for the lives that could have been / Each week we lose a hundred fine young men." Cash's vision of blackness is not an embrace of nihilism, but a fascination with those discarded by institutions and systems of power. Moreover, "The Man in Black" would come to symbolize a call to revolution against the political establishment that Tex Ritter would celebrate a year later. Rather than thanking Nixon, Cash not so subtly excoriates him.

But outlaw men did not just assert an ownership over the luminosity of what made country music exceptional, they also argued for a dirty kind of authenticity. They sought to transform country music by taking control back from large recording studios and reframe the genre by reminding contemporary country producers of the value in old styles, genres, and artists. In 1977, at the height of the fame of *Wanted! The Outlaws,* Tompall Glaser recalled that a motivating factor for the artists of his generation was reclaiming value in "worthless" old artists no longer valued by big recording studios, who "quit programming Ernest Tubb, so they made him obsolete. They put him on the scrap-pile before he died. But he's not obsolete. There's a market for him" (Bane 216). In short, outlaw artists weren't so much nostalgic for old times and traditions as much as they wanted to reclaim those thrown on "the scrap-pile." Glaser offers Tubb as one of those luminous artists shining in the wasteland of country recording. Although these attempts to locate an origin story for the "roots" of country music had appeared before, outlaw country men would uniquely define the value of the obsolete (what has been surpassed) as a model for the future (what could be achieved). The seeming inconsistency led one critic to label them as "the tradition minded rebels" (qtd. in Ching 121). By reframing country music on the trail of broken traditions abandoned in an embrace of pop sensibilities and political silent majorities, outlaw country sought to illuminate the trash and debris left behind and embrace the way "Hank done it."

Outlaw country was not only transformative for the genre, it was also transportive as it sought to trouble country music's obsession with Nashville and offer other sites and spaces without the same commercial baggage Music City, USA, had accumulated during the 1970s.[27] Several regions heavily associated with genre music actively fought against the establishment: the folk music of Greenwich Village in the 1960s, the counterculture jangly rock of San Francisco in the 1970s. But these sites of contestation were not part of the establishment; in fact, Greenwich Village or Haight-Ashbury in San Francisco were spaces of marginalization embracing their disconnection from the symbolic urban cities to which they were attached. In the wake of the outlaw country music of the 1970s, the turn away from the dominance of the Nashville Sound began with Glaser's founding of Glaser Brothers Productions at 916 Nineteenth Avenue South, Nashville, in 1970, the same year when *Hee Haw* was becoming a smash hit. The studio was, in effect, a small building where the Glaser Brothers sought to empower musicians to have more artistic control over their sound, image, and studio musicians than major labels would offer at the time. Declared "Hillbilly Central" by a *New Yorker* writer exploring the new wave of country music emerging in 1974, the production studio would become a site that announced itself as both the marginalized (Hillbilly) and also empire (Central).[28]

But, as outlaw country artists redefined authenticity and exceptionalism through a dirty aesthetic of the figure of the rebel or outlaw, their reconciliation of both what is authentic and what is exceptional really took place in the celebration of a space outside Nashville altogether. Outlaw artists found their authentic and exceptional home in the state of Texas, birthplace of Willie Nelson and home to both urban and rural sites that would come to define substantially different modalities of authenticity for country music. Starting in the early 1970s, Willie Nelson's annual Fourth of July picnics in Austin became huge events for those in and outside of country music's establishment. At the concerts, which were almost "a country counterpart to Woodstock" (Ching 120), one found both "hip young fans" intermingled with "rough edged rednecks" without breaking into fist-fights. By 1976, the town was so synonymous with outlaw country that public television launched *Austin City Limits*—a sort of anti–*Hee Haw*—focused solely on performances of live music with no comedy or Opry filler.[29] The first episode starred hometown boy Willie Nelson.

And yet, Austin was not the only potential site of value for outlaw country artists. In Luckenbach, a small Texas town to the west of Austin and northwest of San Antonio, outlaw artists found another marker of authenticity in the guise of a hip small-town community of artists. Inspired by the convergence of country musicians in such a small town, the song "Luckenbach, Texas," on Jennings's 1977 album *Ol' Waylon*, is a rejection of both Nashville and the fame that it offered young artists. "I don't need my name in the marquee lights," Jennings grunts in one of the opening lines of the song; later, he adds, "So baby, let's sell your diamond ring / Buy some boots and faded jeans and go away / This coat and tie is choking me / In your high society you cry all day." In "Luckenbach," Jennings' rejection of the aesthetics of modernity is transformative for the singer, who notes that he and his woman need, simply, to get "back to the basics," but in order to do that, they have to reject not just their way of living but the very place they live in.

"Let's go to Luckenbach, Texas / With Waylon and Willie and the boys," the singer offers in a strange meta-name-check wherein Jennings sings as a character of himself as a singer worthy of emulating. Unlike Nashville—or even Austin—with its suburbs and high society, Luckenbach offers the basics of what every country boy or girl might desire; moreover, it is a space rife with both tradition ("Between Hank Williams' pain songs") and the hippest music of the moment ("and [Nelson's] Blue Eyes Cryin' in the Rain"). In "Luckenbach, Texas," one finds a fantasy of country music's past coming to terms with its current dirt. The singer asks his partner to throw away what the establishment thinks is valuable (diamonds, houses, fancy cars) and embrace the forgotten and dirty things and spaces (faded jeans and small towns). For outlaw men, dirty music could only shine in marginalized spaces.

One of the central ironies of the outlaw country movement is that, while artists like Nelson and Jennings were "drawing upon a diverse array of musical sources and reaching out to new audiences, they did more to preserve a distinct identity for country music than most of their contemporaries" (Malone 405). In fact, the popularity of these "tradition minded rebels" is a testament to the way in which outlaw artists successfully redefined notions of authenticity, exceptionalism, and place in the genre of country music. Beyond the 1970s, outlaw country music morphed into a series of images, themes, and rhetorical markers that still retained a kind of authentic vernacular within a genre of music struggling with image. By 1979, Waylon Jennings had become such a popular originator of the outlaw myth that the television show *The Dukes of Hazzard* enlisted him to write their theme song and act as narrator for the program following two "outlaw" cousins on probation for selling moonshine as they thwart *Hee Haw*–esque corrupt buffoons of local law enforcement. The show was a tremendous success and ran for over six years.

However, many of the original outlaw musicians did not retain their commitment to progressive revolution and rejection of the establishment. As they became more popular, outlaw men increasingly embraced conventional political identities and more conservative agendas (most notably, a figure like Hank Williams Jr., who has, at this point, become better known as a right-wind pundit than a performer).[30] This shift shows how a focus on what is dirty, what has been neglected, reviled, or left behind, can break both ways, especially politically. After all, lost causes are the breeding ground of right-wing political movements. If "traditional rebel" is a paradox, so is "radical conservative." Outlaw country men embraced the "revolutionary" while the American right wing began to be more tuned in to challenging established American institutions than the left. For every Willie Nelson on the left with Neil Young, there is a Hank Williams Jr. offering the outlaw persona as a figure of conservative value structures. We can't forget that, even though outlaw country artists were quick to reject some of the conventions of country music, their investment in the dirtiness of it still had troubling connections to the music's sexual politics, regional exceptionalism, and political conservatism. Those who broke politically right could still claim to be revolutionary, if only in their resistance to progressive values.

Regardless of its political influence, outlaw country's renegotiation of what was once valueless into that which shines still frames discourses of authenticity surrounding country music artists well into the twenty-first century. For a genre of music that still finds itself anxious about connections to popular music, even the most widespread commercial successes of country still use the figure of the trashy outlaw as a rhetorical marker symbolizing authenticity. Superstar Garth Brooks's chart-topping "Friends in Low Places" was the runaway commercial hit of 1990 and made the musician a significant amount of money, but the song configures the authenticity of the singer in connection to those he knows "in low places / where the whiskey drowns / And the beer chases my blues away." One can't help but read Jennings's image of a hard-drinking, good-timing, unkept man into Brooks's celebration of a man who is "not big on social graces."

Moreover, outlaw country continues to guide a somewhat marginalized but hyper-unified audience of listeners hungry for artists and musicians that embrace the dirty aesthetic and ethos defined by Nelson and Jennings. In May of 2004, the satellite radio company SiriusXM launched an "Outlaw Country" channel on their popular streaming service.[31] Defined by Steven Van Zandt, the producer of the channel, as "a sanctuary for the freaks, misfits, rebels, and renegades of country music" ("Outlaw Country [SiriusXM]") the programs that comprise the schedule emphasize old-school outlaw country from the 1970s as well as new artists inspired by Nelson and Jennings, including Waylon's son, Shooter Jennings, bands like the Old 97s, and artists such as Steve Earle, Lucinda Williams, and Margo Price.

The show's popularity, especially with a demographic of baby boomers who would have been in high school or college during the height of the movement in the mid-1970s, even inspired a cruise where fans and artists could interact during the day and hear concerts at night. Among the acts booked on the cruise were Waylon's widow, Jessi Colter, as well as Shooter Jennings and his band, Waymore's Outlaws. Jennings and his outlaw contingent continue to guide conversations about country music's authenticity and exceptionalism, whether in various guises of "real country," "alt-country," or "Americana music."[32] It's clear the initial celebration of the dirty aesthetic of the outlaw—trashed by smoother and more popular sensibilities—continues to remain luminous half a century later, when Jennings first demanded a change.

WHAT YOU REALLY KNOW ABOUT THE DIRTY SOUTH?

Considering contemporary connections to musical artists who attempted to renegotiate genre definitions for "exceptionalism," "authenticity," and "place" through a lens of the luminous throwaway and a dirty aesthetic, I am compelled by hip-hop artists collectively unified under the phrase "the dirty South." In fact, I find much of the same rhetorical positioning of outlaw country artists in the 1970s in the rise of the dirty South hip-hop movement at the turn of the twenty-first century. Unlike country's structural dominance in one city, dirty South hip-hop emerged during a time in which East and West Coast rappers fought each other (sometimes literally) for recognition of true authenticity. In 1994, at the height of the coastal battles, the duo OutKast released their debut album, *Southernplayalisticadillacmuzik;* comprised of rappers André 3000 and Big Boi, OutKast introduced and repositioned the South from its marginalized space in the hip-hop world to an authentic and exceptional epicenter.

There are numerous connections between outlaw artists and OutKast. Like Glaser's "Hillbilly Central," OutKast's first album was recorded and produced in a "throwaway space" not part of the establishment: producer Rico Wade's basement, referred to as "the Dungeon." Wade's production company, Organized Noize, had been influential in remixing material from mainstream acts like TLC, and their work on the album *Ooooooohhh . . . On the TLC Tip* helped to land OutKast its first record deal from TLC's production company, LaFace Records. Together, OutKast and Organized Noize went to work in the Dungeon and began reworking old demos from material they had experimented with since 1992. The resulting album would be unlike anything the hip-hop world had heard; it would celebrate the South's potential for creativity and vibrancy—by first asserting and affirming its dirtiness.

It wasn't just aesthetics that changed the hip-hop world: the cadences, voices, slang, and performances of André 3000 and Big Boi already set *Southernplayalisticadillacmuzik* apart from the other hip-hop albums of the 1990s. André 3000's distinct voice was different from major rappers of the era like Tupac Shakur or Dr. Dre, but Big Boi's voice and manner of rapping was more conventional. Like Buck Owens and Roy Clark, the duo balanced each other out, and their back-and-forth on the album feels less like the grand formality of Biggie Smalls or the offhand squirreling of an artist like Eminem, and more like a conversation among friends. There was a familiarity with each other immediately obvious to listeners. However, what marked *Southernplayalisticadillacmuzik*'s difference from contemporary hip-hop albums was its instrumentalization and regional discursivity. OutKast did not rely on samples from mainstream music, digitized beats, or synthesizers the way most hip-hop artists operated during the decade; instead, the duo favored recording actual guitar riffs, live drums, and other instruments to give the album an organic feel. The music's sense of urgency and vibrancy was met with critical and popular acclaim, but the duo's rhetorical positioning of Atlanta as a site of authenticity and exceptionalism is really what connects *Southernplayalisticadillacmuzik* to an album like Waylon Jennings's *Dreaming My Dreams,* both as transformative and transportive for their respective genres.

Southernplayalisticadillacmuzik is both a debut album for OutKast and a debut album for Atlanta (and by extension, the American South) as site of a new exceptionalism for hip-hop; OutKast introduces the city to a public that has only scant familiarity with it. On the fourth track, OutKast features a short skit entitled "Welcome to Atlanta," which uses the framing device of an airline pilot landing a plane at Atlanta's Hartsfield-Jackson International Airport. As they descend closer and closer to the city, the pilot points out various spots in Atlanta that are well-known, including sports venues and concert halls. For instance, the pilot asks his passengers to look out the window and locate the famous "Georgia Dome," where many national sporting events and championships are played. As the passengers look, the pilot reminds them that the building "still flies the Confederate battle flag." By beginning a comic interlude with an articulation of Atlanta's connection to a national imaginary, OutKast then seeks to reframe the site not simply as the city of sports teams—"the home of the Atlanta Hawks, the Braves, and the Falcons"—but as a space of borders and lines deeply connected to racial identity.

However, the racial lines border segregated areas where there are new sites of discursive creativity. Unlike the city's past of Confederate flags and white-supremacy power dynamics, OutKast's reconfiguration of Atlanta recognizes the city as a mecca for Black artists and musicians quickly changing the way the world sees the major urban area of the South and prophesies that Atlanta will one day be known by its affiliation with the group:

> Atlanta has been called the new Motown of the South
> And is the home of LaFace Records
> Organized Noize Productions
> If you look to your far right, you can see Decatur
> And below you, to the right, is East Point and College Park
> Home of the red dogs, rap cats, and robbin' crew
> And home to the player, the 'Lacs, and the motherfuckin' OutKast.

The rhetoric of "Welcome to Atlanta" is not just braggadocio; it is, in fact, similar to the work of the outlaw country artists of the 1970s who argued that their music and the new spaces it offered as potential sites of vibrancy and luminosity were mostly compelling because they were throwaway "outcasts." Even in the duo's very name, they position themselves as the isolated trash of a movement and a genre that refuse to validate them.

Hip-hop scholar Regina Bradley notes that "Welcome to Atlanta" "sonically emphasizes Atlanta's urbanity. . . . the focal points of the captain's tour blend past and present monikers of southern blackness," and she finds the "intentional 'dirtying' of the south via pairing references to the controversial Red Dog police program."[33] She argues that the program's "bullying of working class Black communities alongside recognizable white southern iconography like the confederate flag grounds Atlanta not only in its contemporaneity but also a recognition of the lingering effects of the racial trauma still inflicted on Black people in the south." By positioning Atlanta as part of a continuum of white-inflicted Black trauma—in a variety of guises such as economic, physical, political, and judicial—OutKast invites the hip-hop listener to locate within the city the struggles that have animated hip-hop music since its inception. No longer just a sports town or the blighted and backward country marginalized from a bicoastal genre, Atlanta for OutKast is the epicenter of much of the fertile "dirt" that Bradley connects to both "literal red clay, dirt, or mud, the term also connotes the dirtiness of the treatment of southern black folks, even in the post–Civil Rights Era, which de-romanticizes the belief that the movement ended the racial and social-economic tensions facing southern black communities." By welcoming hip-hop listeners to Atlanta, OutKast created a new vision of the city that suddenly became very compelling to popular audiences. In a short amount of time, many artists offered their own version of "Welcome to Atlanta," a title affiliated with hip-hop performers such as "Jermaine Dupri, head of So So Def Records . . . a remix featuring Sean Combs, Murphy Lee, and Snoop Dogg shouting out their respective home towns . . . [and] 'New Atlanta' with a new generation of Atlanta rappers including Migos, Rich Homie Quan, and Young Thug" (Bradley 10).

If Atlanta was transportive for hip-hop, OutKast suggested it was also a site of exceptionalism and authenticity throughout *Southernplayalisticadillac-muzik*. In the eponymous track, Big Boi widens his regional lens to include not just Atlanta but the entirety of the American South: "Well it's the M-1 crooked letter coming around the South / Rolling straight Hammers and Vogues in that old Southern slouch." Unashamed of his southern accent, he proudly boasts, "Deep, the slang is in effect because it's Georgia." In articulating the broader region's exceptionalism, Big Boi reclaims pejorative affects that mark the place as antithetical to the genre's popularity and reclaims them as exceptional. André 3000's verse connects southern exceptionalism to "soul food," which he argues is a spirit or spark absent in bicoastal hip-hop: "Like collard greens and Hoecakes, I got soul / That's something that you ain't got." Slang and soul food might not be the most obvious objects to praise during the decade of slick East Coast–West Coast lyrical battles, but it is precisely because country accents and greasy foods are so contested and dirty that OutKast find them worthy of celebration. By repositioning throwaway topics in hip-hop as luminous trash affirming the ethos of the genre, OutKast reclaims an identity without cleaning it for mass consumption: being dirty is the appeal.

Claiming the South and its regional culture as a space of potential value—especially in how they embody the very "soul" of hip-hop—obviously connects with the outlaw movement's embracing of Luckenbach and Austin as sites through which those marginalized from Nashville's corporatism could reclaim their exceptionalism and notions of authenticity. And like outlaw country in the 1970s, OutKast's promotion of the region eventually eclipses popular artists from both the East and the West Coast. A year after *Southernplayalistica-dillacmuzik* debuted, rapper Cool Breeze, another Atlanta hip-hop artists recording with Wade and Organized Noize, coined a term describing much of what OutKast and other Atlanta artists were doing.

Wanting to come up with a phrase that expressed an emerging genre embracing their southern hometown's disposability, Cool Breeze went into the Dungeon to write a hook, and came out with the now iconic question: "What you really know about the Dirty South?" Breeze described the hook and the phrase "dirty south" as a purposeful jeremiad to the hip-hop community, one that embraces its dirt and takes pride in its marginalization.[34] "We wanted to make y'all eat this Southern fried chicken," he says. "Not chicken cordon bleu. Not pineapple chicken" (Rehagen). A rhetorical "dirty South" asked hip-hop artists on both coasts—whose claims of authenticity hinged on lawless drug dealing—to reevaluate everything they've heard about the South. Much of the lyrics of "Dirty South" argue that it is the South, not Los Angeles or New York, that is the site of the original gangsta culture: Breeze explains, "I'm about to let you know that we're up on our game about the politics and drug units. . . . What you're doing, we're doing too. You're thinking we're country. You're thinking we're slow. But we're one up on you" (Christina Lee).

"Dirty South" was such a powerful term in the hip-hop world because it articulated, owned, and celebrated marginalization. Like the "outlaws" who resisted and denied the smooth cadences of the Nashville Sound, dirty South hip-hop artists embraced the grittiness of their world—"It's about the red clay and the dirt roads," says Wade—and claimed it as a point of pride. The ownership of marginalized status made appeals even more compelling. Dirty South artists were almost oxymorons in the larger community of the hip-hop world; Wade explains, "It means we country. But we ain't country" (Rehagen). As one music reporter explains, "If *Southernplayalisticadillacmuzik* spearheaded a movement, 'Dirty South' branded it. Casual shout-outs from artists like Timbaland led to countless others adopting Cool Breeze's no-nonsense dope boy perspective for themselves" (Christina Lee). Taking Breeze's hook, Wade and the other producers at Organized Noize turned the short rap into a larger song and gave it to their newly formed hip-hop collective known as Goodie Mob. The song would appear on an album likely inspired by André 3000's praising of "hoecakes" and "collards" on *Southernplayalisticadillacmuzik: Soul Food.*

The explosive popularity of dirty South hip-hop only increased after the release of *Soul Food.* At the Source Awards—the major venue for the world of hip-hop—OutKast won "Best New Artist" in 1995. The East and West Coast rappers in attendance loudly booed as the group came on stage to accept. At the microphone, André 3000 addressed their disdain with a now-famous response: "But it's like this though, I'm tired of them closed minded folks, it's like we gotta demo tape but don't nobody want to hear it. But it's like this. . . . the South got something to say." Bradley notes that "It is important . . . that André's rally called to the entire south, not just Atlanta. This is significant in thinking about southern experiences as non-monolithic, the aural-cultural possibilities of multiple Souths and their various intersections using hip hop aesthetics" (15–16).

In shouting out the entire region, OutKast offered dirty South hip-hop as a vehicle for other African Americans in the South to craft a voice and a style that rejected the bifurcated coastal battle happening in the 1990s. Big Boi remembers that the criticism from the Source attendees was motivation for the duo: "From that point forward, all that hate was just motivation for us. So we went into the studio, and it was just me and Dre together. We were working at Dallas Austin's studio, DARP, and we were working at *Stankonia* studios, the studio we have now. And we just started recording record after record, and one day Dre called me and was like, 'I got the beat! I got the beat!' and it was the beat for 'Rosa Parks'" (Samuel).[35]

"Rosa Parks" would end up being the first single for OutKast's next album, *Aquemini;* it became hugely successful, charting at number 55 on *Billboard's Hot 100 Chart,* a rare achievement for a southern hip-hop duo. OutKast's popular success both inside and outside the hip-hop world was the defining feature of dirty South hip-hop for the rest of the decade and into the next century. When asked why the South suddenly became a viable region for hip-hop, rapper TI explains, "OutKast, period. OutKast. That's when it changed. That was the first time when people began to take Southern rap seriously" (Max). By the time OutKast released their next two albums—*Stankonia* in 2000 and *Speakerboxxx / The Love Below* in 2003—they had become, quite simply, the most popular musicians in America and one of the best-known duos in the history of popular music. You could hear their music on the radio, on television commercials, on *Saturday Night Live.* Their success would reinvigorate the South as a site of exceptionalism within the hip-hop world.

OUTLAW SHIT

In positioning these two revolutionary musical genres—dirty South hip-hop and outlaw country—as rejections of spaces and discourses of establishmentarian commercialism that eventually redefined the genres of their respective music industries, it's critical to acknowledge the debt that artists like OutKast and Waylon Jennings owe to their embrace of dirt, debris, marginalization, refuse, and trash. Whether its Jennings's black-suited robber persona grumbling about the glowing aura of the lowlife or André 3000 celebrating the vibrancy of a hoecake, outlaw country and dirty South hip-hop both celebrate the luminous trash left in the wake of commercial and conventional investments in popular music. They both offer dirt as an ethos and an aesthetic with potential value in reframing and even revitalizing their respective genres, but also, the unqualified success of OutKast as well as Jennings and Nelson show how compelling such an aesthetic of dirt is with popular audiences, who find in the dirty rhetorical markers authenticity and exceptionalism, even as they ask their listeners to imagine other spaces and places outside of the fixed realm of country and hip-hop music.

And yet, though I have kept a tight focus on the reinvention, resignification, relocation of a genre in a context of commercial pressures—the alternative images of the South—the revaluation of dirt in these musical genres offers something to the national imaginary about the region at large. Certainly, artists who mine dirt, who pay attention to what has been neglected or excluded, will prove innovative in their chosen field of endeavor, but beyond being just a method of revitalization or transformation of a genre, Jennings's and OutKast's innovations do cultural work beyond the purview of their chosen field. In both outlaw country and dirty South hip-hop, musical innovations of celebrating dirt and disposability position the South in a profoundly ambivalent way, as a space of both trash and value, of danger and play. Similar connections exist between cultural and literary texts from the 1970s and those of the twenty-first century, showing how dirt continues to operate as shorthand for dangerous or radical work that valorizes marginalized spaces and people.

The compulsion to focus on the South, then, offers a way for consumers and audiences of respective genres to identify with the outlaw or the marginalized, without having to "own" any of their dirt. And that investment without ownership has real cultural consequences, whether it is the garbage sexual politics of outlaw country as it morphs into neoconservative ideology or the fraught complications of celebrating lawlessness in dirty South hip-hop. If we examine a fuller accounting of costs/benefits in relation to this national investment, we locate the way in which dirty South hip-hop and outlaw country reveal a larger American scene where disposable bodies (mostly Black) proliferate and the self-destructive path of outlawry (especially drug addiction, but other forms, including white militias) eventually seem the only available option to so many. I don't want to uniformly offer either genre as somehow revealing an inherent authenticity or its innovations in positioning dirt solely as a new kind of exceptionalism. Instead, I want to ask why their claims of authenticity and dirtiness are so compelling, even decades apart and with a vastly different demographic of consumers. I'd like to think that attention to dirt could offer different ways of understanding and mining its potential by finally offering alternatives to outlawry and its costs. After all, very few people get to cash into being outlaws, but they are not being offered any other alternative role to play in a society that ignores them except when it exploits them or reviles them.

Those skeptical of connections between hip-hop and country music are understandable. It's no understatement to say that country music has long been connected to white authorship and spectatorship, and, as recent examples show, country has always had a difficult time integrating its audiences or recognizing and celebrating performers of color. Hip-hop audiences, however, have been far more open to white emcees and rappers, and it appears far easier to break into the world of hip-hop as a white musician than as an artist of color who wants to find success in country music.[36] As a result of hip-hop's flexibility, white artists have found a space in the subgenre of dirty South hip-hop; known colloquially as "redneck rappers," artists like Colt Ford, Rittz, Yelawolf, and Struggle Jennings—the step-grandson of outlaw artist Waylon Jennings and the grandson of Waylon's widow, Jessi Colter—have been able to find visibility within a genre that acknowledges both their regional identity as well as issues of class disparity. Struggle's 2011 song featuring Yelawolf is titled "Outlaw Shit," in which he samples from Jennings's 1978 song about being arrested for cocaine possession.[37]

Waylon Jennings's voice sings the titular line—"Don't you think this outlaw shit has gotten out of hand? / What started out to be a joke, the law don't understand"—that anchors Struggle's song; in it, he raps about his various run-ins with the police and time spent in prison. Struggle's understanding of what it means to be "dirty" or an "outlaw" comes from both a mixture of the rebellious streak of his grandfather but also a life spent in poverty and dirt. Growing up, he argues, going against the law seemed noble; being an outlaw was in his blood: "I grew up thinking it's part of the game / Them outlaws always taught me bad guys we're the fed's." Significantly, he samples Waylon's refrain as a way of articulating a frustration over both the limits of the outlaw life and the real-world consequences of living in a "dirty South":

She said storms will never last
So I'm looking out the window like, when's it gonna pass
I need some cash, I did the math, it keeps ending in subtraction
Is it fate or just the laws of attraction? I'll never know
Pa's tracks, fast lane, cocaine dealer
Tryna ease this pain with these painkillers
I don't want my soul to be stained to obtain my wealth
I couldn't learn from his mistakes, I had to make 'em myself.

In presenting his story as being critically connected to two different genres of music that privilege exceptionalism and authenticity through dirt, Struggle Jennings offers a profound critique of how a potential for transformation can also be disfiguring.

His rap is an indictment of the "outlaw" mentality that offers transgression and criminality as avenues for success outside the establishment but denies or naively refuses to acknowledge the real consequences of poverty or economic marginalization. And just as Waylon's "Are You Sure Hank Done It This Way" or OutKast's "Southernplayalisticadillacmuzik," Struggle's song is a meta-genre attack on both outlaw country and dirty South music's dangerous conflation of thug, outlaw, and gangster life. Struggle Jennings's collaboration with Waylon and Yelawolf serves as a kind of bridge between two musical genres; outlaw country and dirty South hip-hop might find commonality in their embrace of the dirt and debris with which their respective genres color them. But, in the end, whether it's the outlaw music of a new generation of Americana artists, or the evolving world of dirty South rappers, it's critical for artists within both scenes to respond dynamically to real-world consequences of renegotiations of authenticity that define outlaw values as exceptional—to put it in Waylon's words, it's easy for that shit to get out of hand.

The contrast between *playing* at outlawry and *practicing* outlawry can be seen in one of the most terrifying figures of the 1960s: backwoods or redneck white vigilantes. Waylon Jennings's white outlaw dressed in black and hearkened back to an old school cowboy or western stereotype—a rambling man moving from town to town, answering only to himself and living for the journey. Such a figure was disconnected from the decade's true southern outlaws: white mobs of rural and suburban southern men who rallied in force to attack progressives, Freedom Riders, and African American protestors. National anxieties over these real "vigilantes" played out in a number of different media, from television shows to movies to novels. And while Jennings's outlaw called his audiences to embrace a dirty rebel aesthetic by turning away from the "same old tune" of his "fiddle and guitar," an author like James Dickey would make his readers shiver in terror to the trilling sound of what is arguably the oldest school of all country instruments: the banjo.

CHAPTER 2

LET US NOW PRAISE HILLBILLY JUSTICE

Deliverance and Dirty Elegies

Some people may conclude that I come from a clan of lunatics. But the stories made me feel like hillbilly royalty.... My people were extreme, but extreme in the service of something—defending a sister's honor or ensuring that a criminal paid for his crimes. The Blanton men, like the tomboy Blanton sister whom I called Mamaw, were enforcers of hillbilly justice, and to me, that was the best kind.

—J. D. Vance, *Hillbilly Elegy* (2016)

IN THE VORTEX

As the 1960s ended, President Johnson's commitment to his "War on Poverty" appeared more and more fruitless; civil rights leaders began to imagine a way to reconcile African American and white working-class or poor citizens, an idea that was particularly threatening to the entrenched segregation of the South. During the final years of his life, Martin Luther King Jr. was in the process of attempting to unite African Americans throughout the South with their brothers in poverty through what he termed the "Poor People's Campaign."[1] King never got to see the realization of his attempt to unite white and Black poor people; he was assassinated on 4 April 1968. In his final sermon, he stressed that the goal of fighting poverty was of equal importance to poor African Americans and whites throughout the nation; he invited them to come together to resist their common oppressor as an act of profound radicalism: "You know, whenever Pharaoh wanted to prolong the period of slavery in Egypt, he had a favorite, favorite formula for doing it. What was that? He kept the slaves fighting among themselves. But whenever the slaves get together, something happens in Pharaoh's court, and he cannot hold the slaves in slavery. When the slaves get together, that's the beginning of getting out of slavery" (Carson 210). By widening his focus to economic enslavement, King was providing a compelling (and, to white southerners, supremely threatening) rhetoric. But it wasn't just rhetorical: the month before his sermon, King had brought together disparate and multiracial unions to the South. In Atlanta, King and the assembled workers talked about their similar goals; the first order of business was to march to Washington, where they would build a small biracial village on the National Mall. Dubbed "Resurrection City" by organizers, the space housed over three thousand protestors who set up residence there by the spring of 1968. On 19 June of that year, more than fifty thousand protestors joined them for the Solidarity Day Rally for Jobs, Peace, and Freedom.

During the summer of the Resurrection City encampment, James Dickey was living and working in Washington, DC, as the poetry consultant for the Library of Congress. Primarily known as a poet thanks to his 1965 National Book Award for *Buckdancer's Choice,* he had begun to write his first work of sustained fiction, a novel first titled "The Deliverer," which later became *Deliverance,* his most famous work. The two years he spent in the middle of the explosive turbulence of the 1960s in Washington, DC, dramatically affected him. In conversation with John Logue in 1971, Dickey spoke of the profound terror of the violence of the civil rights era—the marches, the protests, the assassinations—as an inescapable daily reality while writing his novel:

> I worked some more on *Deliverance.* We were going to come back East to be writer-in-residence at Hollins in Virginia . . . [but] we were offered the consultancy at the Library of Congress. . . . So we went and lived in Washington for two years [1966–68], during the last part of the Johnson administration and also during the time of all the troubles after the death of Martin Luther King: the riots, the March of the Poor. . . . Boy, I *mean* I was in the vortex. Was it frightening too. Terrifying. (Baughman 59–60).

Dickey's time in the terrifying vortex of the District of Columbia during the end of the civil rights era deeply affected the author, who was not just from the South but working on a novel about men from the suburbs of Atlanta who take a canoe trip in the mountains of rural North Georgia; during their vacation, the suburbanites are viciously attacked and forced to retaliate when one of them is murdered by a backwoods hick. As anyone who has even a cursory knowledge of *Deliverance* (either the novel that Dickey eventually published in 1970, or, more graphically, John Boorman's 1972 filmic adaptation), the villain of the piece is all too familiar for audiences who lived through the decade during which Dickey had composed his story: the vicious southern hillbilly. Clearly Dickey was tapping into American anxieties over poverty, violence, and southern rurality, all associated with the recalcitrant vigilante whose emphasis on local values and interpersonal justice frustrated the progressive march toward emancipation, freedom, and desegregation. In *Deliverance,* James Dickey was articulating the shared national anxieties of the civil rights decade.

And yet, we don't read *Deliverance* as a civil rights novel—despite connections to both the historical moment of its composition and the novel's relevant themes. One reason we don't connect those dots is because Dickey was anxious enough about the novel's reception that he agreed to scores of interviews to promote it; once it was clear the novel was going to be a success (not to mention a major motion picture), Dickey capitalized on the fame and attention he received by making public appearances on television and talk shows. In turn, there is a rather large public archive of Dickey's commentary on *Deliverance,* but the substantial volume of the author's remarks is not necessarily a good thing for critics and scholars.

For one thing, Dickey was a notorious liar, especially when it came to writing. His biographer, Henry Hart—whose subtitle for his book is *The World as a Lie*—quotes the author as saying, "Yes, I lied. But what has truth to do with me? I'm an artist. I MAKE the truth" (457). It is a well-known criticism leveled at James Dickey throughout his life: he lied about many things. Writing about *Summer of Deliverance*—Dickey's son Christopher's memoir of his father— one reviewer notes, "James spun all sorts of tales about hand-to-hand grappling with black bears in the forest, about his imaginary diseases, about his conquests of women." In that same review, we get the following description of the author: "James Dickey was not diffident. Imposing, swaggering, and fearsomely intelligent, he put himself forward, a bullyboy in poetry criticism, granting interviews and even improvising self-interviews by way of staking a claim for his literary ambitions" (Davison 107). Considering his reputation, anything Dickey has said on record about *Deliverance* must be carefully considered in the context of an author who was, above all else, attempting to promote himself and his book and willing to stretch the truth to do so.[2]

Partly due to anxiety about his reputation as a poet, Dickey took the lead in conversations about *Deliverance*'s literary merit; he alternately argued for the novel's prosaic universality and its straightforward survival narrative. Sometimes he would stress his composition of *Deliverance* as a retelling of mythic narratives; other times, he argued it was simply a rollicking adventure story.

And in still other moments, he would claim that *Deliverance* was, at its heart, a crime novel. As a result, we do not really know what James Dickey was thinking of when he wrote *Deliverance*.[3] Perhaps because so many early critics found *Deliverance* to be a series of meditations on universal themes, Dickey offered support for their readings; he would describe his fascination with myths and archetypes foundational to human nature, such as the inherent and destructive violence universally present inside of all humans. He writes in one letter about *Deliverance*, "there is a lot of violence in people that doesn't get a chance to come out in the pleasant circumstances of suburban living, and . . . this violence takes the form of a kind of unspoken yearning, an unfulfillment in people—men mostly—and then turns into a kind of poison that they have no way to get rid of" (Bruccoli 202). Regardless of the mythic zeitgeist to which Dickey was anxious to attach his novel—the evil at the base of humanity, the demasculinization of civilization, the human capacity for survival—Dickey's proposed themes suggested that *Deliverance* was unanchored to any historical moment, suspended ahistorically as a kind of parable. As a result, most early critics tended to analyze the novel alternately as either an exploration of nature's indomitable will versus man's determination (a survival novel) and/ or a meditation on man's inherent capacity for violent depravity when the constraints of social obligations are dissipated (a novel interrogating social ethics).[4]

Early readings of *Deliverance*—usually supported by Dickey's own burgeoning recognition of the novel's popularity—invite myopia about cultural and historical connections. Such reviews ignore the political and social upheaval James Dickey experienced during the writing of his book. His story was not ahistorical, and his plot invited connections to the time in which it was written. After all, *Deliverance* was written by a southerner abroad in the nation's capital experiencing daily the terror of civil rights marches and assassinations. In fact, as he was editing *Deliverance,* Dickey was sure he was going to be killed by violent mobs.[5]

Even still, some of the reasons we refuse to engage with the book's connection to the historical moment of its composition are obvious: we just don't *see* it. There are virtually no Black people in Dickey's novel.[6] His main characters are neither activists nor racist members of mobs attacking protestors; the four canoers are well-off men from the suburbs of a city not connected to racial protests or tensions—Atlanta.[7] The protagonists of the novel are not poor; they work numbingly mundane but well-paying jobs. Dickey does not spend any time exploring their political or racial views; there are no descriptions of protests, activism, marches, or racial violence of any kind. In short, Dickey's own confessions about his ideas for the novel,[8] the subsequent movie version, and, indeed, the history of critical analyses all elide significant connections *Deliverance* has to the historical moment in which it was written.[9]

It is time for us to rethink how *Deliverance* fits within the multiple times and spaces in which it was written and set as well as when it was consumed—as a novel composed by a southerner about the violence of the rural South in the 1960s and edited and revised extensively during the end of the civil rights era. Whether imposed by the author or by our own fantasies of consuming *Deliverance* (including watching or not watching the film), these resistances to read the novel connected to its historical moment foreclose some critical connections about national and regional anxieties over the atrocities of the civil rights era. For me, it is impossible to read *Deliverance* and not locate the vortex of terror that Dickey feels in the potential violence of the decade's central villain: the hillbilly.

More crucially, it's useful to examine how Dickey uses terror as a tonic of vitality, effectively rewriting the hillbilly as a symbol of abjection, trash, and dirt into a figure of tremendous (if receding) importance for the non-rural (and white) suburbanized southern man, who, in the end, recognizes the immediacy of the hillbilly's instinctive understanding and performance of "justice." It is a recognition that suggests all kinds of troubling connections with violent attacks against civil rights activists and African Americans in the 1960s. If we read the novel in its historical context, I believe we might find that, beyond being a novel about the anxieties of the civil rights era, *Deliverance* is an elegy for the dirty trash of the civil rights decade, the southern hillbilly and his inherent violent enactment of vigilante "justice," (r)ejected by American exceptionalist discourses in the service of progressive nation-building enterprises. Further, Dickey's dirty elegy proves a model for southern writers over the next fifty years to articulate value in the hillbilly without having to own any of his history.

SOMETHING IMPORTANT IN THE HILLS

Reading *Deliverance* in the context of the decades in which it was written and consumed—the 1960s and 1970s—one is first struck by its popularity. The book skyrocketed to the top of the bestseller list to the number two position, just under Erich Segal's romantic melodrama *Love Story*. At first surprised by his success, Dickey admits, "There's also an enormous element of luck in it. I wrote the right book at the right time" (Plimpton 207). It was the "right time" for readers living during what one critic calls "a time of anguish that Americans were suffering over the Vietnam War, culminating in the spring of 1970 in horror at the massacre at Kent State"; Dickey's exploration of the vicious deliverance of hillbilly violence was important in no small part because of its meditations on "What violence did to men and to American values [which] was a burning issue of the times" (Kizer and Boatwright 111). Another critic describes the novel as "an unsettling book that arrived, as if on cue, at an unsettled time. In its primitive violence readers caught echoes of Vietnam, the Sharon Tate murders, even of John F. Kennedy's assassination. In its elegiac lament for a disappearing river, the book chimed along with America's budding environmental movement" (Garner).

But if critics were, by and large, willing to read the novel in concert with the beginning political and cultural revolutions of the 1970s, they resisted connections to the decade in which it was composed, the 1960s.[10] I want to begin a conversation about *Deliverance*'s relevance to civil rights violence in the South by offering Dickey's hillbilly as an ambivalent figure of fascination and dirty value who offers potential for suburban men like Ed Gentry to problematically reclaim a blunted masculinity.[11] Significantly, the hillbilly value that offers the most vital potential is a teleological reading of (white) vigilante violence. For Dickey, this ambivalence to violence enacted outside of the boundaries of law is not a sickness to be cured but a dirty lesson the hillbilly can teach his (sub) urbanized brother. That hillbilly justice is supposedly vanishing from the modern "civilized" world only makes the immediacy of the dirty value more vital and, paradoxically, less threatening to its taxonomy as a uniquely southern and American vice. Dickey achieves this dirty elegy by positioning his main character, Ed, as a skeptic to hillbillies' value, and *Deliverance* subsequently narrates his gradual conversion, a spiritual awakening through the interlocuter of the "terrible beauty" of hillbilly violence (Monk 262). In this way, Dickey sees violence as sacramental, a pathway to insight or even transcendence. That Dickey displaces transcendent violence onto white-on-white violence is a factor of his displacement of a variety of southern issues in his novel and should have no bearing on our reluctance to read his book as a civil rights novel.

Though the novel deals with four men, each with distinct personalities, Ed Gentry and Lewis Medlock are Dickey's focus. They are not alike in any way: Ed remarks, "Lewis and I were different, and were different from each other"

(19). It is clear early in the novel that Dickey means Ed and Lewis to be foils for one other: both suffering through the same sense of a "principe d'insuffisance" that is one of Dickey's epigraphs.[12] Ed feels a sense of melancholy that numbs him completely. Working at his job, he experiences "the feeling of the inconsequence of whatever I would do, of anything that I would pick up or think about or turn to see" which he feels in his "very bone marrow" (28). "How does one get through this," he asks himself, but his answer is unsatisfying: "By doing something that is at hand to be done . . . that and not saying anything about the feeling to anyone." Later, he confesses to Lewis that he survives the mundane by disconnecting, sliding: "living antifriction. Or, no, sliding is living *by* antifriction. It is finding a modest thing you can do, and then greasing that thing. On both sides" (51). Ed buries himself in mundane matters and refuses to change. In fact, half-buried might be the most apt description for Ed, who goes through life like a suburban zombie: he regards his life as a husband, father, executive, and friend as a role he must play; moreover, he interacts with his colleagues and the other member of the canoe trip with a detached and ironic sarcasm.

While Ed is numb at his job as an art director and disconnected from his role as father and husband, Lewis is hyper-engaged—he works out incessantly and constantly goes on extreme trips; Ed lacks Lewis's "drive" and "obsessions." Instead of sliding like Ed, Lewis puts his body through extreme forms of survival, "almost as though the burden of his own laborious immortality were too heavy to bear, and he wanted to get out of it by means of an accident, or what would appear to others to be an accident." Lewis's drive to test his body, "to rise above time," precipitates the tragedy of the novel, for it is Lewis who goads the other three men to travel to a remote part of the Georgia wilderness. Early in *Deliverance,* Ed marvels at Lewis's determination, his ability to give "himself solemnly to the business of survival. . . . What kind of fantasy led to this? I asked myself" (52). For his own part, Lewis confesses to Ed that he almost wishes that the world would explode and force him into a situation where violence was the only means to survive: "I wouldn't mind if it came down, right quick, to the bare survival of who was ready to survive" (53). Ed wants to escape the daily grind of the office, his wife, his kids, but Lewis is after a spiritual awakening that can only come from an "authentic" experience with the land and its people.

One of Lewis's "obsessions" is the rural mountain men of North Georgia. Though he certainly pines for the purity of uninhabited wilderness, Lewis conflates his romantic ideas about the forest and river with the people who live there. For Lewis, such individuals are to be admired and respected. Driving to the place where they will leave their vehicles, Lewis makes it clear that this trip is more than a vacation for him:

"Funny thing about up yonder," he said. "The whole thing's different. I mean the whole way of taking life and the terms you take it on."

"What should I know about that?" I said.

"The trouble is," he said, "that you not only don't know anything about it, you don't *want* to know anything about it."

"Why should I?"

"Because, for the Lord's sake, there may be something important in the hills" (50).

What is "important" up in the hills for Lewis is not just landscape—rivers, trees, animals—but people who make their home on that land; like the terrain they live on, the great accomplishments of the hill people are completely unknown to progressive civilizations. "Do you know . . . there are songs in those hills that collectors have never put on tape. And I've seen one family with a dulcimer."

In Lewis and Ed, Dickey gives us two different perspectives on hillbilly value. For Ed, such an identity is as ludicrously unimportant as the numbing work he does in his zombified suburban life: "I don't give a fiddler's fuck about those hills," he tells Lewis at the beginning of the novel: "If these people in the hills, the ones with the folk songs and dulcimers, came out of the hills and led us all toward a new heaven and a new earth, it would not make one particle of difference to me," he confesses. But for Lewis, the hillbilly is the quintessential essence of sincere and untroubled masculinity; Lewis sees their way of life as the ultimate rubric for survival when "the machines . . . fail, the political systems . . . fail, and a few men are going to take to the hills and start over" (51). Lewis admires the hillbilly not only for a commitment to tradition but for his potential to narrate a fantasy of an unspoiled, uncorruptible future; when the apocalypse hits, Lewis knows where to go: "That's where I'd go," he tells Ed, "Right where we're going. You could make something up there" (53).

Dickey highlights the disconnection of perspective between Ed and Lewis; Lewis has sympathy and respect for the hillbilly and truly believes the figure has value to offer men. Ed Gentry, however, does not share the same kind of obsessions Lewis has with the rural South. As they drive towards Aintry, he remarks on the divide between the suburbs and the wilderness with sarcasm:

The change was not gradual; you could have stopped the car and got out at the exact point where suburbia ended and the red-neck South began. I would have liked to have done that, to see what the sense of it would be. There was a motel, then a weed field, and then on both sides Clabber Girl came out of hiding, leaping onto the sides of barns, 666 and Black Draught began to swirl, and Jesus began to save. . . . From such a trip you would think that the South did nothing but dose itself and sing gospel songs; you would think that the bowels of the southerner were forever clamped shut; that he could not open and let natural process flow through him, but needed one purgative after another in order to make it to church. (48)

Ed is a suburban worker bee, so his perspective on "the red-neck South" is largely described through the language of his profession, advertising. He understands what spaces mean by reading roadside advertisements, but his dismissal of the southern redneck as a serially constipated, Jesus-loving freak would have been consistent with many popular conceptions of southerners in the 1960s.[13] Most noteworthy in his humorous dismissal of the redneck southerner is Ed's commentary on the "bowels" of such a man: they are closed perpetually, resistant to the "natural process[es]" needed to "flow through him." Instead, the backwards hillbilly's openness *must* be forced by "one purgative after another." For any readers of *Deliverance* in 1970, Ed's articulation of the hillbilly's staunch resistance to open himself to "natural" processes had to remind them of brutal resistances to the political progress to end segregation and for the enfranchisement of African Americans throughout the region. Ed reads the resistance through the language of popular culture and advertisements, but the rhetorical underpinnings of his analysis remain consistent: the hillbilly southerner is a closed system; to break him open requires an outside (and, he suggests, violent) purging.

Dogged recalcitrance and resistance to letting natural processes flow don't just emotionally and spiritually constipate the hillbillies of the region; they reveal a startling capacity for violence in pursuit of interpersonal justice. Dickey knew well stories of the Freedom Riders, who were trained to be aware of violent southern outrage and its consequences. When a colleague, Ken Kipnis, approached Dickey to ask his advice as he prepared for just such a ride in 1964 in Mississippi, the author's only response was, "Be careful; there are a lot of dangerous people down there" (Hart 293). And yet, Dickey was drawn to those dangerous people, even if he may have been repulsed by their actions. It is precisely this ambivalent fascination and fear, seemingly contradictory impulses that are inextricably connected, that Dickey redeems throughout *Deliverance* both for Ed, and I would argue, for himself.

LET US NOW PRAISE HILLBILLY JUSTICE

Before the men are attacked for the first time, Lewis warns Ed that, while hillbillies are "good people," they can be very violent, especially to outsiders: "They're awfully clannish; they're set in their ways. They'll do what they want to do, no matter what. Every family I've ever met up here has at least one relative in the penitentiary. Some of them are in for making liquor or running it, but most of them are in for murder. They don't think a whole lot about killing people up here. They really don't" (55). Beyond the obvious reference to the Ku Klux *Klan* in Lewis's description of the hillbillies of North Georgia, the inferences he makes to their indifference to human life and their perspective on murder had to remind a reader in 1970 about the murders and violence perpetrated by mobs of white men throughout the South in the 1960s. The same thing that marks Ed and Lewis as "lesser men" (57) in the eyes of Lewis also lends a kind of macabre value to the life of this rural southerner. Though they are loyal and dependable—"the kind of life that *guarantees* it," Lewis tells Ed—the hillbilly's special devotion to clan and community is passionate and dangerous. Somehow it is the dirtying of that kind of man's values that appeals to Lewis. It is not clean; it's marked. When he tells Ed the story about a hillbilly boy who locates and rescues his broken-legged friend, Shad, in the wilds of the forest, Lewis makes it clear that it is both "his values . . . his old man and his old man's way of life" and the endless dirt of "superstition and bloodshed and murder and liquor and hookworm and ghosts and early deaths" that make such an identity exceptional to him. "I admire it," he tells Ed, but, more importantly, "I admire the men that it makes" (58).

Lewis's obsession with the dirty value of the hillbilly stems from the seemingly contradictory notions of devotion to one kind of system (family, clan, community, region) and rejection of others (social, political, national, ethical). That dissonance reveals a special value, a dirty one predicated on the privileging of a local (regional, familial) structure of beliefs over a more universal shared system (ethical, social), especially the policing of the former through violence. Lewis finds in that dirty value a source of power, and I believe Dickey finds it as well, for it seems as though the more violent, disturbing, or disfiguring the articulations of those dirty values are, the more compelling they become for Ed. Lewis's valorizing of hillbilly violence spills problematically into Dickey's narration, for as one critic notes, he "has expressed the belief that volatile and violent qualities are an inherent and sometimes desirable part of the human condition, while the loss of aggressive, instinctual urges is a form of castration which cuts off access to the full realm of experience" (Keesy 105).

Lewis fetishizes the hillbilly's violent qualities, including his articulations of pain and delight. He advises Ed to listen closely to the noises of the hills because he is "liable to hear the most God-awful scream that ever got loose from a human mouth"; he's not trying to frighten his friend but rather alert him to the potential of listening to something exceptional, like a rare birdsong: the hillbilly yowl. Mostly, the screamer is just an "old guy up here who just gets himself—or makes himself—a jug every couple of weeks, and goes off into the woods at night. . . . he doesn't have any idea where he's going. . . . When he gets drunk enough he starts out to hollering" (Dickey, *Deliverance* 61). Though Ed remains detached from the spectacle of being drunk enough to scream, he has to admit that he's hoping to "go through some fantastic change" once they hit the river—maybe he, too, can hear the inarticulate and bestial yawp of his id?

Ed gets his wish. And, like the dividing line between city and country, the change in him is "not gradual." The language Dickey uses to describe Ed's change is steeped in the discourse of conversion. At first, Ed is the skeptic; he has trouble locating any kind of the dirty value in the redneck, small-town southerners that Lewis so idolizes. When "an old man with a straw hat and work shirt" appears in front of the car, he looks "like a hillbilly in some badly cast movie, a character actor with too much in character to be believed. I wondered where the excitement was that intrigued Lewis so much; everything in Oree was sleepy and hookwormy and ugly, and most of all, inconsequential. Nobody worth a damn could ever come from such a place. It was nothing, like most places and people are nothing" (64). Even the mannerisms of the country bumpkins surrounding Ed don't seem particularly unique: they are characters in a movie, figures on a television screen. When an old man's hands tremble as he talked, Ed imagines he "was deliberately making them do it" (65). Dickey's division between Ed and Lewis in the opening sections of the novel make clear that Lewis is the acolyte and Ed is the skeptic. Lewis can read the sacred texts of hillbilly bodies and find transcendent meanings while Ed can only see physical difference. The dirty hillbilly body is grotesque to Ed, who thinks, "There is always something wrong with people in the country," whether it's the "missing fingers" or "some form of crippling illness." The men surrounding you in the rural South were not "physically powerful" though "you'd think farming was a healthy life." As the skeptic to the world of the purist hillbilly, Ed can only think of disfigurement as another kind of stereotype and advertising cliché. He finds himself desperately wanting to escape "from the country of nine-fingered people" (66).

Dickey shares Lewis's admiration of the hillbilly. Critically, the novel started out in a style far different from the one that Dickey eventually published. We know from Dickey's letters that original drafts of the novel were "more in the style of James Agee" (Calhoun and Hill 110), in that they were "written in a very heavily charged prose, somewhat reminiscent of" the author (Van Ness 6). However, I also find Agee's location of spiritual fulfilment in the poor, white tenant farmers he documents in *Let Us Now Praise Famous Men* the true influence on *Deliverance*. According to critics, Dickey considered it "his favorite book" (Hart 258), and in his *Self-Interviews,* he writes, "I would argue that his [Agee's] book, *Now Let Us Praise Famous Men* [sic], is exactly what Lionel Trilling said it was, the greatest moral document of the time. But to me it's a great deal more than a moral document. . . . it's an example of the human sensibility to go very deeply into life, not just brush along the surface of it and have nothing left but a few scattered sense impressions" (75). Jameson likewise finds in *Deliverance* the motivations for Lewis's canoe trip out west when they encounter the violent hillbillies, and he references *Famous Men* in his essay: "it is an eerie experience . . . to come across these ghosts from an older past, from the Dust Bowl and Tobacco Road, faces that stare at us out of the old Evans and Agee album. . . . it was the Thirties [Dickey's protagonists] went forth to meet" (Jameson 56).

In the hills, there exists potential for Ed's spiritual awakening, a conversion to a way of seeing that Agee describes in his photo-documentary some thirty-five years before *Deliverance.* For Angie Maxwell, "this influence [of Agee on Dickey,] specifically the unique moral conscience that pervades Agee's work, which Dickey referred to as Agee's 'complete participation' with his subject— explains Dickey's inconsistent representation of the poor white South, a subject that figured prominently in his work" (135). An "inconsistent representation" or ambivalence over the hillbilly marks the contestation of readings of the figure offered by Ed Gentry and Lewis Medlock, but the true deliverance of the novel's title is not the survival of Ed, Bobby, and Lewis from the redneck world of missing-fingered folks, it is, in fact, Ed's slow and gradual revelation that indeed there is, to borrow Lewis's phrasing, "something important in the hills," something, to borrow Agee's words, to be "praised." And once he sees violence as sacramental, he becomes nothing short of a monster.

DIRTY CONVERSIONS

Like Flannery O'Connor, Dickey uses a moment of profound violence to signal an episode of grace necessary to redeem his narrator from zombified complacency, but it is a kind of violent and dirty grace that can only be bestowed upon men, one that comes by the forced opening of something meant to remain shut.[14] I am speaking, of course, of the scene of the novel now metonymic for both novel and film—the rape of Bobby, the interrupted (arguably sexual) assault of Ed, and the murder of the first hillbilly vigilante. It is a disturbing scene that greatly frustrated Dickey's editors, who tried multiple times to get him to excise it (or, at least, tone down its gratuitousness).[15] Dickey refused in no small part because Bobby's rape represented a climax for his main character, Ed Gentry, and his gradual belief in the redemptive potential of violence.

Just as in a conversion, Ed comes to the scene as a skeptic, unable to read any meaning onto the men or the land they inhabit. When he first encounters the two hillbillies in the woods, Ed can only see them as disfigured freaks; one of them has a face that "seemed to spin in many directions" (Dickey, *Deliverance* 115). The other man's eyes "peered as though out of a cave or some dim simple place." Unable to read the men, Ed reverts to popular-culture stereotypes to understand them: "'Escaped convicts' flashed up in my mind on one side, 'Bootleggers' on the other" (116). Until Bobby is raped, Ed cannot find any hint of significance to the hillbillies; they are completely baffling to him. At no time do their movements or language facilitate an understanding of their interior selves. The two men look at each other, but "either something or nothing was passing between them" (116); when the hillbillies tell Bobby that the two of them "ain't never going to get down to Aintry," Ed is not sure what they mean because they speak "without any emphasis on any word." Hillbillies are texts that Ed cannot read, and he admits as much: "I don't know what you're talking about" (117), he tells them weakly.

The two hillbillies' actions are similarly bizarre and confounding. At first, the smaller of the men casually reaches over to touch Bobby's arm with a "strange delicacy" (118). The terror of the moment is clear: this is not the way men touch each other. When Bobby pushes back, the man levels the gun. Still not understanding what's going on, Ed decides to half-raise his "hands like a character in a movie" (119). The men tie Ed to a sapling tree and threaten him with a knife, but even with his life threatened, Ed desperately clings to a detached, sarcastic (civilized) persona:

"You ever had your balls cut off, you fuckin' ape?"

"Not lately," I said, *clinging to the city.* "What good would they do you?" (120, emphasis added)

The threat of castration is an act of supreme dominance among the men in the forest, but it, of course, reminds any reader of the violations of genitals that attended the spectacles of lynching in the South, and the language of the hillbilly—especially the coded racialized word "ape"—similarly references racist epithets.[16] Beyond that connection, the talk of "balls" morphs into potential sexual violations. The violent interaction among the four men quickly becomes erotic, a matter that Ed tries to laugh off, but cannot, especially when the men turn to Bobby and tell him to drop his pants. Ed feels the visceral threat first in the squeezing of his most physically interior spaces: "My rectum and intestines contracted."[17]

The moment the men begin to force Bobby to undress, effectively emasculating and humiliating him ("them panties, too," the men say when Bobby has taken off his trousers), Ed begins his profound transformation; we can first sense change by a shifting inability to read his friend Bobby: "I could not imagine what he was thinking," he tells us (121). The crucial shift between Ed's familiarity with the interior world of the white, suburban male and his gradual deliverance into the world of hillbilly justice crystalizes as the men rape his companion. The sound of Bobby's screams, "a sound of pain and outrage" (122) connect to the articulation of the drunk hillbilly Lewis reveres: at the moment of orgasm, vocalization and voicelessness reverse as the man assaulting Bobby responds with a muted yell, lifting "his face as though to howl with all his strength into the leaves and the sky." But there is no sound made by the man assaulting Bobby; the exchange of voices is significant here: the first time in the novel we hear the pure articulation of something primitive, not from the rural hillbillies of the Georgia wild but from Bobby's response to being sadistically violated.[18]

Lewis and Drew interrupt the attempted sexual violation of Ed; Lewis shoots one of the men with an arrow. Though one hillbilly escapes, the other, wounded one remains alive for several minutes. As he slowly dies, he moves closer to Ed, who, up to this point, has been skeptical of hillbilly exceptionalism and finds his experience in the woods like watching a bad movie. The dying hillbilly stumbles towards Ed as though he has wisdom to impart; he holds his hands out. Significantly, Ed describes his posture as being exactly "like a prophet" (125). But what prophecy does the dying hillbilly offer, and what deliverance does this violent confrontation offer Ed? We are drawn, of course, to Dickey's title and meant to ponder: delivered from or into what? If violence is a means of escape, to survive, it is equally for Dickey, a deliverance into a new kind of ontology, one that turns Ed into a different, darker person.

The same dirty value Lewis finds in the hillbilly as well as the seeming importance of the rural southerner's imminent extinction is what animates the men to go on the trip in the first place. It is no coincidence that Ed's awakening to the "prophet"-like teachings of his hillbilly assailant comes through a forceful challenging of both Bobby's and Ed's masculinity through sexual violence. The kind of importance that Dickey finds in the hillbillies' system of values is always-already dirty, tied in with a resistance to modern or progressive ethical ideals as well as a hyper-masculine refusal to feel shame for desires or actions. "There was no need to justify or rationalize anything," Ed says of the men as they take Bobby deep into the woods, "they were going to do what they wanted to" (121). Hillbillies are "men who follow their impulses without vacillation" (84), and in his fascination with their indifference, Dickey exposes what one critic calls "the hollow core that exists at the heart of this novel" (Eyster 470). When Ed is delivered into the new version of himself, he ceases to be whole.

But to ignore for a moment the moral and ethical implications of a belief that the force at the core of life "exists; it is indifferent and it demands, on occasion, blood sacrifice," I want to come to the core question that one critic poses this way: "what concerns us in reading *Deliverance* is . . . less the question of too much or too little violence (or of any other form of the 'irrational') than the question of the religious sanctioning of violence" (Tschachler 82). The curious lessons the men teach Ed through their actions are that violent sexual acts are the provenance of men of power.[19] Though Lewis commits murder for the first time, it is Ed who has been transformed. The values he adopts turn out to be the dirty ones privileged by the Georgia hillbillies and the white mobs of the civil rights era. A dirty kind of value suggests one that is both disfigured and disfiguring. The novel describes the gradual evolution Ed undergoes in which he is converted to a deeper understanding of the potential for meaning in the hillbilly code. But the conversion of Ed to hillbilly values really comes when he adopts their means of justice: vigilantism.

Realizing the escaped hillbilly knows the dirty secret of what has happened in the clearing and that he is a member of a community to whom the other men are outsiders, Ed and Lewis decide the best course of action is to follow the dirty rules of the region: over the protestations of Drew, they decide to cover up their murder by burying the man deep in the woods and heading for Aintry, the safety of civilization. However, before they can get there, Drew is murdered, shot at from high in the hills. In the ensuing panic, Lewis is gravely injured, and Ed is the only one of the three survivors relatively unharmed. Alone, he is forced to climb up a cliff, find the man hunting them, and, in an act of pure vigilantism, murder him before he can round up a posse. Settling on the course of hillbilly vigilantism, Ed takes note of his shifting conversion when he hears the echo of his voice tinged with the language and mannerisms of a hillbilly:

> "We can do three things," I said, and some other person began to tell me what they were. "We can just sit here and sweat and call for our mamas. We can appeal to the elements. Maybe we can put Lewis back up on the rock and do a rain dance around him, to cut down the visibility. But if we got rain, we couldn't get through it, and Lewis would probably die of exposure. Look up yonder." I liked hearing the sound of my voice in the mountain speech, especially in the dark; it sounded like somebody who knew where he was and knew what he was doing. (159)

Much like an acolyte learning from a prophet, the first step to Ed's deliverance comes through speaking in tongues, talking like "some other person," but he quickly moves from adopting the tenors of hillbilly speech to mentally trying to inhabit the man whom he hunts.

Ed's transformation from suburban professional to dirty hillbilly monster is most crucially achieved during the episode when he stalks and murders the man he believes shot Drew from the cliffs above the river. As he begins to ascend the cliff to find him, Ed realizes, "Everything around me changed" (167); his feelings of his old identity gradually disintegrate as a new one emerges. Trying to think like the man he's hunting, Ed finds his personality gradually eroding until he becomes the hillbilly he stalks, and the language of his transformation into the man is saturated with violent sexual imagery, tinged with ambivalence, and ringed with references to dirt:

> I had thought so long and hard about him that to this day I still believe I felt, in the moonlight, our minds fuse. It was not that I felt myself turning evil, but that an enormous physical indifference, as vast as the whole abyss of light at

my feet, came to me: an indifference not only to the other man's body scrambling and kicking on the ground with an arrow through it, but also to mine. If Lewis had not shot his companion, he and I would have made a kind of love, painful and terrifying to me, in some dreadful way pleasurable to him, but we would have been together in the flesh, there on the floor of the woods, and it was strange to think of it. Who was he? An escaped convict? Just a dirt farmer out hunting? (186)

There is an elegant longing—romantic even—on the part of Ed to connect intimately and profoundly with someone who might be, significantly, a "dirt farmer." Ed's connection with the hillbilly murderer in *Deliverance* mirrors for one critic "the same moral values of terror and violence which in [Dickey's] best poetry philosophically bind the killer and victim in ambivalent oneness, as necessary to each other, as co-performers in a ritual enactment of salvation through sacrifice" (Eyster 470). For the first time, Ed's obsession with the hillbilly supersedes Lewis's. For Lewis, the importance of the hillbilly is philosophical, a fantasy about men clinging to their dirty system of values that transcend suburban, progressive, or civilized ones. Ed's fixation with the hillbilly is far darker; he has little interest in their codes or communal ethics but in their vast "indifference" to the world outside their desires. It is impossible to read this section of *Deliverance* and not find Ed's transformation from buttoned-down suburban ad executive dragged along on a trip with his buddies to a cold and calculating monster as a change facilitated almost entirely by fantasies of penetration, intimacy, and rape, all imagery associated with the brutal scene in the clearing.[20]

When Ed finally locates the man he thinks is responsible for Drew's murder, he recognizes they share a "peculiar kind of intimacy" (197). Part of their intimate connection is vigilantism, interpersonal violence that displaces systemic justice; it is an intimacy of philosophy binding the men into a brotherhood. When Ed finally shoots him with the arrow, the man gives "up his blood like a man vomiting in the home of a friend" (200). But in the murdering of the man, Ed, too, is injured; both men are pierced by arrows of the same quiver. And with the connection of blood and pain, Ed finds that "there had never been a freedom like it. The pain itself was freedom, and the blood" (201). Coming back to consciousness, Ed follows the trail of blood to the body of the hillbilly; he is, at first, sad to see the man dead primarily because their subconscious connection must, too, disassociate. "His brain and mine unlocked and fell apart," Ed notes, "and in a way I was sorry to see it go. I never had thought with another man's mind on matters of life and death" (205). For a few moments, Ed experiences the mourning of the loss of their intimate connection.

But as he decides what to do with the body, he finds darker elements of his new identity emerging. He has become the monster he stalked, and in his increasing ambivalence to outside ethics, he contemplates other dirty vigilante atrocities. "This, also, is not going to be seen. It is never going to be known," he tells himself. Like Milam's confession of murdering Emmett Till in *Look* in 1956 or the murder of civil rights workers in Mississippi in 1964, Ed's indifference to the body of the victim he murdered stems from his belief that what he is doing is justified, that the act is sanctioned retribution, a dirty justice. Such a freedom from visibility gives him license to do "What? Anything . . . you can do what you want to; nothing is too terrible." It's not surprising that his instincts, borne from hillbilly vigilantism, are connected to lynching imagery: "I can cut off the genitals he was going to use on me. Or I can cut off his head, looking straight into his open eyes. . . . I can do anything I have a wish to do." Lost inside of his fantasies of violence, Ed finds himself dizzy as "the ultimate horror circled me" (206). But the feeling is not unpleasant; in fact, as he contemplates what terrible atrocity he can commit, Ed begins to sing softly to himself.

Moments later, Ed notes with fury that Bobby has not followed his directions; the realization leads him to a frenzied rage that culminates in contemplating shooting his friend. As he imagines shooting Bobby from the cliff, his language is cloaked in connections to Bobby's sexual violation and emasculation:

> You're dead, Lewis, I said to him. You and Bobby are dead. You didn't start on time; you did everything wrong. I ought to take this rifle and shoot the hell out of you, Bobby, you incompetent asshole, you soft city country-club man. You'd have been dead, you should've been dead, right about exactly now. . . . I walked back and picked up the gun, and my craziness increased when I touched it. I sighted down the barrel and put the bead right in the middle of Bobby's chest. Do it, the dead man said. Do it; he's right there. But I got around it by opening my fingers. . . . I didn't want to put the thing to my shoulder again; it had been close; very close. (207–8).

Ed's transformation is now complete. He has not only adopted the hillbilly code of vigilantism, he has also critically integrated the hillbilly's greatest value, ambivalence to violence in the pursuit of interpersonal justice. Bobby has failed to follow the rules, and his punishment should be death. The dead hillbilly's voice returns one final time to haunt Ed's conscience: *"do it. Do it."* In Ed's imaginative embrace of ambivalence to systems of power outside the hillbilly world, we find a complete conversion to his dirty values. The trajectory that describes his gradual evolution starts with a rejection of the people in the hills, skepticism about Lewis's obsession with them ("I don't give a fiddler's fuck about those hills"), violent revelation in the means of a brutal sexual assault on Bobby (and an aborted attempt on Ed that he secretly fantasies about it later), and finally adopting an ethos of hillbilly justice that gives him a sense of tremendous freedom. The freedom Ed feels is liberation from the social strictures of civilized suburban Atlanta, but the main value such a personality offers him is the freedom to operate outside the rules of conventional ethics and morality.

HILLBILLY JUSTICE

If *Deliverance* both probes national anxieties over the civil rights–era South as well as explores Dickey's fascination with white vigilantism, I'd like to consider Dickey's eventual celebration of the "justice" of white vigilantism. This deracinated hillbilly justice can operate on the margins of the civil rights movement; because there are no Black characters in the novel, Dickey does not have to deal with the thorny issues of a white author representing violence to Black bodies, or, indeed, the long history of southern atrocities done to African Americans in the name of "justice" or "law." And yet, a central ethical question throughout *Deliverance* clearly resonates with the history of southern murders of Black and white civil rights workers: what concept of justice do men pledge allegiance to when their individual understanding of fairness is threatened by the very systems meant to protect it? Framed in this way, *Deliverance* provides a profound, if terrifying, acknowledgment of the potential to achieve balance, to be "delivered" into redemption, absolution, and freedom by operating outside of systems of justice through individualized, interpersonal, messy, dirty justice.

In his 1959 essay "Notes on the Decline of Outrage," Dickey explores the burden the 1954 *Brown v. Board of Education* has had on a generic white southern man, who "after the supreme court decision on segregation, and with the admission of Negroes to buses and street-cars on equal footing with whites . . . knows he will have to assert himself one way or the other" (272).[21] Dickey's 1959 essay must have felt positively prophetic by 1961, when the country had seen just how violently the white men of the South would assert themselves on the question of forced desegregation. Though it is one of the traits of the hillbilly that Lewis admires—"They'll do what they want to do, no matter what"—it also marks them as outside the law: "Every family I've ever met up here has at least one relative in the penitentiary." The violence in *Deliverance* is predicated by white men and solely inflicted on white men, but the reality of white vigilante justice in the 1960s was just the opposite: overwhelmingly, victims of mob attacks, lynching, and other forms of vigilante violence were African Americans. Dickey's portrayal of solely white-on-white violence elides and cloaks the realities of white-on-Black violence throughout the 1960s.

The crime committed by the hillbillies—not just sexual assault, but sodomy—requires that it be answered by violent lawless retribution: Lewis's murder of one of the men by arrow. But what remains is the problem of how to deal with the consequences of that action, a complication further exacerbated for men in an unfamiliar land with strange (and primitive) customs. Trying to figure out what to do next, the men have a conversation that reveals what happens when systemic justice fails and must be replaced by the interpersonal, when punishment is meted out by individuals rather than institutions. Their eventual decision to hide the dead man's body as well as Ed's decision to climb the cliff and murder the other hillbilly are affirmations of a species of rhetoric that facilitated lynching and the disciplining of Black bodies through threat, intimidation, and violence throughout the twentieth century, but most specifically in the 1960s.

After the murder of the first hillbilly, the men debate the ethics of law, values, justice, coverups, and criminality, and they fall into different camps about what is best practice. Drew, the most morally pure of the men (as he approaches the subject with Bobby, Lewis, and Ed, he is significantly "washing his hands with dirt"), argues, "There's not but one thing *to* do. . . . Put the body in one of the canoes and take it on down to Aintry and turn it over to the highway patrol. Tell them the whole story" (128–29). Drew believes in the systems of policing and justice; under such circumstances, the actions of the men are "justifiable homicide." But the men aren't clear on how exactly to argue that the murder of the man (through an arrow to the back) might hold up in court. Even though he believes in the rule of law, Drew has "been on jury duty exactly once" (130).

For Lewis, the problem isn't the system but the interpretation and execution of the law by hillbilly men, whose "clannish" connections to region and community supersede fidelity to larger ideals. Distrustful of the hillbilly's allegiance to American democratic ethics, Lewis argues, "We not only killed a man, we killed a cracker, a mountain man. . . . There's not any right thing." Lewis's acknowledgment that institutions representing dominant systems of power do not view all citizens with the same degree of value is a recognition of the unequal power distribution that African Americans protested during the 1960s; it posits that, especially in the rural South, the life of a hillbilly is worth infinitely more than the lives of men and women outside their community, a lesson that did not need to be taught to southern Black men and women at the time.

Lewis continues to pick apart the black-and-white "boy scout-ish" perspective of Drew, and offers another reality of the Jim Crow South: the frustration of justice by jury trials. He says,

> We ought to do some hard decision-making before we let ourselves in for standing trial up in these hills. We don't know who this man is, but we know he lived up here. He may be an escaped convict, or he may have a still, or he may be everybody in the country's father, or brother or cousin. I can almost guarantee you that he's got relatives all over the place. Everybody up here is kin to everybody else, in one way or another. And consider this, too: there's a lot of resentment in these hill counties about the dam. There are going to have to be some cemeteries moved, like in the old TVA days. Things like that. These people don't want any "furriners" around. And I'm goddammed if I want to come back up here for shooting this guy in the back, with a jury made up of his cousins and brother, maybe his mother and father too, for all I know.

Lewis's understanding of how southern justice gets ensnared by the very systems it creates, even as they promise parity, reminds readers of the jury trial of Bryan and Milam or of the men responsible for the murder of civil rights activists in 1964; there is no justice to be found in a jury of peers when the peers are hillbillies.

In the face of such a damagingly hollow system, Dickey offers that the only true justice is fidelity to one's own understanding of it. This dirty justice becomes not just a hallmark of the hillbilly culture—Lewis notes that, if the man that escaped comes back, "he may bring *somebody* back here, though . . . it won't be the law" (134)—but the sense of fulfillment and a satisfactory answer for the wrongs that the men have been forced to suffer in the clearing. Moreover, the kind of vigilantism that the men undertake can only happen in certain spaces—its conditional, spatial justice: "These woods are full of more human bones than anybody'll ever know," Lewis says, and then, in a horrifying line that must remind readers of the murder of Freedom Riders and African Americans from Emmett Till to Medgar Evers, "people disappear up here all the time, and nobody ever hears about it" (136). The rural South, Lewis argues, is not a lawless place; it is a space where people, not systems, decide what's just: "We are the law" (137), he tells Drew.

The question of the justifiable vigilantism certainly fascinated Dickey, who, in an interview with Givens, says,

> My father was a lawyer. We used to talk a lot about this question when I was a small boy. My father was a rather unsuccessful lawyer, a born loser, a gentle, sweet person. He revered the profession of law—not the letter of the law and the legalistic paraphernalia of the law, but the ethical qualities of the law. My father did not believe that laws were really lawful—the kinds of laws that exist. He believed that justice was very seldom done. He had his own ideas about what constituted justice. A lot of that debate business in *Deliverance* was based on conversations I had with him when I was a little child. (Baughman 214)

Moral implications of vigilantism aside, what fascinates Dickey in the debate about vigilante justice is the inherent satisfaction of men deciding matters interpersonally as opposed to structurally. "I'll tell you what I really tried to do in 'Deliverance,'" he tells one interviewer, "My story is simple. There are bad people, there are monsters among us. 'Deliverance' is really a novel about how decent men kill, and the fact that they get away with it raises a lot of questions about staying within the law—whether decent people have the right to go outside the law when they're encountering human monsters" (Plimpton 222).[22] What right do "decent men" have to "go after monsters?" Dickey asks, and we may well ask, what right do men have to define what is "decent" and what is a "monster." For Dickey, the question is not difficult to answer: "I think there is a hard and fast rule operating there, as to whether you ought to be extremely vigorous in your notions as to what constitutes abstract justice and the law. Or whether there is, in fact, anything but a provisional set of rules made by men, which may not apply to certain situations. . . . Lewis is saying, men made the law that Drew wants so desperately to stick to, stay within, and they are also men, they can make *their* law" (Anthony 109). There might be men of the world like Drew who wring their hands over ethics and morality, but Dickey firmly sides with the immediacy of hillbilly justice: "I suppose the book might raise the question of what makes people do what they do to preserve themselves and their friends and families . . . [but] anybody comes after me and my people, I'll blow his head off!" (109).

However, Dickey's protestations here do not square with the kind of individual his main character becomes once he is indoctrinated into the sacrament of vigilante violence, and the only character in the novel to literally get his head blown off is Drew, Dickey's font of moral and ethical purity. Even more significantly, Drew's death—being shot from above—connects to the assassination of John F. Kennedy in 1963.[23] Drew, who represents in *Deliverance* the moral imperative of systemic and institutional justice, might be, as Ed says later, "the best of us . . . the only decent one; the only sane one" (225–26), but, for Dickey, Drew's naive and innocent beliefs are not compatible with the realities of place: the rural South is not a spot for idealism. Like the assassination of Kennedy, King, and Medgar Evers,[24] Drew's murder confounds the community of the men who survive him. In the wake of the tragedy, Ed fully turns to his belief in the dirty justice of his actions to get the remaining men home. He invents a story, sinks Drew in the lake, murders a hillbilly on the cliff (who is possibly not guilty of anything), and goes about coldly and methodically covering up every morally and ethically dubious action the men have taken. In keeping with Dickey's dirty obsession with the peculiar value that comes from hillbilly justice, it turns out that Lewis was right: every mountain man they encounter *is* an officer of the law. The man Ed kills on the cliff "was an honorary deputy sheriff of Helms County," though Ed supposes "everybody in the hills . . . was an honorary deputy sheriff" (209), and the actual law enforcement that turns up when the men make it to town is, indeed, skeptical about the motivations of four suburban men paddling downriver in their backwoods town.

Of all the terrible things that occur throughout *Deliverance,* perhaps the most horrifying is Ed's wholesale embrace of hillbilly justice, which causes him to lose any connection to his actions. As he tells his rehearsed story to the officer, "I made it a point to try to visualize the things I was saying as though they had really happened. I could see us searching for Drew, though we never had . . . for me, they were happening as I talked; it was hard to realize it had not taken place in the actual world; as I saw him taking them into account, they became a part of a world, the believed world, the world of recorded events, of history" (240–41). The most chilling part of Ed's transformation from suburban father to vigilante monster is not that he finds himself capable of murder but that he feels a numbing indifference to violence. Ed effectively rewrites the history of the events of the three days on the river, obscures the terrible violence inflicted onto multiple bodies, and creates a narrative in which he and the other men are hapless heroes. The substitution of narratives of veneration for a history of atrocities is also the purview of a white consciousness that seeks to frame itself as the emblem of virtue even as it obfuscates its crimes. If Dickey has any indictment for white culture's easy squaring of its atrocities with its sense of justice, it might be that Ed ends the novel as cold a monster as any dirt-farming hillbilly in the north Georgia woods. "Going back was easy and pleasant," he tells the reader, ghoulishly adding, "though I was driving a dead man's car" (273). Maybe Ed hasn't been saved at all, Dickey suggests; perhaps in becoming a monster to survive, he has been delivered to a darker plane of human existence.

Or, alternately, perhaps Dickey doesn't view Ed's transformation as a descent into primitivity as much as an ascent into self-actuality. In the end of the novel, adopting the dirty values and practicing the dirty justice of the hillbillies proves to be the force that delivers the men back home safely—except for Drew, whose innocence, Dickey suggests, was his hamartia. All three survivors are changed by the encounter: Ed, specifically, finds "the river and everything I remembered about it [had become] a possession to me, as nothing else in my life ever had" (281). Part of the reason that Ed recalls his memories of the river so wistfully is that the flooding of the forest ends up destroying the physical existence of it: "It pleases me in some curious way that the river does not exist, and that I have it. In me it still is, and will be until I die." A nostalgia for a drowned past and veneration of the dirty, yet sincere, life of the hillbilly is not just the end of *Deliverance* but the beginning of a tradition of speaking about the value of white working-class and poor southerners through the discourse of eulogization and elegy.[25] To praise the dirty, one must first claim that they are dead, or quickly dying out. It is what allows Ed to possess his memories of the river and numbingly obfuscate the ugliness of his deeds, and it is also what animates the force of a genre I call the "dirty elegy."

DIRTY ELEGIES

The rhetoric of the elegy has consequences for the author and the figures or ideals being mourned. If *Deliverance* is a novel that problematically valorizes the dirty value of hillbilly violence as aspirational for white, suburban southern men, Dickey can disavow the real consequences of advocating for white vigilantism because he attempts to claim they are *gone or fading,* relics of a time, space, and identity no longer concomitant with contemporary values and systems of order, ones either receding or vanished entirely. Lewis praises the hillbilly's cultural achievements (the dulcimer and the folk song) not necessarily because they are masterfully written works of art (they aren't) but because they are likely never to be heard again. And Ed's gradual conversion to a hillbilly ethos is a powerful personal possession because the river has destroyed the sacred space where he was converted. It has vanished, disappeared, and will never return.

I do not think it's a stretch to claim that *Deliverance* is an elegy for a fading space and people, but I am interested in the rhetoric of *Deliverance* as elegy. Not only does the elegy as a genre suggest, first, a hard ending to a kind of history (a death or a series of deaths), the elegy provides a rhetoric suggesting the figures or ideals eulogized have receded into the past (and thus are not subject to contemporary critique); in turn, the value which Dickey gives these figures and ideals can remain pure. *Deliverance* operates rhetorically as an elegy for the fantasy of a vanishing white hillbilly culture or system of values that, for Dickey, has meanings to offer contemporary men who feel as lost and numb as Ed Gentry. Though Ed at first scoffs at Lewis's sincere belief that "there may be something important in the hills," he realizes, by the end of the novel, there *was,* indeed, something important, something vital, to his sense of self (as a man, as a lover, as a southerner, as a person) that he could have gotten from no other space and no other people.

If we call this value dirty—which I feel I've argued sufficiently that we should because it is contested, violent, violating, disfiguring, ambivalent, messy—I want to connect its ontological dirtiness directly with the insistent assertions by Dickey's characters that the culture, people, and the very land itself are soon going to be extinct forever. The novel ends by melancholically asserting that all the pure "unspoiled places" (283) are going to disappear, sooner rather than later.[26] Even at Lake Cahula, Ed believes "there are still a few deer around . . . but in a few years they will be gone," just like the river and land on which his four companions met their greatest challenge. "Soon they will be gone" could be the plaintive slogan of Dickey's novel insomuch as it offers an elegy for the loss of something of great value, even if it is a bit dirtied by association with the hillbilly.

The modern elegy of *Deliverance* offers its rhetoric as one of the few ways to mourn the un-mournable, both because hillbilly culture is not vanishing and because the values of white vigilantism are contested, hybridized, dirty. If *Deliverance* wants to posit a re-approximation of value in the central identity of fear and anxiety for the nation in the 1960s—the backwoods southern hillbilly—that kind of public valuation can only be discursively claimed in postmortem: to engage in lamentation, one first pronounces the figure or ideal's expiration. Then, the work of mourning obscures much of the terror or the presence of anxiety: what do we have to fear from that which is gone? But the truth of the matter is that the ideals of white southern vigilantes—especially those framed by Dickey as worthy of understanding as crucial to unlocking the secrets of *white* masculinity, self-sufficiency, justice, and self-actualization—never went away. Instead, what *Deliverance*'s elegiac rhetoric offered was a model for how to frame the hillbilly or redneck or white working-class southerner's "value system"—whatever that might be defined as for different authors—as a piece of something valuable that we might find rummaging through the graveyard. Dickey's trick here is that the culture he mourns is still vibrantly alive and active, but the discursive elegy cleanses praise for something that is, at its heart, dirty, violent, and repugnant.

Dirty imaginaries in the 1970s gave birth to a species of discourse persisting into the twenty-first century; for the dirty elegy, one needs only to look to the historical moment of 2016 to see how *Deliverance*'s dirty rhetoric re-emerged after the election of Donald Trump.[27] In the wake of the stunning loss of Hilary Clinton, liberals and progressives throughout the nation argued that a refusal to valorize white working-class individuals was critical to the campaign's failure. There was much ink spilled over the importance of reconnecting rural white voters to a progressive agenda, but many commentators worried that the problem largely was a failure of imagination: how can you get someone to see your point of view when you cannot validate or understand them? Someone had to emerge like Lewis to explain to the Ed-skeptics across the nation why there was, indeed, something important in those hills. Enter James David Vance, former resident of Ohio and venture capitalist with a white working-class past. Written when Vance was thirty-one, his memoir *Hillbilly Elegy* immediately became one of the central texts that political pundits and academics alike turned to for an "authentic voice" to explain what we were missing by refusing to engage with the hillbilly.[28]

Hillbilly Elegy offers the same kind of rhetorical cleansing of the hillbilly that *Deliverance* does, only Vance's work is less complicated because the 2016–17 interest in the mind of the white working-class was a far more favorable moment for the hillbilly than the late 1960s. Even so, Vance acts as the Lewis character to Ed Gentry, the diffident and sarcastic coastal liberal "elite." Arguing first that "there may be something important in the hills" to value for political gain in the next election cycle, Vance excoriates progressives for what their lack of interest has done to poor and working-class whites. Like Lewis, who tells Ed that his problem is "not only don't know anything about it, you don't *want* to know anything about it," Vance argues that only by *wanting* to know about hillbillies can one truly begin to appreciate their value.[29] His description of the people he recognizes as "his people" is almost paraphrased from Lewis, who praises the hillbilly's love for community even as he recognizes the pejorative consequences of their devotion to their own clan. Vance opens by noting his background: "The Scots-Irish are one of the most distinctive subgroups in America. . . . This distinctive embrace of cultural tradition comes along with many good traits—an intense sense of loyalty, a fierce dedication to family and country—but also many bad ones. We do not like outsiders or people who are different from us, whether the difference lies in how they look, how they act, or, most important, how they talk. To understand me, you must understand that I am a Scots-Irish hillbilly at heart" (3). Vance's rhetoric here is not unique: Dina Smith notes that, during the rise of "white trash studies," many of these semi-"memoirs" had strange connections to narratives of enslavement—from bondage to freedom: I was white trash, but I escaped to become an authority that is now authorized to translate its value to audiences.[30] Vance similarly tries to define himself as authentic and authoritative. "I was one of those kids with a grim future," he confesses, then sentences later, "today people look at me, at my job and my Ivy League credentials, and assume that I am some sort of genius, that only a truly extraordinary person could have made it to where I am today" (2). Though he is a "hillbilly at heart," Vance is one who escaped from the spaces and the confines of his class; he was born a hillbilly but just got "lucky."

Vance sees his role as simultaneously translator and eulogizer; he writes his book, in part, to help Americans "understand what happens in the lives of the poor and the psychological impact that spiritual and material poverty has on their children," but he also wants to speak for those who cannot speak to us because they either do not have the language to do so, lack the visibility, or are on their way to total extinction. Part of the lack of hillbilly visibility is that as a group, Vance argues, they are "more socially isolated than ever, and we pass that isolation down to our children (4). Echoing Lewis's commentary that Georgia hillbillies are "awfully clannish . . . set in their ways," Vance finds his community under the threat of extinction. No longer able to exist in a progressive world that denies their voices, Vance's hillbillies retreat to spaces more and more socially isolated from any kind of diversity. Alone and threatened, the hillbillies face an obvious peril: they are always *just* on the cusp of vanishing altogether. The rhetoric of Vance's translation-elegy argues for a reinvestment in the world and perspective of the hillbilly before it is too late. If *Deliverance* uses the survival novel as a Trojan horse to celebrate vigilantism, *Hillbilly Elegy* uses the elegy genre as a Trojan horse for a profoundly angry jeremiad. It is a book that starts and ends in dirt, first with his grandparents, "dirt poor" (8), and finally with a cast of characters that can only be described as a dirty dozen: "Nearly every person you will read about is deeply flawed. Some have tried to murder other people, and a few were successful. Some have abused their children, physically or emotionally. Many abuse (and still abuse) drugs" (9). But, for Vance, they are not "villains . . . just a ragtag band of hillbillies struggling to find their way."

If you're hearing Lewis's voice in Vance's, you could be forgiven; much of what Vance says throughout his memoir reads as a frank confession of his love of the dirtiness of the hillbilly, carefully cleaned through misdirection and purple prose. What emerges in the pages of *Hillbilly Elegy* is a critical reworking of the shame one might feel at identifying with a hillbilly into a point of pride that very delicately separates itself from the associations with racial violence, injustice, and the history of white disenfranchisement of people of color. Vance places his authorship above that kind of reading and begs his readers to try to appreciate "how class and family affect the poor without filtering their views through a racial prism" (8). And yet, many of the values that Vance finds praiseworthy in the hillbilly are what Lewis admires about the Georgia cracker of *Deliverance.*

Both Vance and Lewis find a kind of dirty value in the hillbilly's penchant for taking matters into his own hands and correcting injustices of the legal system through violent criminal acts. As Vance lovingly remembers his family, his descriptions of them are almost always connected to violence: Uncle Teaberry, who made a game of carrying a switchblade and chasing Vance as a boy; Vance remembers fondly how he would threaten to feed his ear to the dog; Uncle Pet who, in a memorable anecdote, took offense to an insult by dragging a man from his truck and "beat[ting] him unconscious" but not before running "an electric saw up and down his body" (14). And for the finale: "Mamaw *had* nearly killed a man" (15), he gleefully gloats. Vance believes it was because his grandmother "loathed disloyalty" and especially "class betrayal," when one poor member of the community would steal from another.

The stories of his family's violence are ones on which Vance was raised, but, by and large, the kind of violence enacted in his community was not prosecuted. As with the hillbilly assailants of *Deliverance,* the law mattered little. Uncle Pet does not spend a night in jail for his vicious attack on the man who insulted him, because his victim "was also an Appalachian man, and he refused to speak to the police." Yet all the stories that Vance grew up on "involved the kind of violence that should land someone in jail" (16). Vance finds an odd comfort in his family and their community's response to what they felt were challenges to morality and shared ethical systems. One "of the most common tales" he hears as a boy is about a man who was accused of raping a girl; the man never makes it to trial because, before he can stand accused, he is found "facedown in a local lake with sixteen bullet wounds in his back." No one ever investigated the murder, Vance concludes proudly. "Some people may conclude that I came from a clan of lunatics," he confesses, "but the stories made me feel like hillbilly royalty, because these were classic good-versus-evil stories, and my people were on the right side" (17). *Hillbilly Elegy* seems to be a part of what one critic calls *Deliverance:* "that small body of writing which finds that the administering of death can be aesthetically principled."

Though Vance dives deeply into his family's secrets and offers some glimpses into how hillbillies have been misrepresented in popular culture (not to mention political culture), his stories of pride in violence owe the most debt to the dirty elegy of *Deliverance.* Praising hillbillies for responding to inequities of justice by taking the law into their own hands is naive at best and monstrous at worst. The sense of pride is even muddier because of the history of white violence against African Americans throughout the twentieth century, but certainly most poignantly and vividly in the 1960s. And yet, Dickey's novel and Vance's memoir renegotiate much of that shame by positively deracializing hillbilly justice as complicated interpersonal balances of individualized justice, by white people aimed at white people. By offering hillbilly justice as a fading ideal, as Dickey does, Vance can present these "stories" as potential tall tales that a child might hear growing up that suggest a deeper dirty value. "My people were extreme," he concludes in the section about violence, "but extreme in the service of something." Like Dickey, Vance never sullies that "something" by naming histories of racial intolerance, lynching, the murder of protestors, massive cover-ups, and systemic disenfranchisement. The species of "hillbilly justice," as Vance finally calls it, is completely unbound from the history of the civil rights era, and because of the negotiations that Dickey makes in *Deliverance,* Vance can argue that it is exceptional, "the very best kind."

Vance's work is not alone in making an argument for a re-approximation of the hillbilly; numerous literary texts, from Allison's *Bastard Out of Carolina* (1992) to Hochschild's *Strangers in Their Own Land* (2016) use the figure of the hillbilly or "white trash" southerner as a metonym for authenticity and value whose dirtiness can be both a marker of a misrepresented history and also, critically, an emblem of pride. But I choose Vance as the heir to Dickey precisely because he follows the model of *Deliverance* so clearly to answer the anxieties of a progressive audience with real concerns about any text that praises the redneck or hillbilly: the first step of such a model is to whitewash the world in which the characters live; second, they must frame the hillbilly's value as always contested, dirty. Finally, a dirty elegy like *Deliverance* or *Hillbilly Elegy* must craft a rhetoric that envisions the potential value of the hillbilly as a species of eschatology. These movements obfuscate motives beyond offering praise for an individual or community, such as celebrating a larger regional or national history intimately bound to the deaths of countless African Americans—because to offer a plain and public celebration of the white southerner of 1970 to 2020 would not be an elegy, it would be a manifesto.[31] Moreover, by dismissing white violence as bordered (as Trump did in Panama City) or dying (as Dickey and Vance do), the rhetoric of their value animates real monsters, such as J. W. Milam and Roy Bryant in 1956 or the El Paso murderer from 2019.

Any attention to the dirty South is going to tangle with the whole question of violence, especially white violence—in a nation that keeps believing, against all evidence, that nonwhite communities are the primary source of violence. The attention to whiteness, then, is important only insofar as the South (of the 1960s and 1970s) is a violent region, with a racialized society grounded in violence. And this unending elegy for violence and the white monstrosity it engenders surface in a similar way in the cultural texts that best explicate a culture's anxieties during specific historical moments: horror films.

Such films locate the consequences of a rhetoric of eschatology in connection with the hillbilly. Socially isolated, as Vance calls him; awfully clannish, as Lewis argues; only in the Panhandle, as Trump claims: the hillbilly monster of the 1970s to the present day exists completely separated from the progressive world of his moviegoing audience. He lies in wait for victims that come to him through a breakdown in mobility, in the nowhere spaces between somewheres. If Dickey's *Deliverance* asks us to find a dirty value in hillbilly justice that is slowly fading away, horror films like John Borman's adaptation of *Deliverance* (1972) or Toby Hooper's *The Texas Chain Saw Massacre* (1974) literalize that constant erosion. In doing so, these films argue that, far from being dead and buried, hillbilly whiteness *still* exists; it's out there. We cannot say that it is alive, because to do so would be to acknowledge a vibrancy that must be refuted, especially for post-racial discourses of American exceptionalism. But one thing we can do is narrativize its always-dying, to tell and hear the story of its constant resurrection. Because the truth of the matter is that species of vicious whiteness never actually died: it is undead.[32]

CHAPTER 3

GTFO

The Violation of Sunken Places

It made $46m, the No 5 film that year. And it's entered the language, as poor Ned Beatty can testify. Wherever he went, people would say: "Squeal like a pig!" It went on for years.
   —**John Boorman,** *How We Made* Deliverance

In the movie—it was becoming what the movie was about, it was the thing everybody was going to remember. "Squeal like a pig!"
   —**Christopher Dickey,** *Summer of Deliverance*

Leatherface . . . didn't really talk, though he did grunt and squeal like a pig at times. Could I squeal like a pig? I would learn.
   —**Gunnar Hansen,** *Chain Saw Confessional*

THE RISING HAND AND AMERICAN NIGHTMARES

At the end of his 1972 film adaptation of Dickey's *Deliverance,* John Boorman includes a scene not in the original novel; safely back at home and surrounded by his family, Ed Gentry (Jon Voight) sleeps peacefully next to his wife. Gradually, the scene shifts back to the North Georgia wilderness, the site of Ed's deliverance from the banality of his suburban life and home to vicious backwoods hillbillies. There is a faint ripple of movement underneath water—a result of the flood making way for the new dam. Softly at first, we hear a strange, dark, and foreboding cacophony of music steadily increasing in volume. The water breaks, unnoticeable at first, and suddenly, we see the hand—albino white and sleek—of Drew Ballinger (Ronny Cox), the murdered companion of Ed, Lewis Murdock (Burt Reynolds), and Bobby Trippe (Ned Beatty), as it rises ethereally. Startled by the sudden nightmare, Ed awakens. He pauses for a moment, then sighs: it had only been a nightmare. As the credits roll, he lies still, holds his wife, and his eyes blink hard open, fixed squarely on a spot far in the distance.

The terror of Boorman's final nightmare sequence is clear: though Ed has been delivered back to the safety of civilization and family, his mind is drawn ceaselessly back to the horrors of the river and forest, of what was done to him and what he did to survive. He finds himself haunted by the prospect that memories of that time will continually resurface; his acts will not stay buried but rise again, always on the edge of his memory, lurking, hidden, ready to pounce. Drew's ghost hand sticking up out of the water represents more than just the trauma of the woods and the monstrous acts Ed committed, it represents the existential threat of what we bury deep in our consciousness, things that must remain locked away from public view, dirty secrets that threaten the stability of safe, suburban life. For one critic, Boorman's final nightmare scene is the most significant moment of the film because Drew's hand rising is less a meditation on Ed's inability to repress his memories of violence and terror than haunting reminder of the buoyancy of the primitive:

> The intermittent "surfacing" of the barbarous, however, ensures that the work of repression is never done. In the final scene, Ed awakens from a nightmare beside his wife (Belinda Beatty), haunted by guilt, which his dream work manifests as the lifeless hand reaching out from the stagnant lake that was supposed to inter the three corpses forever. But the water cannot contain this groping hand, which reaches for Ed and longs to entangle him once again. The film, too, is unwilling to contain Ed's trauma. Rather than fading to black to enclose its own narrative, the film's credits roll over Ed's sleepless, haunted face. Beaded with sweat, the face addresses us urgently as if to question where our allegiance lies and indeed whether we would have done things differently. (Narine)

Ed's nightmare at the end of the film suggests that the things we lock away, flood, or bury in dirt always have transgressive potential to come back, and when they do, we may no longer able to square the cleanliness of our identity with the foulness of our monstrous actions.

Boorman's final beat in *Deliverance* becomes a trope for horror movies that come after it—the hand rising from the depths signifying (sometimes violently) a refusal of what should be dead to stay dead, a persistent undeadness that threatens us: in the rising hand, we see the dogged permanence of what we tried to eject refusing to be thrown away; the hand rejects its grave, its place of rest, its hidden and buried space, and rises, sometimes threatening, sometimes gently waving, as if to hauntingly remind us that we are never to be rid of it. Whether it's Drew's gentle ghost hand emerging from the flooded North Georgia forest, the vicious grasp of Carrie (1976) from the grave, the monstrous

The poster for Sam Raimi's horror film *The Evil Dead* (1981)
depicts an undead hand grasping at a woman who is dragged
into the dirt.

creatures that attack the women in *The Descent* (2005), or a zombie hand pull-
ing a woman into the grave on the poster for *The Evil Dead* (1981), the trope remains horrifying because it reveals the perpetual existence of our fears inside
of us regardless of how deeply or fervently we bury or deny them.[1] Perhaps in
the image of the unburied, grasping hand, there is a metaphor for fear itself,
of the futility of ignoring anxieties.[2] Whatever we do to fool ourselves into believing we are not threatened by our fears, the truth of the matter is, they con-

tinue to rise from the depths within us, to touch us, to wave at us, to remind us of their presence, even as we rhetorically narrate their invisibility. The hand reminds us it can still grab us at any time, any place. Maybe—because it rises from a sunken place—the hand is dirty.

Drew's bloated hand at the end of Boorman's film does not just explicate a terror specific to Ed Gentry, but rather a universal anxiety over the fragility of the repressed to remain buried in the unconscious. But *Deliverance*'s final beat also examines a cultural terror of the reemergence of the things we have metaphorically buried in the sunken landscape of the American South. The film version of *Deliverance* as well as the movies it inspired—most notably Toby Hooper's immensely popular 1974 *The Texas Chain Saw Massacre*—explore terrors lurking in the hidden, secret, invisible, and concealed spaces of the American South; these film excavate literal horrors from the debris of a space repressed by American culture, and the anxieties they reveal—crime, murder, poverty, mechanization and automation, mobility, injustice, or histories of violence—are literalized into imaginative spectacles of repeated (and graphic) violations that displace or obscure national ownership.

But the effect of these imaginaries pushes beyond the conventional notions of a "Southern Gothic" aesthetic and more in line with what the editors of *Undead Souths* term "undeadness": one "rooted and routed through a surprisingly dynamic physicality" (3). Boorman's and Hooper's violent imaginaries localized in a specific region (the American South) present themselves as visceral authenticity, virtually ensuring the terrors they narrate must be repressed again and again, obscuring them only to rise and terrorize in a horrific cycle.[3] By disturbing the tenuous spaces and monsters of the rural American South, victims in these two films sound a warning to those who dare trespass in the dirt of the South: what's buried here cannot be disturbed, and the consequences of disrupting these sunken spaces is nothing less than a disfiguring and violating touch, threatening inviolate fantasies of the nation.

Horror movies like *Deliverance* or *Chain Saw* present the South as a site of America's nightmares, which makes sick sense, for according to Allison Graham, southern states represent "creative paralysis": "The American South, it seems, is frozen at its eroticized apex and nadir, relegated by tacit national consensus to a heaven-and-hell diptych of social types . . . rampaging crackers and hillbillies of the Benighted South." Graham explains that, post–World War II, the region ceased to offer dynamic possibilities for art and culture and became instead "the 'dark' underbelly of the nation, the reversed image in the mass-media mirror, the South was and is America's repellant yet all too compelling Other" ("South in Popular Culture" 335). Of course, confining dirt to a specific region (the South) is another strategy of repression, one that works alongside "burying."

Dislocation involves moving dirt somewhere else, to separate it from "normal" life. America can believe in its own righteousness by saying its evils (racism, of course, prime among them) are only a southern problem. Such a dark and dirty otherspace offers the perfect setting for exploring America's nightmares, and Boorman's *Deliverance* clearly struck a chord with the American public in 1972. His film was every bit the phenomenon that Dickey's novel was; it was nominated for five Golden Globe Awards, three Academy Awards, and was in the top five of highest-grossing films of the year. Part of the popular appeal of the film was how, in the words of one critic, it concretized "the major anxieties that afflicted Americans during the late 1960s and 1970s . . . including those between social movements . . . [and] race-driven anxieties" (Narine 452). And yet, unlike the novel, the film rejects many of the novel's "ambitions," especially Dickey's "yearning sense of cultural valorisation of the backwoods tradition" (Blake 133).

Even though the novel is somewhat different from the film, Dickey remained determined—sometimes, comically so—to be involved in the process of translating his book to the screen, and like the novel, *Deliverance* haunted audiences.[4] In fact, the film's two most horrific scenes were so memorable that they eventually replaced the story itself. Writing a few years ago, critic Benjamin Murphy writes, "Mention *Deliverance* and there are two responses you might expect: someone will begin vocally trilling a bluegrass banjo melody or someone will grimace while recounting that line from the rape scene: 'Squeal like a pig!'" (205). For another critic, "all that really sticks in the mind" about the movie are the "two elements that do not appear in the book: the insistent refrain of the 'Dueling Banjos' theme" and "two of the most invidiously stereotyped hillbillies imaginable" ordering Bobby to "squeal like a pig!" (Blake 133). Surely those two scenes were centermost on the mind of an early reviewer of the film, who singled out the visceral brutality of Boorman's narrative by emphasizing the movie's presentation of "images that refuse to sink out of sight but remain horrifyingly in our view until there is no option but to accept their existence" (Strick).

The bizarre musical collaboration between Drew and the "banjo boy" (Billy Redden) as well as the shocking, brutal rape of Bobby by two dirty vicious hillbillies remain the central, haunting scenes of the film, both of which have virtually eclipsed any other cultural understandings of *Deliverance* that Dickey or Boorman intended. The visual rhetoric of these scenes suggests that perversion is banal for the rural South, a space mostly hidden from civilized and popular imaginations; when the city men stumble onto the banjo boy or the monstrous hillbillies in the clearing, they are shocked to see a space and people less physical than mythical; these are places and folks meant to be forgotten. The result of the wounding disruption of the city men's presence is the awakening of forces they do not totally comprehend. In upsetting the tranquility of what remains invisible to "civilized" eyes, the city men unleash a violence; whether the violence manifests as an orgy of music or bestial orgasm, it is a similar explosive reaction to the terror of witnessing, of seeing what was meant to be buried.

The city folk of *Deliverance* or the road trippers of *Chain Saw* unwittingly victimize the hillbillies in these films by witnessing them—as objects, symbols, not as people—and thus become a part of unconsented intimacies. In retribution, the hillbilly monsters of both films avenge themselves with their own violating and unconsented intimacies by moving from sight to touch—from a somewhat distanced "witnessing" to more intimate (and terrifying) contact between bodies. This violating touch reflects the violation of visibility forced on them by the heroes of the film—in short, the consequence of witnessing is a brutal act of violent touch. The revenge of the repressed is always connected to the threat of disfiguring touch from a hand rising from a sunken space.

The two scenes that have kept Boorman's film peculiarly culturally relevant are rhythms of terror mirroring the waving and grasping hand rising from the dirt. In the dueling banjos and "squeal like a pig" scenes, we have two instances that follow similar patterns: the abrupt revelation of a physical and metaphysical terrain that resists visibility and consumption; an ecstasy of violence whose expression is fundamentally connected to witnessing, and finally, a disfiguring, avenging touch reminiscent of Drew's dead hand rising from the depths at the end of the film. The scenes both end with a ritualistic closing of the opened space, obscuring the terrain as a kind of trap for potential victims who inevitably and cyclically will end up disturbing it again. By manifesting how these metrics of horror ask viewers to witness an unwatchable trauma, *Deliverance* establishes the rural American South as a potential imaginary in horror films upon which to graft other traumas—economic, racial, national, global, political, sexual—and thus articulate a contained terror, one bordered, and thus pleasantly threatening to audiences outside the region. Such a containment of traumas and horrors in one space presents the spectacle of terror and the power of its transgressive potential as a dirty regional imaginary that allows national imaginaries to remain inviolate.

I'M LOST

In the scene between Drew and the "banjo boy," we are introduced to the dynamic of seeing something not meant to be consumed by outsiders. Boorman begins with his protagonists at a gas station; Drew softly strums his guitar, and a boy with a banjo on a nearby porch plays the same chords. Startled by the sound, Drew looks up to find from where the strange echo is coming. Emphasizing watching and seeing, Boorman switches between closeups of the eyes of his main characters—Drew looking from his guitar to the boy, and the boy, whose squinted eyes are locked on Drew. We are drawn to the spectacle of the boy both by Boorman's camerawork but also by his deadlock stare; Dickey—who agreed to write the screenplay for the film—writes that the boy's "peculiarly bald head and pallid skin [are] made even stranger by the low angle side-lit shots that capture his aged and inscrutable face" (Dickey and Boorman 132).

Other characters' sight lines are equally important: the fixed stare of the banjo boy, hypnotic in its static directness, contrasts with the blurred and interrupted focus of the other protagonists. Lewis's eyes dart all over the place; he interrupts the song by asking the gas station attendant questions. However, the man looks beyond him, dancing side to side to see what's taking place between the boy and Drew: "the old man leans this way or that, restoring his view" (15). Ed's eyes—which become the central consciousness of the film and often a stand-in for the audience—dart back and forth between the boy, the other townsfolk, and Drew. When the song begins, Drew's eyes remain fixed on his instrument; Dickey notes in his script, Drew "does not look up from the guitar keyboard" (15), but the boy, on the other hand, significantly does not need to look at his instrument: even though they are improvising a song, the boy has such a mastery of the banjo that he does not need to see what he is playing. Not to put too fine a point on it: the focus of all the townspeople's eyes is on the performers, one by his car, the other on the stage-like porch. The protagonists, on the other hand, look everywhere but at the two instrumentalists. For the hillbillies, the connection being made between Drew and the boy is a sight to behold; something is happening that requires spectatorship: *it must be seen.*

What the audience sees, however, is something whose visual dynamic either is invisible (bordering on unseeable) or resists spectatorship. First, the central focus of the scene is not on seeing but hearing. Second, in emphasizing the visual dynamic of performing, Boorman reveals the asymmetry of his protagonists in this strange space. The city men look out of place, unsure of their authority over the place or their instrument. The country folk, on the other hand, are self-assured. The characters' aesthetic is similarly important: the men from the city are, to put it plainly, movie stars.[5] Reynold's Lewis is a font of hypermasculinity and vitality with "mountain ranges . . . [for] muscles" (15). As a contrast, the albino banjo boy looks unfamiliar and sickly; it is, of course, the reason he was cast.[6] However, even though the banjo boy looks different, his aesthetic gives him a familiar context, a "historical reality" connecting to "the depravation and economic marginality endured by the rural poor." Such an economic wound manifests bodily in a profoundly unhealthy, sickly, deformed figure: "the physically deformed /disfigured or mentally challenged local" (Murphy 158).

The contrast between the protagonists and hillbillies is even more acute when Drew approaches the boy on the porch and asks him to play a song using the chords they have been echoing back and forth: "C'mon, I'm with you," Drew says as he walks into the same frame as the boy for the first time. The two launch into a full-scale version of "Dueling Banjos."[7] The rest of the performance takes place with Drew on a sunken plane: the boy above him, while Drew performs below; an angle that is "the classic horror-movie fashion for filming monsters" (Creadick 67). The boy might be a genius at the banjo, but his appearance and hypnotic stare mark him as a compelling and mysterious figure. The camera shifts between an upper view of the back of the boy's head as he looks down at Drew, and then back to Drew as he looks at his guitar from a sunken vantage point. The placement of the boy and Drew in the same frame emphasizes the power of the boy over the man who literally performs at his feet. The banjo boy fixes Drew with his gaze while Drew watches his fingers. The reverse perspective of the scene is apparent: for the hillbillies, the city folk are exotic figures to be visually consumed.

The air disturbed by the chords of the boy and the man, we get a slow shift in camera angles frenetically moving back and forth from faces; it builds: the song begins to overtake the moment. By and large, Boorman gives us images of unrestrained pleasure. In Dickey's script, he writes that the boy's "face has the beatific vision of the idiot doing what he loves" (16), and the men from the city watch "with growing fascination" (15). Gradually as the song increases in speed and tempo, Drew simply cannot keep up; he finally raises his head and fixes the boy in his frame of vision to offer a confession: "I'm lost." The gleeful boy continues to play in an unrestrained orgy of notes, his fingers a blur as he picks all over the neck of the banjo, while Drew is forced to simply watch in rapt awe. The pleasure the city men derive from this performance is voyeuristic, getting lost in song, seeing something usually invisible (the sound of music) in a space that is "forgotten" or "never-discovered," what Dickey calls the "unseemly" (13). The power of the scene is clear: Ed, Bobby, Lewis, and Drew are lost in witnessing the unwitnessable in a setting that is undiscovered. That the aesthetic of this voyeurism is "unseemly" or disfigured or "weird looking" or causes Drew to get "lost" is significant; the pleasure derived from their initiation into the invisible "forgotten" world of the hillbilly is tinged with terror of losing themselves. Just as in Dickey's novel, Boorman uses a (filmic) language of conversion: to find themselves, the men must first lose themselves.

Throughout *Deliverance,* the act of seeing, of witnessing, is always violating. While the boy and Drew play, the music acts as a signal to the country folk surrounding them; Dickey writes that "three or four weird looking hillbillies have materialized out of the weeds. . . . this ill-assorted group clusters around these two musicians" in what Dickey calls "a dusty, forgotten or never-discovered filling station, way off up in the mountains of Appalachia" (15). The enjoyment of the song by the city men is further differentiated in the aesthetics of asymmetry of Boorman. While the city men sarcastically laugh and smile in complete stillness or mock glee, the hillbillies dance in strange staccato bursts of movements unrecognizable to Ed and Bobby, the latter of whom laughs haughtily at their gyrations. The very pacing of the scene feels downright pornographic in its unrestrained iconography of faces in ecstasy, the slowly pulsing build to climax, and the orgiastic delight in a collaborative act of unrestrained pleasure.

By the end of the song, Drew believes that he and the boy have made a profound connection through their increasingly feverish and chaotic collaboration; they are lovers who, at the end of their lovemaking, can celebrate a co-equal recognition of their shared intimacy. But Drew makes a critical mistake: he offers appreciation by reaching out to shake the child's hand. The tenor of the scene shifts dramatically as the boy refuses even to hold Drew's gaze. By refusing even to look at Drew's hand, the banjo boy rejects any recognition of connection between his music and Drew (or, indeed, his body and Drew's). In

Drew Ballinger (Ronny Cox) offers his hand to the "banjo boy" (Billy Redden), who turns his head and refuses to even look at him.

a scene so focused on visual consumption, it is a significant moment as the boy denies Drew not only his hand but his eyes. His refusal makes clear what the audience already knows: Drew was not his collaborator; he was his competitor, and the city man has been vanquished.[8] With the song over, the city-man Drew and the country-boy have no connection with each other; in fact, the presence of the city men witnessing the intimacy of their song is no longer a collaboration but a violation. The "weird looking" hillbillies seem threatening and strange, and the boy, who had offered his intimacy through song, clearly rejects any meaningful connection with his once-collaborator. "Do you wanna play another one," Drew asks hopefully. The boy does not answer.

In his move to touch the boy, Drew has misread what has taken place and violated the rules of this space; his reaching violation marks a closure that cannot be opened again. "The door has closed," Dickey writes in the screenplay; "There is no way in except through the music" (16). It is no coincidence that Drew's hand is refused, the same one rising ghostly out of the water at the end of the movie to remind Ed and the audience of the threat of that which refuses to remain buried. Drew's hand is symbolic of terror attending the disrupting witnessing and violations of hidden spaces, and the refusal of it by the banjo boy in this scene marks the audience's first glimpse of how the potential for touch can be a physical, sexual, metaphysical, or disfiguring violation. Witnessing the lack of acknowledgment of Drew, Bobby advises his friend to give the boy "a couple of bucks," a condescending gesture of class superiority; by making the refusal to shake his hand an economic issue, Drew and Bobby have further upset the balance of difference between the boy and the city men. The moment is passed; the boy is unresponsive. The wounding of the intimacy and the violation enacted is closed over, masked, lying hidden for the next hapless city men who come along.

The banjo scene connects to the potential for sexuality (in the orgy of music and pleasure) and violation (in witnessing and a refused touch), but sexual violation is ontologically present in the very figure of the boy, who is, as Dickey problematically describes him in his screenplay, "probably a half-wit, likely from a family inbred to the point of imbecility and Albinism" (13). As an individual defined by his family's "dirty secret" of inbreeding and incest, the albino banjo boy becomes a symbol of sexual impurity that is, ironically, a result of an isolated (perhaps, in one sense, pure) sexual history.[9] Bobby's offhand and sarcastic comment to Ed when the boy begins playing—"Talk about genetic deficiencies, isn't that pitiful?"—references the city men's reading of the banjo boy as disfigured as a result of his dirty inbreeding. But, as Creadick argues, his "disability, apparently a consequence of some prior forbidden sexual act of incest, keeps him a boy forever, though a boy-genius when playing the banjo."

The dirty sexuality of supposed inbreeding is a kind of exceptional history for the banjo boy, for it offers both the potential for disability and hyperability. His inbreeding also marks the boy rare, another kind of exceptionalism, for his uniqueness in the eyes of the city men, can be simultaneously compelling (Drew) and disgusting (Bobby). In Borman's visual presentation of the albino boy scene, we find useful connections to Kristeva's "crying out" of the abject to compel and repel us, as well as Douglas's claim that dirt marks a fundamentally impure threat that simultaneously invites us to be thrilled by its dangerous potential for transgression. One critic offers: "In ... Deliverance ... hillbillies have intermarried themselves out of the human race, turning into a new breed of mutants whose Lil'-Abner–type dialect is neither quaint nor picturesque but only a sign of their inability to express themselves like human beings. If the taboo against incest is, as modern anthropology taught us, the hinge between nature and culture (descent/consent), its violation by the 'hillbillies' places them at the far side of the culture/nature barrier" (Portelli 36). The hillbilly stereotype is an always-already emblem of sexual violation and diseased disfigurement: "the locals are unkempt, toothless yokels, many of whom seem to have physical or mental disabilities," one critic offers. The boy's very body reveals the duality of his potential importance. As a result of his family's inbreeding, he is an albino with skin is so white it is "luminous in the shadows" (Murphy 13), what Creadick calls "hyper-whiteness" (67), but it is the curious reversal of purity in what is supposedly the font of impropriety and dirty sexual history; it is, in fact, the purest color of all.

The next time Drew's floating outstretched hand will be seen onscreen is at the end of the movie when it reaches out, not to shake hands with or make some kind of connection between city and country, but instead rises from the water in Ed's nightmare to threaten and disrupt his suburban serenity. Significantly, at the point in the nightmare when Drew's hand rises from the depths to terrify Ed, it has shifted from its normal color to that of the most ivory white, reminding us of the albino boy's skin. The hand first offered to the banjo boy, refused as a violation of Drew's disturbing misreading of what has transpired, thus rises again cloaked in the very (pure) color of a boy who has come to represent so much of the movie's symbolic dirt.

The song Drew and the boy play together—"Dueling Banjos"—has since become iconic, not just as soundtrack for the banjo scene but for the very tenor of *Deliverance*'s horror, especially as it connects with the scene of Bobby's rape (even though it does not play during the scene). The song is of the boy, and both the scenes are the most strikingly memorable in the movie.[10] The same anxieties that the banjo boy scene exposes are actualized in the rape scene. Strangely, it is the grafting of authenticity onto this banjo scene that offers a starker reality to the rape scene, for the overall terror of both scenes comes, in large part, from their appeals to realism.[11] Even though the actor who played the boy (Billy Redden) didn't play the banjo, audiences believed his performance was genuine. So, it is no surprise that, when writing about the banjo scene in *Dueling Banjos: The Deliverance of Drew,* the actor who played Drew, Ronny Cox, asserts, "*Dueling Banjos* has sort of become in the vernacular for all kinds of things that happen in the South" (41). "All kinds of things" reads as an ominous phrase to anyone familiar with the horrors in *Deliverance,* for some of the things that happen in the South are vicious acts of sexual perversion—dirty incest, inbreeding, and rape.

SQUEAL LIKE A PIG!

Faded fragments of "Dueling Banjos" make up the soundtrack of *Deliverance.* We hear faint echoes of the song after the gas station scene; it haunts our ears, reminding us of all the terrors it hints at: sexual perversion, dirty hillbilly disfigurement, disease and poverty, and the horrors that come from disturbing what should stay buried. In the original script, Dickey inserts a scene in which the men reencounter the albino boy as they canoe down the river before they are attacked. Going under a bridge, the men see several faces looking down at them, and Drew notices one of them is the boy with whom he played the banjo: "He waves up enthusiastically and getting no answer from the boy, holds his paddle like a guitar and pretends to play it. The boy stares but makes no response" (27). As the men cross under him, he continues to watch them until the canoe drifts out of sight. At this point in the script, Dickey's albino boy is less a character than a figure from a horror movie, a ghost whose presence haunts the men and reminds them of the terror buried in the hidden world of the forest. After the scene in which Drew reaches to touch him and the boy turns away, his gaze has become terrifyingly prophetic, promising violation and disfigurement. We do not need Drew's next line to understand why Dickey brings back the albino boy right before the most intense scene of the movie, for his haunting and glazed watchfulness is enough for us: "Spooky kid."[12]

The spooky banjo kid gives way to the real monsters of Boorman's movie minutes later; Bobby's rape, as iconic as the banjo scene before it, follows a trajectory similar to the banjo scene. Like the city men who pull into the gas station, Ed and Bobby unwittingly stumble into a space not meant to be witnessed. The men wind up in the clearing because they have lost both their way and their fellow travelers. The initial beats of the scene take their cue from the ending of the banjo scene, especially Drew's final admission to the boy during the song—"I'm lost." Ed is forced to admit to the hillbillies that they do not know where they are; Bobby offers weakly that they are going to Aintry, to which one of the hillbillies replies, "You done taken a wrong turn somewhere. This here river don't go nowhere near Aintry" (40).[13] Ed at once realizes that the men are intimidating, and he reads their movements as attempts to protect their land. Believing that maybe Bobby and he have stumbled onto a secret site for making whiskey, Ed tries to appear as innocent and unthreatening as possible, "Hell, we sure don't want any trouble. If you've got a still near here, that's fine with us. We could never tell anybody where it is, because you know something? You're right. We don't know where we are" (40).

In his script, Dickey describes the hillbilly men in the same language as the banjo boy: "If there were ever any degenerate red-necks, they are these two" (39). Like the boy with his albino skin and squinty eyes, the bearded hillbilly's mouth reveals "awful stumps of teeth, orange and broken" (39); when the tall hillbilly talks, his voice is described as "very toothlessly" (41), and just as in the banjo scene, Bobby and Ed have trespassed on ground that is "undiscovered." Their very presence is a violation.[14] By disturbing the ground of the sunken space of the clearing, they have disrupted an intimacy between the two men and possibly between the dirty, secret relationship that the hillbillies have with the clearing (which might be a space of outlaw behavior). Now, a new kind of intimacy must be established, one that is both connected to the uncovering of what was meant to be hidden and the violating touch Drew offers the boy at the end of the song.

Boorman's terrifying intimacy begins with the first and possibly most threatening kind of touches between men—tenderness. Dickey's screenplay describes the first act of violation in the slightest terms, as "the tall man reaches over and feels Bobby's arm, in a strangely delicate gesture" (41). In Boorman's film, the hillbilly instead touches a place far more intimate with a gesture that is vaguely romantic: he grazes Bobby's face lightly with his fingers. In the most terrifying moment of the film to this point, Ed is forced to witness a gesture diametrically opposed to the kind of touch sanctioned between men—especially in movies. The hillbilly does not pistol-whip Bobby or punch him in the face; he reaches out and delicately touches his cheek. Only when Bobby reacts violently by jerking away do the men become aggressive. Even as we revert back to an acceptable and familiar spectacle of men violently touching each other, the delicate touch that opens the scene signals a violation of normal laws governing intimacy between men.

Just as Ed and Bobby uncover what was not meant to be seen, the hillbillies ritualistically strip their victims of their clothes; Dickey's screenplay notes that, first, "very deliberately, the tall man takes hold of the zipper to Ed's coveralls, and, with a quick movement, like tearing Ed apart, he zips it down to the belt" (42). A few seconds later, the hillbillies order Bobby to undress—"Now let's you just drop them pants . . . them panties, too" (43–44), he tells him. Slowly, the hillbillies enact a vicious mirroring of the same violation of uncovering that the city men have performed on their clearing in the woods. What was not meant to be seen, what is covered and secret, is laid bare. In the vulnerability of their nakedness, the violating touch that Drew first uses as a gesture of connection gets reinscribed as an act of sexual violation; it is a sexual violation mirroring the same language of degeneracy and impurity that Bobby and Ed read into the banjo boy.[15] With Bobby now naked and cowed by the gun they carry, the bearded man acts. In Dickey's screenplay, the description of Bobby's rape is not necessarily graphic, but in Boorman's film, the scene is a grotesque carnival of perversion as the man bizarrely and playfully chases Bobby around various trees and wrestles with him, a twisted form of roughhousing. Playfully riding on Bobby's back, the man gleefully smacks him and implores him—in the most famous line of any southern movie since *Gone With the Wind*—to "squeal like a pig!" Reduced to the role of an animal captured by a hunter, Bobby is brutally raped.

The line "squeal like a pig" was not originally in Dickey's novel or screenplay, but, in the light of the earlier scene with the banjo boy and its connection of witnessing with violation, it makes sense that Boorman and his actors would discern that this moment of revenge for the violation of a sacred space would use not only the city men's same crime of uncovering and violating what should remain secreted but traffic in the language and actions of the hyper-primitive: not just primitive man, but bestial, prelingual. What terrifies audiences about Boorman's presentation of the rape is not, as is so often argued, the terror of male rape (already an act that strains visibility) but the playful way in which the rape unfolds, first with a gesture of romantic intimacy, then in a silly though ritualistic uncovering, and finally, in a comic wrestling role-play. One thing my students routinely note when we watch the film together in class is how disturbing the omnipresence of laughter is; the hillbilly men take gleeful pleasure—just as they did with the banjo boy's music—in performance. While the men hold positions of dominance and power that suggest their re-violations of the Atlanta men are a kind of revenge, both the banjo and the rape scene show the pleasure of improvisation and roleplay, of the intimacy of call and response.

That the central act of this playful scene is sodomy makes sense; violations in *Deliverance* are always connected to closed spaces being forced open.[16] The men infiltrate the woods, and, more specifically, the clearing where the hillbillies are, opening it up to eyes that are not meant to see it. In order to close the wounding of that violation, the hillbillies instinctively sense the power of the act of sodomy—of forcing themselves without consent onto and into openings not meant to be seen or entered—as a ritual that will close the space of intimacy for good. The men enact a vengeful kind of forced voyeurism on Ed (and, by extension, the audience), which connects with the witnessing of the banjo boy's performance and the violation of witnessing the clearing. Just as in the banjo scene, where characters look is immensely important; one critic writes, "the men are positioned so that Ed is compelled to watch Bobby's molestation; though he is tied and cannot help Bobby, he is vertical while Bobby is bent over a log. This rhetorically lessens Ed's humiliation in comparison to Bobby's. Further the audience's gaze is directed at Bobby. We can read the subject and object of this scene easily along a Mulvian paradigm: we are looking at Bobby, the men are looking at Bobby, Ed is looking at Bobby, and we are looking at Ed looking at Bobby" (Farmer 113). We are drawn back to the importance of seeing, just as in the banjo scene, but we are also affected by the rupture of sound. The symbolic weight of witnessing Bobby's rape affects the audience of *Deliverance* on many levels, but the myriad responses to the act boil down to one sentence—"Squeal like a pig!"—and Bobby's pitiful moaning. The sight and sound require a response: the touch denied in the banjo scene now comes back—first as a tenderness whose possibility is then foreclosed and replaced by roughhousing (a more acceptable form of male touching) that morphs into graphic violence. By the end of the scene, there can be no doubt that the genre Boorman chooses for *Deliverance* is not adventure or thriller, but horror: Bobby's rape haunts audiences not solely because it is an indictment of the hillbilly, effectively turning him into a vengeful demon who polices his spaces with an inhuman ferocity, but because it borrows the tenors of the banjo scene to effectively describe an insidious terror rising from the depths. Buried deep but rising, like the hand at the end of the film, the scene refuses to retreat from our memories. More than one of my students has confessed to me, "I can't get that scene out of my head."

DELIVERANCE ON STEROIDS: THE TERRIBLE SPACE

Boorman's two infamous scenes bleed into other filmic conceptions of the American South as a bordered space that can only be crossed with careful self-reflexivity. Two years after *Deliverance*, Tobe Hooper's *Texas Chain Saw Massacre* (1974) found popularity largely by replicating Boorman's hillbilly-redneck monster; Hooper centers on a terrifying family of backwoods cannibals, especially the central villain, Leatherface. Writing in *Chain Saw Confessional*, Gunner Hansen, who plays the monster, explains that, while the movie was nominally inspired by the serial killer Ed Gein, Hooper was motivated to make a film that explored the horrors of the country hillbilly:[17]

> Beyond using Gein as the inspiration for Leatherface's mask and his family's home décor, Tobe said, he and Kim had decided to just fill the movie with

everything that had ever scared them in horror movies. One of those elements was the urban fear of country folk, who, to the city dweller, stood outside of civilization and its strictures. "I'm pretty sure we were convinced that if our cars ever broke down between cities, the rednecks would just have their way with us," Daniel Pearl [the cinematographer] says. "I always thought this film was sort of an extension, this was sort of taking that paranoia even just one step further, where they would wind up eating us. Sort of *Deliverance* on steroids."

Deliverance on steroids might be a good slogan for the film, for it recognizes the debt that *Chain Saw* owes to Boorman's film but also the pornography of excess that Hooper adds to the terror of the hillbilly. There are obviously similarities between the two plots: in both movies, characters from the city travel into the dark heart of the rural American South only to be viciously attacked, murdered, and violated by weird hillbillies; the crux of both movies is the dramatic imagining of how our protagonist(s) might enact a desperate escape to the familiar terrain of the city from the dark and primitive rural landscape of the South.

Moreover, the presentation of the rural spaces and those shadowy figures that inhabit it connect *Deliverance* and *Chain Saw* in a dirty and horrific imaginative brotherhood. And yet, the depiction of the hillbillies in the two movies is not identical. For one critic, the hillbilly monster in *Chain Saw* "differs significantly. For instance, in Boorman's film one can see, despite the harrowing ordeal undergone by his quartet of weekend warriors, a certain degree of sympathy towards both the soon-to-be-flooded Georgian wilderness as well as those who live in it (toothless rapists aside). . . . By way of contrast, from the outset, the monstrous clan who terrorize the college kids in *The Texas Chain Saw Massacre* are depicted as terrifying embodiments of chaos, disorder, and malevolence. Although the setting in rural Texas is obviously important—it is . . . a variation on the frontier horror story" (Bernice M. Murphy 148).[18] If *Chain Saw* is *Deliverance* on steroids, the hyperagression and puzzlingly bizarre actions of the hillbilly family in the former marks an extension of Boorman's reading of hillbillies as intellectually impoverished and degenerate. The hillbilly rapists in *Deliverance* are intent on enacting a perverted revenge on men who unwittingly wander into their land, but the hillbilly monsters of *Chain Saw* do not just want to violate their victims, they want to consume them.

My reading of *Deliverance* makes clear that I consider it to be, like *Chain Saw,* a horror movie. Carol Clover's reading of *Chain Saw*—one of the more popularized analyses in the scholarship on horror movies—finds central differences between it and *Deliverance* in the presentation of their monsters. For Clover, *Deliverance* is essentially "urbanoia"; Boorman presents men from the city who approach "the country guilty" (128). Because the suburban men are aware of the destructive potential of the city on the country, they experience a dizzying "nervousness of having to face directly those they recognize, at some level of consciousness, as the rural victims of their own city comfort" (129). Clover's reading of *Deliverance* makes it clear that she finds it a rape-revenge horror movie (explicating an urban-rural divide). On the other hand, Clover considers *Chain Saw* a "slasher film," with all the attending tropes of that genre.[19] But, while the family of cannibal murderers in *Chain Saw* are "slashers"—the ones stalking the young victims—the real monster of the movie is its setting.

The title of the film invites audiences to conflate place with violence: each word (*Texas–Chain Saw–Massacre*) is of coequal importance, but each significantly can be read as interchangeable. To be in Texas is to be massacred; to wield a chainsaw, one must reside in a place of both mechanization and primitivity. There is no getting around it: even in its title, *Chain Saw* suggests that the real terror lies not in people but in places.[20] In thinking broadly about place, I want to connect the setting of Hooper's movie to one of Clover's main categories of importance in slasher films: the "terrible place." For Clover, the "terrible place" is most often a structure; in *Chain Saw*, Clover offers "the decaying mansion" (30) of the cannibal family as a good example. The house's terror comes from the existence of "Victorian decrepitude" in the middle of a rural landscape. Decay is a horrific aesthetic—no longer viable but, nevertheless, extant in between other recognizable features of a small southern town; this is a space that should be dead but is still living: the undead mansion.

Our understanding of Clover's terrible space can be broadened by using her imagery of structures (with borders) to think beyond the concept of "place" not as structural but spatial, regional. This terrible space "may at first seem a safe haven, but the same walls that promise to keep the killer out quickly become, once the killer penetrates them, the walls that hold the victim in" (31). Clover might be talking about a house or tunnel or shed, but she could be articulating the terrors inherent in the bordering of the American South itself. Established by imaginary cartographies (such as the Mason Dixon Line), the U.S. South acts as a splitter, quite literally a sunken space of American geography and imagination, and Texas is one of its most geographically southern states, thus even more potent as a space of terror. In *Texas Chain Saw Massacre,* the terrible place that traps the young victims *is* Texas, a stand-in, of course, for the generic rural expanse fixed in national imaginaries of the American South—a nowhere space that exists only between recognizable civilized spaces.

In the original script for *Chain Saw*—titled *Leatherface*—Tobe Hooper and Kim Henkel present their Texas as a place of unforgiving desolation. At the opening of the film, "It is midday and midsummer . . . and the brutal southwestern sun blasts the choking landscape" (1). We follow the iconography of the road; there is the presentation of a carcass of a dog, roadkill, infected with maggots, guts streaming from the open wound. As if to alert us to the trope of open wounds and violated disfigurement, the first image we get is of the sun, a literal hole burning in the sky, and the next the opened belly of the dog. We soon see a van driving along the blistering asphalt crossing into a small town, which "has seen better days. Much of the business district is boarded up and a number of the residences are vacant" (2). After the emphasis of the visual wound, the next images presented to us are of a van traveling south; Hooper clearly plays with the imagery of driving and riding south, which suggests several things about his film.

First, in a movie that meditates on driving—a kind of "road movie"—the van represents the privilege of mobility; a vehicle suggests an affiliation with class both in its ability to transport but also in its connection with leisure travel. The small town the van passes through connects with the roadkill dog hemorrhaging on the side of the road; they are spectacles to be seen, or not, and if they are, easily forgotten. The dog itself is also, quite literally, a victim of driving. And dead towns are also, often, a victim of driving—both of a highway now bypassing them or of the fact that mobility has emptied out rural spaces. The van being full of young people is also significant in that it reminds us of the Freedom Riders of the early 1960s. Both the opened body of the dog on the road and young people in a large vehicle traveling through the rural spaces of the American South signal to us familiar horrors of the 1960s: dangerous things happen when you turn down a dark rural road in the South. If the iconography of the Freedom Riders is too subtle for viewers, just a few scenes later in Hooper and Henkel's script, we get a local redneck—"swarthy, beer-bellied," and "pock marked"—dismissively suggesting that civil rights protesters should be murdered. "I wouldn't give you jack shit for ever one o' them turds," he tells a character known only as "cowboy": "And don't give me none of that civil rights crap. Civil rights my ass" (6).[21]

The local men live in spaces in between recognizable towns (where our group of riders are going); these people are another part of Clover's presentation of the terrible place: "terrible families" (30). Clover calls the redneck monsters of *Chain Saw* an "outlaw brood," and both words are fitting for the kind of white vigilantism that waited for the Freedom Riders in 1961. Indeed, the conversation among the pock-marked man, cowboy, and two new men— an old man and a younger man with a "beer belly"—shifts into praise for the immediacy of violence:

> Pock: I know your daddy and he wipped your butt when you needed it. Ain't that right.
>
> Cowboy: You're right.
>
> Pock: Godamn right I'm right.
>
> Beer Belly: I can remember my daddy taking a stick to my young ass a time or two myself. Didn't hurt me none.
>
> Pock: Done you good.
>
> Old Man: They's some you can't never do nothin' with 'em. (6–7)

Similar to children being whipped into shape, the civil rights protestors are figures to be disciplined; they are outsiders whom you "can't never do nothin' with" but viciously beat. Henkel and Hooper give us our first glimpse of how terrible spaces breed terrible people and how those people see violence as a necessary end in establishing and maintaining order.

The terrible people of this terrible space are defined by a belief in violence that infects not just their views on education or child-rearing but their clannish devotion to land, family, and tradition. Just after we see the men talking, the group of young travelers passes by a slaughterhouse. One of our main characters, Franklin (Paul A Partain) waxes poetic about the profession of cattle slaughtering and—in graphic detail—praises how proud he is of his family's connection to that tradition:

> We have an uncle that works at one of these places just outside of Houston. Look at those buildings. That's where then [sic] kill them. He was the guy that kills them. They even call him the killer. They used to bash them in the head

with a sledge ... hammer or something like that. Half the time it wouldn't kill them the first time and they would start squealing and freaking out and the guy would have to whack them two or three times and then they would skin them sometimes even before they were dead. (12)

Franklin's story is interrupted by Sally (Marilyn Burns), who notes she would "hate to work in a place like that." At first disgusted by the dirty business that takes place inside such a building, the character Kirk (William Vail) replies thoughtfully, "It's probably the only place around here people can work" (12). Sally's innocence as well as Franklin's descriptions of the brutal murdering of cattle clearly foreshadow the ritualistic hunting of the group by the cannibal clan, and they establish that the characters in the van have little imagination for what being working class or poor might mean in a small southern town.[22] Though Franklin tries to soothe everyone with his assurances that slaughtering cattle is done much more humanely now, his description of the mechanization of the process (with a gun) elides the loss of jobs (and money) that comes from humans being replaced by machines. The protagonists in the van lack the ability to understand the cost of automation or their privileges of class.

The people that—unlike Sally—have no choice but to work at the slaughterhouse—those who are laid off because of the processes of mechanization—turn out to be the monsters who attack them.[23] Unable to imagine these unemployed slaughterhouse workers or their lives, our protagonists conjure them: moments later, we meet the first of the family, the hitchhiker (Edwin Neal), who in his very name is emblematic of a lack of mobility. Unlike the young people in the van, the hitchhiker does not own a vehicle and thus must rely only on others for transportation. The group decides to pick him up even though he is, like the hillbillies and banjo boy of *Deliverance*, "weird looking" (14). In fact, Hooper clearly connects the hitchhiker with the albino banjo boy in several ways, but most prominently in how their mental deficiencies manifest in physical ways. Like a Mendelizing characteristic, exterior deformities mark interior ones in Hooper's film, and the young man's "fine boned face is marred by a strange discoloration which begins just below the right nostril and runs, increasing in breadth down the side of his face, under his chin to his throat where it disappears" (15).[24] The skin on his face isn't the only strange feature, for the man has one eye "covered with a thick, milky cataract" and arms "covered with a number of small scabby sores." His visage

The demented hitchhiker (Edwin Neal) from *Texas Chain Saw Massacre* (1974) whose strange facial discoloration marks his mental and moral deformities.

makes it clear: he is a monster; Franklin whispers to everyone, "I think we just picked up Dracula" (15). Like the albino boy in *Deliverance,* the hitchhiker is a spectacle to behold; his monstrous deformity is something that can be *seen.*

COULDN'T YOU JUST WALK?

The scene with the hitchhiker is the protagonists' first encounter with the demented, violent Sawyer family, the monsters of *Chain Saw.* The Sawyers are connected to the town but also the larger region—when the hitchhiker tells them he's heading North, Franklin offers, "You could have fooled me. I thought we were headed due south" (15). We learn that the man is from a family that worked at the slaughterhouse; "a whole family of Draculas," Franklin sneers (16), but most importantly, we learn that the new method of killing cattle has put his entire family out of work.[25] "With the gun and the knocking box they don't need me anymore" (17), he sadly tells the group. "The old way, with the sledge, is better." Hooper uses the hitchhiker scene not just to introduce his characters to a monstrous family of hillbilly cannibals but to manifest how clueless his protagonists are about class. Like the city folk in *Deliverance*, the young people in the van represent a comfortable, privileged class whose casual trip through the wild rural expanse of Texas is an act of leisure. The hitchhiker's immobility (forever stuck both in the town where he grew up and in poverty) is completely baffling to the group in the van. If Hooper wants to emphasize a similar kind of revenge trope as the one Boorman offers in *Deliverance*, we might call it the revenge of the dispossessed over those who refuse to engage thoughtfully or empathetically with the realities of their poverty.

Hooper rewrites Boorman's banjo scene in his hitchhiker one—the only difference is that the city men in *Deliverance* can appreciate the prodigious artistry of the albino boy's skill with a musical instrument, but the group in the van are unable to appreciate the hitchhiker's talents. He is as worthless as leftover cattle parts that litter the floor of the slaughterhouse, but, as he notes, even those trash parts still have value: together, they make up something exceptional, headcheese: "Except for the tongue they boil the head and scrape the bone clean of flesh. All the parts are used; nothing is wasted. The jowels [sic], the eyes, even the muscles" (18). To the urban protagonists, such food is disgusting, but to someone who, like Dracula, feeds off the abject, headcheese is a delicacy. The hitchhiker comes from an impoverished class that must feed off the waste of the middle class. As the most naive of the group, Sally dismisses headcheese as dirty and disgusting; just as she can't imagine why anyone would work at a slaughterhouse, she can't bring herself to imagine what kind of people would enjoy something so gross. "I don't see how anybody could eat that junk," she says, gagging (19).

As an emblem of the waste left over from the work of commodity culture, the hitchhiker critically lacks a singular identity; he is leftover capitalist labor that refuses to stay invisible. But without his job, he does not know what to do or who he is. "My family's always been in meat," he tells Franklin early in the scene. No longer able to square a familial identity with their professional one, the hitchhiker and his family are, quite literally, wasted figures with no purpose. The Sawyer family represents what Zygmunt Bauman labels in his *Wasted Lives: Modernity and Its Outcasts* "wasted humans" in whom the very language we use to describe them—"redundant" or "excessive"—reveals our refusal to recognize their value. As an "inevitable outcome of modernization," one associated with "economic progress," the Sawyer family represents figures that stand in the way of forward momentum "that cannot proceed without degrading and devaluing" their way of "making a living." And yet, the family demands empathy. As unemployed workers, they are dirty "cannibals and maniacs but also victims themselves . . . casualties of technological innovation," one critic explains (Zinoman 128).

Unable to go anywhere or earn money—a wasted man—the hitchhiker no longer works at the slaughterhouse, but is drawn back to it, like a ghost haunting a once-familiar building. Without a paying job, the man decides to become "an artist," a leisure identity, a fantasy of potential upward mobility. A man without a job must be a man of leisure, and so the hitchhiker decides he is a "sculptor." "I work with leather" (17), he proudly tells the group while showing them some of his goods. The hitchhiker is also an amateur photographer. He passes around photos of the slaughterhouse's killing floor and the leftover carcasses of cows. When Franklin is transfixed by the graphic images, the hitchhiker mistakenly reads his fascination as acknowledgment of his artistry. Attempting to make some connection with him, the hitchhiker takes Franklin's knife and plunges it into his own hand. Like the albino boy and Drew, the hitchhiker's and Franklin's attempt at collaboration in mutual performance instead turns into a dark violation.

Unlike the banjo boy—whose talent for music is self-evident even to the civilized city men of *Deliverance*—the hitchhiker's talents are not sources of fascination but repulsion. His "performance" does not offer intimacy but disconnection; there is no value to be found in his actions. His talent for self-mutilation does not impress the group. Sally remains mystified by him: "How can you do that," she asks in disgust (21). In a last, desperate bid for recognition of his skill, the hitchhiker takes a photograph of Franklin. Mistaking Franklin's interest in his photos, the hitchhiker hopes to impress with a portrait, but when the photograph develops, Franklin dislikes it: "It didn't turn out so good," he tells the hitchhiker (25). Like the discolored streak that runs across the hitchhiker's face, the photograph disfigures Franklin. "You look worse," Kirk laughs.

When the hitchhiker asks for money—"You can pay me now. . . . Two dollars. It's a good picture" (26)—Franklin refuses. The connections between the banjo scene in *Deliverance* are obvious, even if in reverse: The hitchhiker becomes Drew, desperate to share collaborative intimacy with someone outside his class, while Franklin becomes the arbiter of value and artistry. It is Franklin now, the city man, that refuses the "touch" of the hitchhiker, who, after he is denied payment, becomes morose and sad. The emotional tenor of the van scene with the hitchhiker mirrors that of the dueling banjos of *Deliverance;*

only this time it is the city folk who deny the potential for intimacy. The reversal is most acute in the request for payment—two dollars—the same price that Bobby advises Drew to pay the shy albino when he refuses to shake hands. ("Give him a couple bucks.")

There are obvious connections between the van and banjo scenes; I find the same metrics of violence indicative of the excavation of hidden spaces in *Deliverance.* In the scene with the hitchhiker, we have the exposure to that which was never meant to be seen—the killing floor of a slaughterhouse— the building of a fantasy of intimacy culminating in violating touch, and the closing of that wound with a masking or marking of the space. The violating touch is both the refusal of the hitchhiker's photograph but also the first true instance of violence in the film when the hitchhiker destroys the photo of Franklin (in a weird contained explosion that feels vaguely ceremonial) and slashes Franklin's arm with his razor. Wounded, Franklin, like Bobby, "squeals" (28), and the hitchhiker is forced out of the van. In a final act of masking, the hitchhiker "tears open his wounded palm with his teeth and smears blood on the side of the van and . . . spews saliva over the side" (28).

The hitchhiker dirties the van with juices from his body—the domain of the abject—and his bloody prints operate both as a marking (unclean) and a masking (a vehicle disguised as a body). He is released back into the rural nowhere whence he came. The riders in the van continue their trip. Though shaken, our protagonists have learned nothing from their encounter with the hitchhiker, are still mystified (if not captivated) by who he was and his motivations. Crucially, their class naivete remains unchallenged. They still don't understand why a person would work in a slaughterhouse, eat dirty and disgusting food like headcheese, stab himself in the hand, and ask for money for a crummy photograph. The hitchhiker's very identity remains a hazy puzzle to the group. Even though Franklin is in a wheelchair and problems of mobility plague him, he does not seem to understand the hitchhiker's own problems of mobility, either in his poverty ("Why would anyone work there?") or in his inability to leave. When the hitchhiker invites the group over for dinner, noting that his house is close by, Sally huffs, "If it's so close, couldn't you just walk?" (24).

A FAMILY WAY: THE INTIMACY OF THE TABLE

The other members of the Sawyer clan are also hauntingly bizarre. "The people are a strange lot," Hooper writes, "It is apparent that they are not quite normal" (30). Despite the Old Man's (Jim Siedow) warning to the group not to go messing around in the woods, the group eventually finds its way to Franklin's grandfather's old house and, later, the Sawyer property.[26] Just as Bobby and Ed haplessly wander into the wrong place at the wrong time, the group in the van stumbles into a hidden house not meant to be seen. Even as they enter the Sawyers' land, they remain naive and mystified by the strangeness of the hillbillies. Franklin spends much of the first part of the film looking at the bloody marks left by the hitchhiker, trying to translate them into something meaningful: "I think it might be some kind of a symbol," he tells Kirk (38). Franklin and the other members of the group are still unable to "see" or interpret the value of the poor hillbillies they encounter. Their exposure to the true world of the poor other comes during a violent and shocking initiation inside the Sawyers' house.

What the group of young riders find in the Sawyer mansion is a house of horrors. Unemployed because of automation in cattle-killing, the family has continued to slaughter, but its work has shifted from cow to human bodies. The violence inflicted on the protagonists comes in large part because of a lack of awareness of issues of poverty and mobility as well as their cultural naivete about the rural South. Speaking about his grandfather's house, Franklin tells Sally, "Uncle Ed lived here a while after Grandpa died. He had to move when they started laying people off at the slaughterhouse. Nobody's lived here since as far as I know. All the people around here know how to do is slaughter cattle. I guess a lot of them had to move away or something" (39). Franklin is, sadly, mistaken: as he and the others are about to find out, no one has "moved away," because no one in the town could do so. Once Kirk discovers the cannibal clan's home, the "terrible place" in which the Sawyers are forever stuck, the remainder of the movie is essentially a systematic punishment of each naive rider in the van. Their complete lack of awareness of issues of poverty, critical lack of imagination for the realities of a small-town life, and lack of connection with the lower class all mark them as victims for the cannibal hillbillies. They are, in the words of one critic, "privileged, shallow, and vapidly pleasure seeking" (Freeland 248), figures of ridicule. We do not condone the violent fates they endure, but we cannot help feeling that they are not entirely innocent either.[27]

The central tormentor of the film is also the character whose name has become synonymous with the movie—Leatherface. Hooper's monster echoes those in Boorman's *Deliverance*. When we first see Leatherface murder Kirk with a sledgehammer—the weapon the hitchhiker used to slaughter cattle before he was laid off—we hear "a high pitched pig like squeal ending in a hysterical whinny" (49). Leatherface is bestial and primitive (the sounds he makes are animal noises), but the "pig like squeal" obviously borrows from the famous line in Boorman's film and the disturbing violation of Bobby's rape in the clearing. In fact, Leatherface's entire language is the "hysterical, high pitched pig like squeal" (51). But perhaps the true terror of Leatherface is his inscrutability, symbolized by his famous mask.

Hooper's description of the mask emphasizes hybridization, human pieces mixed with inanimate materials—skin and string, flesh and metal; his mask covers "the entire head . . . the face of the hood is human but shriveled and leathery. The hair is human hair" (52). The aesthetic of Leatherface's mask suggests white vigilante terror, especially as practiced by the Ku Klux Klan. Hooper is careful to note that what the monster wears is "a close fitting hood rather than a mask" (51–52). Its leathery appearance gleams white. Clearly, the mask's whiteness symbolically references the terrorizing white hoods throughout the South and reminds an audience of the iconography of violence inflicted on the bodies of those who threaten the stability of southern customs. The rippling effect of the mask and its subsequent folding in on itself is eerily reminiscent of the leathery and torn face of Emmitt Till, whose funeral photos were reproduced throughout the late 1950s and into the 1960s.

Like Boorman's albino banjo boy, Leatherface's visage is haunting. Both the banjo boy and Leatherface are nonverbal figures of simultaneous fascination and repulsion. Both are defined by a mask-like, hyper-white countenance. Like his banjo counterpart, Leatherface has a mental illness rendering him mute. If the banjo boy's talent is music, Leatherface's talent is killing. He is a butcher, and he works on bodies—stripping them of flesh, separating their parts—with impressive skill.[28] Like his counterpart, Leatherface is childlike; his attitude towards the other members of the family is subservient and obedient. When Sally runs to the safety of the service station where Leatherface's father is, the monster "is visibly frightened. He ceases his squealing and begins to pad in animal frenzy" (75). When the old man gets home, he beats Leatherface, who is "transformed to a cringing whining child" (83). Perhaps one of the most bizarre and terrifying parts of the movie is Sally's witnessing intrafamilial conflict not meant to be viewed by outsiders. In fact, the nightmarish sequence that begins with the old man, the hitchhiker, and Leatherface preparing dinner with Sally has become, like *Deliverance*'s rape scene, the most iconic of the movie.

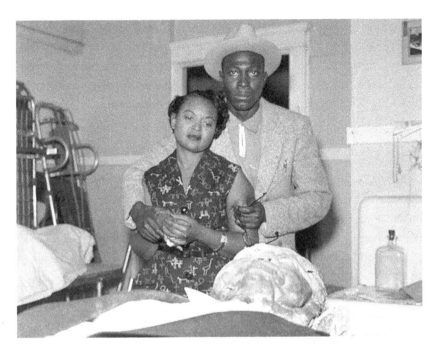

The mutilated face of Emmitt Till at his open-casket funeral in 1956, *top.* The disfigured mask of Leatherface, the central villain in *The Texas Chainsaw Massacre, bottom.* Author's photo of the original mask housed in the Harry Ransom Center in Austin, Texas.

If the scene with the hitchhiker is Hooper's rewriting of the dueling-banjos scene, I believe that the dinner scene deliberately references Bobby's rape in the clearing, especially its trajectory of unearthing violations and ritualistic acts of violence. Sally is already guilty of trespassing in a space not meant to be seen; this "violation of the domestic space," as one critic notes, is a "common feature of the backwoods horror movie" (Bernice M. Murphy 162). Because she has disturbed a place that was meant to remain hidden, she is forced to enact a closing ritual—an act possible only through violating, disfiguring touch. But, if the family's mansion is the "terrible place" that must not be viewed, what she sees in that space is repeated bizarre violations. Hooper writes extensively in his screenplay about the macabre furniture and decorations that adorn the house, things made from human and animal skin and bones. These decorative pieces of undead art made from corpses are symbolic of dead things that continue to exist. The horror of their continued presence is that they are a part of a living world in the most mundane way imaginable.

By forcing her to have dinner with them, the family crafts an intimacy that, on the surface, appears boring and mundane, but is arguably the most disturbing aspect of this scene. It is an intimacy whose ethos is private, meant to be shared only with family. Like Sally, the audience is not prepared to witness the softer, domestic side of the monsters they have come to fear. Perhaps to signal the bizarre discordance of such an intimacy, we learn that Leatherface's stark mask has been changed for dinner. Now he wears one "distinctly different fro[m] the one he earlier wore. It is the tanned facial skin of an elderly woman; it has been stretched over a rigid form to give it the proper shape. It is apparent that behind the mask Leatherface is smiling broadly; there is a flash of filed teeth. He is excited and pleased with himself" (83). For the first time in the film, we are allowed the intimacy to "see" behind the mask. We understand Leatherface as a being capable of pleasure and happiness. We know that he is smiling, that he is happy and excited, but we are also privy to a new mask, one reserved only for his family, a softer and more feminine mask. The new mask is yet another modality of uncovering that which remains hidden.

There is a kind of dirty initiation present in the dinner scene. Sally is privy to a dynamic no one else gets to see, and she is almost welcomed by the hitchhiker and Leatherface, the latter of whom continues to pat her hand and talk to her in calm tones. Yet again, we see another side to Leatherface, even more intimate, even more feminine, an identity reserved only for the dinner table. He wears a mask "of a woman who might once have been beautiful. . . . the mask has been made up with a white powder and has some of the starkness of stage makeup. The lips are heavily ringed with a dark red lipstick" (87). Perhaps echoing Bobby's howl of pain when he is sodomized, Sally howls, and the men around the table join her. She has become, even for a moment, a part of a horrific family, and the hitchhiker even suggests her face might eventually become the new mask for his brother. When the family begins to bicker, Sally is further a witness to a horrific truth that she has been naive to throughout the film: she no longer can be innocent in her imaginings of the people of the town; like Ed at the end of *Deliverance,* she is learning the monstrous, dirty horrors of poverty and immobility, chief among them: that violence is more real than the innocent dreams of the privileged.[29] In the end, it's dog eat dog—as the working class knows, but the middle class refuses to acknowledge, taking refuge in pious fantasies of a good society.

Yet another horror of intimacy awaits Sally: meeting the still-living, decaying patriarch of the family. The hitchhiker brings the grandfather down to the table, and he "still looks dead. He has not moved and does not respond in any way to anything about him" (86). Once the body is placed at the table, Leatherface softens more; he "speaks in a kindly and welcoming tone to the grandfather, approaches the chair and bends to kiss him on the forehead." Just as before, we notice that "he is smiling graciously behind his mask." Now in the most intimate of spaces—where she had once trespassed—Sally is positioned to witness a family dynamic for which she has no understanding. Like the hillbilly rapist who first gently brushes Bobby's cheek with his hand, Leatherface touches the young woman tenderly, "fussing over her" and "occasionally strok[ing] her hair." Gentle touch quickly turns violent as Leatherface "speaks to her in a reassuring tone" and "quickly and expertly" slices her index finger open with a nearby knife (87).

With blood pouring out of the wound, Leatherface places Sally's finger into the most intimate of holes, the grandfather's mouth. We watch in horror as he sucks her blood and begins to come alive. The scene has transformed from a horror examining the vengeance of those whose borders have been trespassed into a cycle of transgressive violations centered on disfiguring touches. There is both a gendered dynamic here as well as a desire for a reconstituted domesticity, that (perhaps) only the woman can enable. The "ruin" of capitalism destroys any vestige of a "normal" family, replacing it with a rapacious one that mirrors capitalism's own rapacity. The poverty has been produced by social forces—and the family must re-form itself in response to those forces. Like *Deliverance*'s hillbilly murders and rapists, a reformed family is capable of a violence that is not solely acts of revenge but rather a crafting of intimacy whose violating potential is positively pleasurable: something entering into a hole not meant to receive it.

When the scene reaches its climax, the hitchhiker suggests the grandfather be the one to murder Sally by hitting her in the head with the hammer, just like he used to do with cattle. According to the old man, the grandfather was the best killer the slaughterhouse ever had, and by giving him a chance to work his magic once more, the men think it might awaken something inside of him. It takes a few tries, but when he does eventually hit Sally, the young woman is transformed into an animal. It is Sally who now "squeals" and writhes around like a trapped pig. She has been transformed from outsider tourist of privilege to the lowest of the social order—not a child or a baby, but an animal to be slaughtered for food. Leatherface treats her like a pet, but she is not to be owned, she is to be consumed. According to Eggertsson, "The symbolism of people as meat is a well-known interpretation" throughout *The Texas Chain Saw Massacre* (Eggertsson and Forceville 444).

When she eventually escapes the house, the hitchhiker runs after her, casually and gleefully slashing her with his razor. As with the hillbillies in the clearing in *Deliverance,* the pleasure of the moment is evident from his laughter and orgiastic fits of giggling. When the two cross a busy road, the hitchhiker is killed by a passing vehicle. Significantly, it is a "loaded cattle truck" (98) that hits him. His death comes, ironically, from a dual symbol of that which existentially threatened him: a fast-moving vehicle and cattle on their way to his old job. Sally's rescue comes from another source of mobility, a broken-down pick-up truck. By this time, she is, like Bobby in the clearing, or Ed tied to a tree, more animal than person; "her cries are no longer human sounds," Hooper writes (99). As she jumps in the back of the truck and is driven off into the distance, Leatherface "squeals and slashes the morning sky"; he is fully in "maniac rage" as he throws "the chain saw with savage, idiot fury" (100).

Though Sally escapes, the rest of her group does not. Jerry (Allen Danziger), Franklin, Kirk, and Pam (Teri McMinn) have all been murdered and will soon be transformed into food for the surviving Sawyers. The movie has been its own slaughterhouse, and the murders of the protagonists suggest that the only means of escape is to get out—unsurprising for a film in which anxieties about mobility are central.[30] Like *Deliverance, Chain Saw*'s final beat is reminiscent of the rising hand, as we see Leatherface's undulating and re-

Lacking a vehicle or any source of mobility, all Leatherface can do at the end of the movie is expend his fury by moving his own body in a weird dance of rage and terror.

petitive raising of his chainsaw in the air; mournfully, he makes mad circles in the dawn. It is, no doubt, an image that will rise again and again to haunt Sally, reminding her of these traumas. But the bordering of Leatherface's domain is clear: he cannot escape his town, his terrible place. There is nowhere to go, no means to leave. He is stuck in his family, his region, his house, his poverty. The closing of the wound of Sally's experience as well as the re-masking of the terrible place is marked by the slow diminution of Leatherface as he fades from Sally's view. She leaves; he remains. And in his slow disappearance, we understand that, though this terrible place recedes from our view, it will remain a hidden trap waiting to punish the next victim that naively trespasses on it, and indeed it does: the *Chain Saw* franchise has sparked many sequels, reboots, and prequels.

Both *Deliverance* and *Chain Saw* present the rural South as a site of terror in constant threat of being uncovered by a careless or naive trespass; the infiltration of a rigid border can only be closed through the ritualized disfiguring touch that creates a wound. Iconic scenes from both of these movies show how the various revelations of hidden spaces do cultural work inasmuch as they connect these uncoverings to disavowed or repressed national anxieties. In *Deliverance*, the anxieties are poverty of intellect and empathy as well as fears of disease and impurity, but in *Chain Saw*, the anxieties are centered on mobility and consumption. These fears threaten the stability of any kind of liberal project of nation building, and thus, are secreted away, hidden. Further, *Chain Saw* as "hixploitation" does cultural work insofar as Herring claims "regionally sexualized hillbillies on film contributed to the cultural imaginary of what we have come to think of as the New Right" and the rise of an anti-queer movement in which even nonmonogamous heterosexuality was viewed as a perversion worthy of punishment (98).

But in hixploitation horror movies, a genre whose very power comes from its ability to articulate hidden fears, we sense the power of what we've repressed to grab us again. It is no coincidence that the major action of *Chain Saw* revolves around a series of grave robberies, or that Boorman ends his movie with the dirty hand of Drew. In both movies, things that should be buried refuse to remain under the earth; what has been repressed refuses to disappear. The corpses remain, openly wounded, masked, disfigured, ejected to terrible places that should be entered into delicately, if at all. Though the movies might offer different imaginaries about how to close such a wound (*Deliverance* questions whether such a wound can ever be closed), the warning to those outside the borders is clear: if you want to be free from such dirty threats, stay away. Both *Deliverance* and *Chain Saw* seem to suggest that the only way to defeat the terrors of the violating and disfiguring touches of the rural South is to GET OUT!

GTFO

Deliverance and *Chain Saw* have become iconic templates for horror movies set in the rural South; they have inspired countless movies, comic books, and other cultural texts about hillbilly and redneck monsters terrorizing (sub)urban victims. A recent interpretation (and critique) is Jordan Peele's hugely successful *Get Out* (2017), which uses the hillbilly monster trope to explore Black anxiety over white ownership (of identity: cultural, economic, racial, etc.), Peele works his critique not through the rape-revenge or slasher genre, but through a clever play on the possession film. His movie follows African American photographer Chris Washington (Daniel Kaluuya) as he visits girlfriend Rose's (Allison Williams) family in upstate New York. Chris notices that Rose's family acts strange, but, unlike the albino banjo boy or the deformed Leatherface, whose external appearances manifest their capacity for terror, the white family is blandly nonthreatening, even mildly attractive. However, Chris finds himself troubled by their unknowable interiority. When he surreptitiously takes a photograph of a Black man (married to a much older white lady) at a party, the man instantly transforms; he grabs Chris menacingly, imploring him to "Get out!" By the end of the film, we learn the reason for the warning: Rose and her family have been stalking talented Black artists, athletes, and musicians, hypnotizing them, and implanting the consciousness of elderly, affluent white people into their bodies. Chris breaks free from his mental and physical confinement, burns down the house, murders the family, and finally manages to escape.

Though Peele does not set his film in the American South, the iconography of it is clearly southern. Peele filmed most of *Get Out* in the Gulf Coast area of Alabama, and Spanish moss oozes off the trees. Also, several accents of the central villains are conspicuously southern. But there is something even more terrifying and insidious about a possession movie in which the terror is not situated in an external "terrible place" but a terrible interior, where its potential to threaten is invisible. The horrors that Peele articulates are symptoms of a national naivete viewing Black anxiety about white violence as a solved problem, a species of the past, a time when, as one of the characters in James Baldwin's novel *Just Above My Head* says, a Black man could look south of the Mason-Dixon Line and scare himself to death.[31] In 2017, however, the naive assumption that African Americans have passed into a different historical moment that obviates the need for their terror becomes a crucial point of horror in *Get Out.*

More than forty-five years after *Chain Saw*, *Get Out* argues that the rise of a post-Obama liberalism, with its rhetorics of post-racial America, is far more threatening than overt violences of demented hillbilly rapists or degenerate, poor redneck families. As Lanre Bakare writes in *The Guardian*, "The villains here aren't southern rednecks or neo-Nazi skinheads, or the so-called 'alt-right.' They're middle-class white liberals. The kind of people who read this website. The kind of people who shop at Trader Joe's, donate to the ACLU and would have voted for Obama a third time if they could. Good people. Nice people." The horrors of Peele's film are not literal consumptions of flesh or perverse sexual violations of revenge but manifestations of "how, however unintentionally, these same people can make life so hard and uncomfortable for Black people. It exposes a liberal ignorance and hubris that has been allowed to fester."

Bakare's summary of *Get Out*'s connection to its historical moment is not tied to the long past—horrific murders like Emmitt Till's or the history of lynching throughout the 1950s and 1960s—but to contemporary instances of violence inflicted on African Americans in the twenty-first century: "The unique history—plus the fascination, fetishization and fear of dark-skinned men—on this continent gives *Get Out* even more punch. After seeing it, I started to think that it might not be a coincidence the film came out almost five years to the day since Trayvon Martin was killed." Moreover, much of the violence inflicted on Black men and women has become increasingly more visible: body cameras and smartphones have helped do the work that statistics never could. *Get Out* recognizes these instances of visible violence even as it tries to grapple with new ways that violence manifests and masks itself. Peele understands that the strategies of disavowal are always shifting, especially when violence is often presented as virtue—or (alternatively) doesn't recognize itself as violence.

Get Out examines an insidious terror untethered to a specific national region, space, or history; it is an American trauma that lives inside the sunken soul of the nation. Peele shows how that dirty soul—a place buried in a cultural and national subconscious—is the perfect terrain to hide true horrors that exist outside of public consumption. Chris's primal fear in *Get Out* is that he will be buried in the muck of the nowhere, a space that feels at once like the graves of the civil rights workers in Mississippi and the countless cells that house Black bodies in prisons throughout the nation. First hypnotized by Rose's mother, Missy (Catherine Keener), Chris learns that she has cast him into what she calls the "sunken place," a site of constant paralysis. The sunken place is not an external terrible place but an internal one. While being stuck or buried prematurely might be a universal fear, Peele claims it as a terror with meaningful connections to Black disenfranchisement and incarceration:

> I always had this concept of the place that you're falling toward when you're going to sleep, and you get that falling sensation and catch yourself. And if you didn't catch yourself, where would you end up? I had this hellish image, and I thought of this idea of, "What if you were in a place, and you could look through your own eyes as if they were literal windows or a screen, and see what your body was seeing, but feel like a prisoner in your own mind—the chamber of your mind?" The moment I thought of that, it immediately occurred to me the theme of abduction and connection to the prison industrial complex that this movie was sort of presenting a metaphor for. It was a very emotional discovery. I remember having so much fun writing it, but at that

Chris in *Get Out,* trapped in the "sunken place," where he is paralyzed bodily but still retains his consciousness of what occurs around him.

moment when I figured out this weird, esoteric, but also emotionally brutal form of suffering to put the character through—I literally cried writing the scene. (Yaniz)

Peele finds catharsis by writing through a literalization of Black experience in the twentieth and twenty-first centuries; Chris experiences a similar catharsis when he first encounters the sunken space: the most iconic image of *Get Out* is Chris trapped in the sunken place, paralyzed, with tears streaming down his cheeks.

The violation is different from the ones in *Deliverance* and *Chain Saw.* In *Get Out,* Peele uncovers a history of wounds inflicted on an entire race; these ruptures are not able to be healed because they are not allowed to be recognized by a dizzying discourse of post-racial liberalism. A national history of wounding Black bodies is refused visibility and thus, crucially, cannot be owned. Chris's wide-eyed and tear-soaked face suggests that, by opening himself up (to borrow a phrase from Clover), he has unwittingly stumbled into a place of vulnerability through which he will, like so many Black bodies before him, be subject to invisible aggressions and systemic violations.[32] Like the iconic scenes of *Deliverance* or *Chain Saw,* the image of Chris's face marks the paralyzing nature of victimization—reminding us that these horrors have not been killed, solved, or exorcised; they have only been hidden, displaced, repressed, sunken. And when they surface again—things that refuse to stay buried—they haunt us with the reminder that grafting terror onto a certain region or class only works to obscure the violations further. There is no space in which Black bodies and Black consciousness are not threatened, no other land to escape, nowhere to GET OUT *to*. *Get Out*'s monsters are not immobile or impoverished monsters like Hooper's in *Chain Saw;* they are upper-middle-class white people who are—and can travel—ANYWHERE; they have no Mendelizing characteristics to warn us of their monstrosity as in Borman's *Deliverance*. And their imaginative perversions are not sexual violations in a clearing: the terror of these villains is the banal and white mask that hides dirty hearts. Unlike the banjo boy or Leatherface, these white, affluent, liberal, post-racial upstate New Yorkers do not advertise the horrors of their heart; they keep it hidden in the most sunken place of all—their soul.

I find myself imagining ways in which "the terrible space" invites connections to anxieties over ground, dirt, and soil that became a national preoccupation in the 1970s. On 1 January 1970, President Richard Nixon made his first official act of the new year and the new decade the signing of new legislation. The National Environmental Policy Act (NEPA) was quickly followed by the creation of the Environmental Protection Agency (EPA) and the celebration of the first "Earth Day" on 22 April 1970, with over twenty million people participating across the country. The crisis of pollution and its effect on the globe became a national problem that blossomed into what Rosenbaum called, "the big bang of U.S. environmental politics, launching the country on a sweeping social learning curve about ecological management never before experienced or attempted in any other nation" (9). During the ensuing tumult surrounding anxieties over pollution and ecology, there was another turn to the South, but this time the connection between dirt and region suggested something far more mysterious and magical, as popular imagination focused on the most sunken of all southern spaces: the fetid swampland of Louisiana.

CHAPTER 4

DIRTY ETHICS
AND SWAMPY ECOLOGY

[The] chemical mingled with my flesh . . . reacted with swamp ooze . . . turned me into . . . WHAT?
   —*Swamp Thing: The Bronze Age,* 1972

The serum you have injected tonight has made you all part of the most significant historical milestone since the taming of fire. . . . we are no longer human beings. . . . we are now so much more.
   —**Mark Landry,** *Bloodthirsty: One Nation Under Water,* 2016

Hushpuppy, quaking with fear, runs through a menacing swamp clutching her medicine jar. The rising winds swirl the marsh grass all around her. . . . Hushpuppy looks around the swamp, unable to understand. HUSHPUPPY (V.O.): Daddy could have turned into a tree, or a bug. There wasn't any way to know.
   —**Benh Zeitlin and Lucy Alibar,** *Beasts of the Southern Wild,* 2012

O n the first day of a new decade—1 January 1970—President Nixon invited reporters to the "Western White House," La Casa Pacifica in San Clemente, California. There, he publicly announced his support—and gave his signature to—the National Environmental Policy Act (NEPA). Nixon proclaimed that "the nineteen-seventies absolutely must be the years when America pays its debt to the past by reclaiming the purity of its air, its waters and our living environment" (Nixon, *Public Papers* 51). Breaking with his previous reluctance to projects of conservation and environmental protection, Nixon claimed that "the decade of the seventies will be known as the time when this country regained a productive harmony between man and nature" (2–3).[1] Just four weeks later—a year to the day after an underground oil well off the coast of Santa Barbara exploded, dumping three million gallons of crude oil into the Pacific Ocean and destroying thousands of marine species—key senators and representatives responded to the dirty accident by gathering to celebrate the first Environmental Rights Day.[2] Buoyed by popular support and legislative momentum, several of the organizers instrumental in planning the event—including Republican congressman from California Pete McCloskey,

Wisconsin senator Gaylord Nelson, staffer Denis Hayes, as well as others—imagined a much bigger movement.

On 22 April 1970, the movement had its first signature event—Earth Day; organizers chose the day to maximize participation by college students who would, in theory, have fewer exams and commitments that week.[3] The participation in the first Earth Day was impressive. According to historian J. Brooks Flippen, it was "a fitting culmination to a popular movement, a demonstration that ecology had achieved political capital as never before" (8). Environmental historian James Morton Turner notes that the event was the culmination of a sense of "new urgency" in the United States about the state of the planet and the role of conservation: "Earth Day was an exceptional event. Millions of Americans took part in rallies, protests, sit-ins, stream cleanups, hikes, and walks on college campuses, in local communities, at state capitols, and in Washington, D.C. Never before had so many Americans joined together to express their concern about issues such as air and water pollution at home, population growth worldwide, the destructive war in Vietnam, and the future of American parks, rivers, cities, and wilderness" (95). Though the environmental movement of the 1970s was not the origin of American interest in or anxiety over conservation, pollution, waste, garbage, and litter, the popularity of Environmental Rights Day and Earth Day crystallized anxieties about the environment in a way that was, for perhaps the first time, uniquely popular.[4] Earth Day continues to be celebrated every 22 April and has become "the conceptual frame through which the media portrayed pollution and other environmental problems" (Dunaway 44).

And yet, even as Nixon and other government officials touted a nascent environmental movement, most of the states that make up the American South reacted with apathy or downright disdain for federal legislation arguing for changes in farming, timber use, and land management. Even as America was moving to declare its commitment to eradicating pollution and cleaning up littered landscapes, the South was content to stay dirty. But what "dirty" meant in the 1970s—especially in concert with the lived lives of poor southerners of color—would get complicated throughout the 1970s by competing political and cultural rhetorics that sought to inextricably tie ecology to ethics.

DIRTY ETHICS

As federal legislation proliferated, the environmental movement employed a deeply personal rhetoric that asked Americans to accept the truth of an "environmental crisis but also narrowed the meanings of environmentalism, too often severing it from questions of power and presenting it as a moralistic cleanup crusade" (Dunaway 46). A key voice popularizing the theory that individual efforts could protect the environment, the "Keep America Beautiful" nonprofit, produced multiple public service announcements throughout the decade focusing on stopping pollution and litter.[5] A year after the first Earth Day, in what has now become arguably the most famous commercial of the decade, the 1971 "Crying Indian" spot for the organization opens with an actor dressed in Native American garb (Iron Eyes Cody) as he lazily paddles a canoe through calm waters in brilliant sunshine.[6] We follow his journey down a river increasingly littered with man-made debris: plastic, aluminum cans, trash. Leaving the water and walking toward the freeway, Cody surveys the garbage-dotted terrain in front of him. Without warning, a blurred and dizzying bag thrown from a passing car arrests our view; its contents explode trash at the man's feet. We follow the line of the man's body to his face where the camera zooms in on what "may be the most famous tear in American history" (Dunaway 79). The scene freezes on the actor crying, and a gravelly narrator scolds us as we watch Cody's stoic, tear-streaked face: "Some people have a deep abiding respect for the natural beauty that was once this country . . . And some people don't." The image of Cody's crying face appeared everywhere; from billboards to magazine advertisements, it became "indelibly etched into American public culture" (80). It suggested that littering the natural landscape of America was not just a disservice to the nation but to the integrity of indigenous people who first inhabited it; moreover, it offered commercial nostalgia for a pristine and pure vision of an America that "was once" and, the ad argued, could be again. The spot suggested that all one needed to change the world was to relearn "respect for natural beauty." In the "Crying Indian's" face Americans had found a symbol of the environmental decade, one that would continue to be rhetorically powerful well beyond the 1970s.

Keep America Beautiful distilled questions of pollution and the importance of conservation and protection into personal ethics. What was a complex, dynamic, and multifaceted conversation was reduced to a simple premise. It was the kind of rhetoric that "sought to interiorize the environmental critique of progress, to make individuals feel guilty and responsible for the degraded environment [by] deflecting the question of responsibility away from corporations" (Dunway 82). Such rhetoric transforms responsibility for natural harmony away from institutions and onto the personal moral and ethical responsibility of individuals. By reframing the issue of environmental ruin as a matter of individual morality—as a personal and moral failing as opposed to a national, economic, or political one—the popular understanding and support for the environmental movement in the 1970s largely hinged on rhetorics of responsibility: "cleaning" littered landscapes or "purifying" polluted waterways were reflections not of a people or a region's economic and political realities but rather a profound revelation of an individual's ethical and moral conscience.

The Keep America Beautiful commercials garnered "genuine public concern over the degradation of the environment, and it signaled the organizational florescence of grassroots and international environmental movements" (Lewis 192). However, by popularizing the environmental movement in the symbol of the Crying Indian, Keep America Beautiful solidified a popular conception of ecological and conservation issues into ethical imperatives that persist well into the twenty-first century. In addition to displacing ownership of pollution and environmental degradation from corporations, governments, or other systems and institutions of power and onto "some people," the defining feature of an environmental rhetoric in the 1970s was a call to recognize the "dirty ethics" of "some people," people whose capacity to pollute and litter our pristine landscape mark them as supremely dirty.

EXCAVATING SOUTHERN ECOLOGICAL HISTORY

Because Keep America Beautiful appealed to Americans' sense of ethical responsibility, the American South might, on the surface, appear as one of the more obvious regions for conservationists to target. It is hard to think of a region of the nation more associated with "primitivity"—in all its stereotypical forms—than the American South in the early 1970s. And yet, the popular understanding of southern savageness did not connect with the same kind of romantic primitivity that Keep America Beautiful privileged. Unlike the "noble savage" purity of the Native American imaginary in the Keep America Beautiful campaigns, the southerner had an unclean, contested, and ultimately impure connection to ecology.[7] The plantation system, with its reliance on enslaved labor and its exploitation of the land, did not just lead to ecological ruination, but racial exploitation and moral degradation as well.[8]

The southern economy was so rooted in the plantation model—both in the nineteenth century and later, through the sharecropping model, into the twentieth century—that the region found itself on the outside of aspirational narratives of multiple movements in the 1960s through the 1970s: the counterculture movement, the ecological movement, the civil rights movement, the American Indian movement. Despite the emergence of the environmental justice movement in the South (including the 1968 Memphis Sanitation Strike and 1979 formation of the Northeast Community Action Group in Houston), throughout the turbulent 1960s the South remained a convenient "other" for all the leftist movements of the time—militaristic for the antiwar movement, traditional patriarchal Christian (Baptist) for the feminists, racist for the civil rights movement, anti-union for what was left of the labor movement, and insensitive polluting for the environmental movement. In short, the popular understanding of the American South as a place with a dirty history and unclean ethics made it a prime target for national displacements of anxieties over ecological concerns; indeed, to the average nonsoutherner of the decade, the South was a region entirely populated by "some people."

As a result—which of course facilitates ignoring wholesale the history of the environmental justice movement among southerners in the 1970s—we tend not to associate the South with either the promotion or the enacting of laws and regulations seeking to preserve, conserve, or protect the natural world; in the 1970s and through the next half-decade, there are precious little histories of ecological conservation in the region. Even though much of the South is comprised of some of the largest and most ecologically diverse areas of the country, the ecological story of the South is more often connected to pollution and landfills—not to mention protection of corporate concerns over ecological ones.[9] In many ways, plotting a history for "environmentalism" or "ecological conservation" in the South is tricky. As Sutter writes in his introduction to *Environmental History and the American South*, "The southeastern United States, despite a long and dramatic history of human-environmental interactions and a growing contemporary assault on its natural landscapes, remained at best a peripheral subject for environmental historians. . . . American environmental history had grown up in the West, and it had spent some time in New England and the Midwest as well, but it had rarely ventured below the Mason-Dixon line" (1).

A dearth of public southern environmental histories is curious for a region whose stories about environmental justice are extant and whose very existence is defined by its connection to environment, the natural world, soil, and agriculture, to say nothing of climate. And yet, "in a disproportionately poor and rural region renowned for being friendly to migrating industries and slow to regulate environmental impacts, southern environmentalists have had a hard time getting traction" (Sutter 4). Though the South is one of the more ecologically diverse regions of the nation, either through ignorance or manipulation, histories of ecological preservation and conservation are lamentably sparse.

Of course, there are histories of southern conservation efforts and environmentalists that reached national audiences, but to explore why the South is often ignored or forgotten in ecological histories of the nation is to investigate disparities of economic realities between poor people of color and the inherent whiteness of the environmental movement throughout the 1960s and 1970s. Eileen Maura McGurty notes that in the late 1960s, when "discussions about the disproportionate impact of environmental degradation and environmental reform on the poor and people of color occurred full force," the South's long and dirty history of racial disenfranchisement (as well as the rampant segregation of the region) vastly complicated efforts to solidify the South's importance in the environmental movement (374). The "common speculation" of national and local movements in the 1970s suggested that "either environmental organizations explicitly excluded the poor and people of color or the environmental agenda simply was not relevant to their lives" (375). Divisions between a national environmental movement and the nascent, but powerful, civil rights movement caused the mayor of Gary, Indiana, Richard Hatcher, to declare in 1970, "The nation's concern with the environment has done what George Wallace was unable to do: distract the nation from the human problems of black and brown Americans" (qtd. in Spears 103). Just as in the civil rights split between Martin Luther King Jr. and the Black Panthers, there was a split between the Sierra Club and more radical players that bifurcated the environmental movement into political camps that longed to be bridged. Much of the emphasis on whiteness, or what McGurty calls "elitism" by national ecological organizations, alienated poor communities of color throughout the South; more specifically, the movement felt grievously disconnected from the struggle for survival and enfranchisement that was continuing to be a problem throughout the Deep South.

Also complicating any momentum for environmental protections were the new techniques for farming that began to be advanced throughout the 1970s, especially methods of automation and industrialization. With increases in technology came new potential for ecological ruin and environmental degradation—soil erosion and depletion, deforestation, and pesticides and fertilizers that caused widespread chemical pollution. In fact, much of the writing on southern ecology and conservation during the 1970s feels more jeremiad than history: for example, a textbook on the ecological history of the American South ends with a chapter describing the decades of the late twentieth century titled "Paradise Lost?" In a summary of the main points of the chapter, the authors write, in part "At the core of the many transformations [in the twentieth century] were technological innovation and social upheaval. In some instances, southerners stemmed abuses of the past, while in other situations, they introduced previously unknown forms of environmental degradation. . . . A rural, agricultural region at the outset of the century, the South retained many agrarian traits, but its residents witnessed accelerating urban and industrial development, pine crops replacing cotton, and an easing of the stifling racism and subjugation of African Americans. Each transition altered how humans dealt with the environment that they lived in" (Saikku et al. 183). Technological innovation helped the region economically transform itself but often went hand in hand with ecological peril. Thus, any kind of history of southern environmentalism in the 1970s is muddied by the region's connection to over-farming, environmental degradation, and rampant segregation and racism. Perhaps the only way southerners found themselves invested in issues of environmental rights was because of leisure activities such as hunting and fishing. or the renewed interest in protecting the coastal waterways of the Gulf of Mexico because of the proliferation of oil refineries and commercial fisheries. In short, the history of southern conservation and ecological concerns throughout the 1970s is dirtied by affiliations with economies of exploitation, waste, and pollution, not to mention corporate exploitation and systematic environmental racism enacted by institutions defined by their connection to masculinity, affluence, and whiteness. Southern ecological concerns always connect to a dirty history.

Because agricultural "modernization" or "progress" in the 1970s South meant greater chances for ecological ruin, southern "environmentalism" remained antithetical to ecological concerns throughout the nation. Just as Keep America Beautiful displaced questions of pollution and purity from governmental or corporate responsibility onto conceptions of an individual's ethical conscience, the South's segregation and violent rejection of racial equality displaced much of nation's ownership of ecological ruination to the region. In order to untangle some of the thorny connections between ecological crises and their moral and ethical interpretations, we must first begin to understand how a conception of southern environmentalism was understood largely through an emphasis on interpersonal moral imperatives and not systemic or institutional failures. If the South had any kind of ecological voice in the American vernacular, it was a dirty one.

And yet, uncovering how systemic racism was complicit in the pollution of the southern landscape exposed Keep America Beautiful's empty rhetoric of individual morality. In fact, the concept of "environmental racism," defined by Dorceta E. Taylor as "processes that resulted in minority and low-income communities facing disproportionate environmental harms and limited environmental benefits" (2), first became popularized through connection to court cases throughout the American South.[10] Because environmental problems in the South were refracted through the lens of moral issues of racism, conceptions of "environmental justice" first became visible in the region. And environmental justice was clearly a step forward from piety about pristine nature and noble savages. Furthermore, a focus on environmental justice pushes toward concepts of institutional racism, and hence away from an individualistic moralism. Thus, linking environmental devastation to racism might have marginalized the South from the mainstream centrist environmental movement, but the focus on how the two go together opens up a more productive (and more accurate) focus on the forces (powers) driving pollution. Here, the (literal) dirty South has something to offer—but in this case, it offers not a dream of a cleansing sacrificial violence, but a concrete grappling with the dirty realities of where pollution comes from and whose interests it serves.

In short, the South has become an ambivalent region regarding national anxieties over ecological preservation, as evidenced by those environmental historians and activists who write about it. Undisputedly one of the nation's most rural (and therefore, seemingly "natural" or "unspoiled" regions), its "agrarian . . . sensibilities, land use histories, and conservation histories" mark it as "an inscrutable place" (Sutter 4). *Inscrutable:* I want to focus on this word to examine the region's dirty ecology, for the South is not necessarily only read as a polluted site—defiled by its people or the backwater of the colonial enterprise—but rather as one that is, at its base, ecologically unknowable, mysterious, muddied, inchoate.[11] The South emerged in the late twentieth century as both a region of tremendous environmental resources and as a site of the exploitation of those resources as well as the attendant consequences of environmental exploitation—pollution, litter, landfills. I want to explore the potential of dirt (physically and discursively) to interrogate just how the South operates as a space of potential for fantasies of ecological transformation. While dirt suggests conceptions of impurity and defilement, it also offers potential for transgression and imaginative play, even within the confines of what might seem, at first, to be a fairly stark and consistent reading of conservation and ecology.

GETTING SWAMPY

To explore the South as a site that simultaneously suggests (dirty) ethical and ecological transgression as well as exceptionalism, let's begin by untangling connections to discourses of protection and conservation through the lens of the region's ecologically unique and most symbolically rich feature: the swamp.[12] Long a site of contested value, the swamp has occupied a unique place in American consciousness; as a space of both ecological wonder and terror, it has represented contradictory tropes of abjection and purity, of decay and rebirth, of protection and disease. The very value of swampland was debated as early as the beginning of the twentieth century: in 1900, the Supreme Court case of *Leovy v. United States, 177 U.S. 621 (1900)* upheld the right of state officials in Louisiana to drain the wetlands surrounding Plaquemines Parish in Louisiana.[13] In their findings, the court summarized the popular perspective of the time: swamps were dangerous spaces that needed to be eliminated: "If there is any fact which may be supposed to be known by everybody, and therefore by courts, it is that swamps and stagnant waters are the cause of malarial and malignant fevers, and that the police power is never more legitimately exercised than in the removing of such nuisances" (Desty and U.S. *Supreme Court* 131). Reflecting the contemporary understanding of swamps, marshes, and other "wet lands," the court decided that, in the words of Royal C. Gardner, that swamps "were dank, dark places that threatened public health and welfare" (5). Moreover, the court recognized that swampland was of no practical agricultural value to the state; "swamps and their ilk were nuisances to be drained, and the newly available land could be put to beneficial, economic use" (Gardner 5). And yet, during the late 1960s and into the 1970s, as "America experienced an extraordinary awakening, . . . a national embrace of the notion that human beings should stop fouling their own nests" (Grunwald 241), perceptions about swamps began to shift.

Though swamps and marshes still retained some connections to disease and decay, they experienced a dynamic shift in appreciation during the environmental movement of the 1970s: "Rather than being viewed as mosquito-breeding nuisances (or cheap land to drain and fill)," southern swamplands in states such as Louisiana and Florida were celebrated for ecological exceptionalism. Conservationists recognized how "wetlands provide important habitat for animals and plants, support the seafood industry, protect homes and businesses from floods, and help improve water quality" (Gardner 2). However, such recognition of the value of swamps often came too late, for conservationists tended to "appreciate the value of wetlands and their ecosystem services only after they [were] gone (or degraded)" (2). Swamplands were routinely destroyed for speculation and development. Indeed, by the early 1970s, "Half the [Florida] Everglades was gone, drained for agriculture or paved for development. The rest was an ecological mess—sometimes too wet, sometimes too dry, always obstructed and convoluted by highways, levees, and canals" (Grunwald 264).

Because most swampland in the nation was in the Southeast, environmentalists and conservationists had a difficult time convincing local and state government—let alone those outside the region—that fetid and dank sunken lands of waterlogged decay were systems in need of protection.[14] Consequently, much of the southern swamps of the early twentieth century simply disappeared; Donald Hey and Nancy Philippi note that, "by the time the nation moved to curb the pollution of the surface waters, in the environmental decade of the 1970s, more than half of the wetlands . . . had been destroyed" (2). The southern swamp was a feature that truly mirrored the dirty and muddied connotations of the region's connection to ecology and conservation.

In his book investigating its cultural and literary importance, Anthony Wilson examines the southern swamp's imaginative potential: the quickly vanishing swamps occupied "an intriguingly complex and liminal space in the Southern and national imaginations" (ix). Echoing Sutter's declaration of the South's "inscrutable" connection to ecological history, Wilson finds the swamp's contradictory connotations offer a rich tapestry for artists: the swamp "inscribes themes of purity and adulteration [which play] out in an array of political, cultural, and psychological contexts." The southern swamp's symbolic potential directly connects to its ability to operate so effectively as conflicting imaginaries. Depending on the historical moment or the rhetorical work asked of it, the southern swamp can be both "the always present but always denied underside of the myth of the pastoral Eden" or "the last pure vestige of undominated but ever threatened Southern ecoculture" (ix).

Southern swamps are a mess of contradictions—both what differentiates the South from other (ecological) spaces in the nation but also what marks its potential danger, as a space of horror and disease. The connection to the swamp and disease creates what Wilson calls a popular imaginary that can be grafted onto the region's dirty history, for representations of the diseased swamp were promoted by "abolitionists [who] applied disparaging images of swamps . . . to describe the moral decadence of the entire South" (xii–xiii). If we are looking for an effective symbol of the paradoxical but transgressively rich potential of the dirty South's place in the ecological movement of the 1970s, we might not find a better image than the southern swamp.

Though Wilson never forgets that the wetlands he examines are a real ecological feature of the South whose vanishings have had dramatic consequences for the region's natural survival and the nation's climate,[15] he focuses on the discursive and rhetorical potential of the swamp as a mythic refraction of dominant (and sometimes subdominant) cultural and historical perspectives that work to reflect powerful, if conflicting, insights into how the region reads—and is read—by multiple constituencies. In its very makeup, the swamp refuses clarity. Wilson marks the swamp's resistance to classification; swampy areas are made up of "land that resists reclamation for agricultural development purposes . . . an area outside of civilization whose geographical features—notably its treacherous mix of water and earth—render it resistant to colonization or agriculture" (xiv). Swampland is trash land—of little to no value for projects of industry and commodity; furthermore, swamps are spaces that resist classification or valuation. As a species of ecological space, swamps can be described as land, water, both, or neither. They are subsequently terrain that remains both hyper-natural but also unnatural, a contested imaginary whose potential for representation is dynamic and multifaceted. If the South's ambivalent connections to the environmental movement needed an image, it has to be the swamp.

It is difficult to imagine a space more contested, more unstable, one whose very definition and existence fluctuated between antitheses. At once an impure location of foul and murky water mixed with rotting land and vegetation—a space of no agricultural or colonizing value—the swamp was also one of the most biologically diverse and ecologically unique features of the nation.[16] Though it took an executive order from President Carter in 1977 to protect the wetlands, it is clear that, for much of the second half of the twentieth century, the southern swamp was prominently on the minds of American environmentalists and artists.[17] Perhaps because of their contested value, southern swamps—or "wetlands" as ecologists and environmentalist eventually renamed them—were slow to gain recognition as ecologically important spaces, even in the "environmental decade" of the 1970s, and quickly began to disappear.[18] And yet, in their vanishing, the swampy areas of the South still represented much of the region's mystique and allure. Swamps were vanishing and omnipresent, of little value but of primary importance.

Because the swamp was such a contested—though discursively rich (paradoxical even)—site, it was prominently used as a setting for fiction, fantasy, horror, mystery, and magic. Most popular examples of the swamp-as-setting emphasized its history of pejorative associations. Gardner explains that "cultural references reinforced the notion of wetlands as public nuisances" throughout the twentieth century; he offers as examples a short cartoon, *The Winged Scourge* (1943), which follows the Seven Dwarfs from Snow White as they work to drain a nearby swamp in order to destroy a breed of mosquito believed to cause malaria.[19] Still other examples in popular culture and literature offer the swamp as a space of potential transcendence and play, a site of mystery and magic: Gardner cites this kind of swamp setting in *The Hound of the Baskervilles* and *The Lord of the Rings*. But for his final illustration of how the swamp offers discursive possibilities, Gardner suggests the popularity of *Swamp Thing*, a comic book originally produced in 1971 and set in Louisiana. *Swamp Thing* and its popularity are worth examining, for the comic and characters' popular appeal dovetails with the shifting perspective on southern ecology as well as the decade in which this study situates its conception of "dirt": the 1970s.

SWAMP THING(S)

The creature known as "Swamp Thing" initially appeared in comic-book publisher DC's anthology of horror and mystery stories *House of Secrets* in 1971; the issue was an immediate success.[20] According to comic-book writer Len Wein, who first envisioned the monster, the popularity of his character came as a shock: "We [Wein and artist Bernie Wrightson] really didn't think we were going to create a legend" (4), he writes twenty years after "Swamp Thing" appeared. Wein was certain his story would be published in the anthology, but he could not have foreseen how captivated comic-book readers would be by a half-man, half-swamp monster. Even by the standards of 1971, the comic's popularity was tremendous. "Sales figures declared it the bestselling DC title of the month," he recalls. "Mail poured in by the sackful, evoking emotions easily as strong as the story itself" (5).

Realizing that the "Swamp Thing" issue was one of the top sellers for 1971, DC desperately attempted to persuade Wein and Wrightson to make a stand-alone series. However, the two had some stipulations: they did not want the new series just to be an extension of the anthology piece in *House of Secrets;* they wanted instead to start over and change key elements of the story to make their character's arc more relevant to contemporary readers—including issues of environmental protection and conservation. Wein's first story had been set close to the turn of the twentieth century in Louisiana, a "period piece, a love story fraught with danger, murder, and, ultimately, revenge." There, in the bayou, scientist Alexander Olsen is murdered by his assistant, Damian Ridge, who hopes to seduce and marry Olsen's wife, Linda. Behind Olsen's back, Damian alters the scientist's chemicals for his experiment; when he runs a new trial using the modified experiment, Olsen is killed in an explosion. Damian then takes Olsen's body and buries it in the swampy waters outside the house. Spurred by his rage to avenge himself on his murderous assistant, Olsen's body—rotted and decayed because of its time in the swamp water—rises again, undead, seeking justice. After killing Damian, Olsen-as-Swamp-Thing finds he is unable to speak or communicate with Linda and must resign himself to the fate of being a restless monster haunting the swamps.

In Wein and Wrightson's 1972 series, however, there are several key changes: first, the main character's name is Alec, not Alex, Holland (though his wife retains the name Linda). Alex and Linda are both scientists working on an experiment that, if successful, might create a chemical that will, in the words of Holland, "be used to create gardens out of sweltering deserts" (21). The new formula they develop will facilitate mass agricultural growth across the world. Holland and his wife are not just scientists; they are ecological humanitarians who hope to use their new chemical to solve world hunger. They work for the greater good of mankind. The two relocate to the swamps of Louisiana, where they rent a large barn to house their equipment, but they are confronted one evening by criminals working for Nathan Ellery, a mob boss who runs an organization known as the "Conclave." The goons that work for Ellery unsuccessfully try to convince Holland to sell the chemical formula to them. When Holland refuses, they knock him unconscious; as he awakens, Holland notices a ticking bomb under his laboratory table—the goons have decided that, if they cannot have his formula, no one will. Injured by the explosion, Holland runs out into the night engulfed in flames. He dives deep into the nearby waters of the swamp, where Linda and Ellery assume he dies. But he does not—not completely anyway.

Something strange and miraculous happens to Holland when his biochemical soil enhancer mixes with the murky, foul water of the swamp; both water and chemical interact with the innate chemistry of his body. Somehow plant and human merge to form a being part swamp fauna and part man; still possessing his human memories and consciousness, Holland rises from the swamp as a creature with tremendous powers but the drives and desires of a human. He confronts the men who tried to murder him, only later to find they have already killed his wife. Aching with a desire to avenge her death, Holland as the Swamp Thing tracks the murderers down and kills them. His thirst for revenge sated, the Swamp Thing slumps down, morose and alone. Even in avenging Linda's death, the monster finds little satisfaction. Saddened by his continued existence in his monstrous form, the Swamp Thing carries forward as an immortal, the simultaneous blessing of invulnerability and the curse of immortality: destined to be seen as only a creature, a monster of the swamps, but inside, a human with memories and desires.

Wein and Wrightson's new series was even more popular than the initial story in *House of Secrets*. Though other comics had presented plant-based monsters before, Wein's backstory for the Swamp Thing was unique.[21] Since the first appearance of the monster, the Swamp Thing's popularity has only increased; currently, the character has at least two stand-alone comics and routinely shows up in crossovers with other major DC characters, such as Superman, Batman, and Green Arrow.[22] Part of the appeal of Wein and Wrightson's character of Alex Holland is that, as readers, we have access to the monster's internal monologue; we—and only we—bear witness to the existential malaise of the creature and his understanding of himself. Wein presents Holland's external struggles for justice juxtaposed with the creature's internal grappling over the memories of the man he was and the painful realization of what he's become. Because Wein gives us access to Holland's consciousness as a human as well as his desire to live in a world that recognizes his humanity, the reader does not see an ecological monster but a superhero.

I believe part of the initial popularity—not to mention sustained endurance—of *Swamp Thing* in the early 1970s connects with the decade's turn to matters of conservation and ecological awareness as well as the comic's connection to the dirty South and the polluted ethics of "some people." In Wein's Swamp Thing, we find a rhetoric similar to the one employed by the Keep America Beautiful commercials: a privileging of narratives of hyperprimitivity that inevitably connects to appeals to personal responsibility, especially related to how we manage the effect of nonnatural objects and materials on the natural world. Both *Swamp Thing* and the "Crying Indian" suggest that there is the potential for something profoundly transformative in humanity's stewardship of the natural world. Both narratives are emotionally manipulative and present stories of ecological transformation through individual (not systemic) interventions. Holland's brilliant formula improves on nature and becomes both his curse and his secret power, as the "chemical mingled with my flesh . . . reacted with swamp ooze . . . [and] turned me into . . . WHAT?"

The swamp's transgressive potential also invites play, and Wein uses it as a space of potential transformation for the human to *become* the environment, and vice versa. Just as the Keep America Beautiful campaign suggests that one person can make a difference, Wein's vigilante narrative suggests that, to fight criminal corruption and exploitation of natural resources, the Swamp Thing (Alex Holland) can save humanity from its ecological ruin. Moreover, both comic and commercial emphasize that these transformations can only occur through what Yaeger calls a "dirty ecology": "the science of halfway practices" where we recycle "a few things while leaking and expending everything else." The leftover "leaks" of man's capitalist or modern endeavors make waste, but it is waste with a dirty value.

Alex Holland is physically and emotionally wounded by the combination of ecology and man-made waste. In becoming the Swamp Thing, Holland manifests the transformative power of a kind of ecology whose mythic potential requires dirty collaboration between nature and the nonnatural. Yaeger argues that such "dirty ecology" pollutes narratives that privilege biological or scientific absolutes: "We must dirty ecology," she writes, "the science of whole environments, with myths, fictions, half-truths, dirty imagery." There is perhaps no better site for "half-truth" or "dirty imagery" than Wein's comic-book swamp, what Will Jacobs and Gerard Jones call the "nexus point [for] the very structure of reality" (qtd. 196) in the American imagination. The chemical formula Holland develops accelerates the natural processes of ecological growth, thereby offering potential solutions for world hunger, but his science is, itself, impure and dirty: manmade chemicals—not biological or organic material— offer exceptional potential to boost natural biological processes. That our conception of the exactness of Holland's scientific feat is mysterious mirrors aesthetic connections to the swamp. Like the swamp itself, Holland's formula is made up of "countless unclassified chemicals" (Wein and Wrightson 28). What happens when the unclassified ooze of something unnatural meets the unclassified ooze of the hyper-natural? Wein suggests that the result can be magic.

Alex Holland's transformation is not unlike many origin stories for comic-book characters, though it is mostly villains who are transformed by chemicals, such as Batman's arch nemesis, Joker, who falls into a vat of compounds and becomes a white-faced freak. But Holland is no villain, at least not in the conventional sense; the monster he becomes—at once unnatural and supremely natural—is a dirty one: not superhero but antihero. Brian Cremins notes that Swamp Thing "spends most of his time brooding over his lost humanity like some moss-encrusted, bayou-dwelling version of the Incredible Hulk" (56), but he does not operate with the Hulk's notorious lack of intellect. Swamp Thing is the bridged consciousness of monster and genius, both sides responding and acting in perfect synchronicity. The magic of Holland's transformation is his retention of his humanity in the face of his unnaturalness.

The popularity of *Swamp Thing*'s dirty ecology reminds us of the appeal of the swamp's murkiness as a popular imaginary for something both fundamentally natural and supernatural. Wein's first run of the monster was positively Gothic, and much of the action takes place on the outskirts of a fetid swamp during a thunderstorm. Images of the swamp are already infected with a Gothic beauty, "the arabesques of its vines and tendrils, the shifting patterns of light that play . . . about its fastness . . . the sultry atmosphere, the treacherous mire, the bewildering vegetation" (David Miller 3).Cremins claims that the immediate and continued popularity of *Swamp Thing* "suggests that the swamp for comic book readers holds the same hypnotic, multi-generational appeal as the fiend-ridden yet romantically compelling moors of Emily Brontë" (56). We are drawn to the swamp like we are drawn to Brontë's moors, for they are contested spaces whose murkiness forces us only to guess at what is hidden beneath their dark waters.

It is no surprise that Wein felt Swamp Thing was a perfect character for an anthology named *House of Secrets,* for his swamp operates as a space whose value is hidden. The popularity of *Swamp Thing* has everything to do with the dirty ecology of the swamp—as contested space of value, as site of decay and rebirth—and its transgressive potential, something obviously connecting to the ethos of dirt. Wein's swamp is a space in which one can experience "violent physical or emotional transformations" (Cremins 56). As David Miller points out, even as far back as the nineteenth century, the swamp was "the domain of sin, death, and decay; the stage for witchcraft; the habitat of weird and ferocious creatures," and yet, even as he acknowledges that "these associations remained current . . . right up to the present," the changing historical moments and cultural awareness of the swamp "imparted mystique to a landscape hitherto shunned" (3). Wein plays on these associations of decay and death by setting *Swamp Thing* in Louisiana, which he defines in the first issue as a site of exoticism and terror consisting of familiar animals with unnatural desires and actions: "This is bayou country: a swampy, desolate marshland forsaken by civilized man—and now inhabited by far less demanding creatures ... screaming herons stretch their sleek wings towards the angry heavens ... mottled bullfrogs sing their croaking night-song in eager anticipation ... great reptiles loll uncaringly beneath the cloaked moon ... and this night, this rainy, wind-swept night, impatient humanity intrudes itself into this primitive region" (17).

Alex Holland and his wife enter the swampland as more than just intruders into the natural world, but as hypercivilized scientists entering untamed spaces. Holland is no mere man; he is a brilliant researcher working on solving the greatest ecological crisis of his time. His experiments lead him to combine chemicals together and, through biochemically manufactured restoration, improve agricultural techniques. His work connects to a muddy history of agricultural progress throughout the region, where automation and chemicals increase farming yields but harm long-term ecology. When you put together all the integers that make *Swamp Thing* successful—the scientist looking to solve a natural crises with polluted chemicals, the murky and Gothic supernaturality of the ecologically ambivalent swamp, the startling transformation of man into vigilante monster through the combination of chemical and ecological elements—it is easy to see why the comic was so popular in the 1970s, for it exposed anxieties surrounding dirty ecology (especially in the South) during a historical moment in which audiences would have been specifically attuned to them.

Though Wein's run of the series ended in September of 1976, the creature continued to make appearances across the DC Comic Universe. When Wes Craven was tapped to direct a film about the creature in the early 1980s, DC relaunched a stand-alone comic. In 1984, British writer Alan Moore—who later came to fame for his complicated graphic novel *Watchmen* (1986)—was tapped to write stories for the series; from that moment on, the creature's ontology more explicitly connected to questions of ecology and dirty ethics. Moore's run of *Swamp Thing* explored American failures of conservation and protection of the natural world. Unlike Wein and Wrightson's origin for the monster, Moore's scientist dies in the explosion inside his lab, but the chemicals somehow preserve his consciousness which mysteriously synthesizes with the bayou world outside.

No longer a magical mixture of Holland's mind, body, and the essence of the swamp, Moore's *Swamp Thing* is a product of a natural world impregnated by human thoughts, memories, and sentience. Qiana J. Whitted remarks of Moore's reboot of the character that he was, essentially, "living vegetation in the shape of a man, one whose 'humanity' operated like phantom limbs on a mossy, hulking frame" (187). Like other plants, the Swamp Thing could die and be reborn in different places and spaces, a perennial monster chained to Earth, rooted in land. But the Swamp Thing's charge changed from righting personal wrongs and avenging injustices done to Holland and his family; instead, Moore's creature does not fight for justice for humanity but rather on behalf of the ecological world. Whitted sees Moore's Holland as "an aberrant presence among his human neighbors" but a creature who was, at his base, a "deeply compassionate guardian" of nature (187).

In Moore's *Swamp Thing,* the swamp ceases to be only the resting place of Holland, a space of refuge and calm, but the very essence of the pristine natural world. In its inchoate murkiness, Moore's swamp achieves a spirituality that is neither human nor supernatural but hypernatural. Moore makes clear that his main character is not Holland or the creature but the swamp itself. In the teaser for his series, titled "This is the place," Moore asks his readers to imagine not a man-as-swamp but a swamp-as-spirit: "At night you can almost imagine what it might look like if the Swamp were boiled down to its essence, and distilled into corporeal form: if all the muck, all the forgotten muskrat bones, and all the luscious decay would rise up and wade on two legs through the shallows; if the Swamp had a spirit and that spirit walked like a man" (Bissette and Totleben 28). For Moore the swamp is not just "a territory for alternate realities, magic, and carnivalesque social satire" (Cremins 29), as it is for Wein, but rather a metonym for the spirit of the natural world, a world fragile, constantly on the verge of fracturing beyond repair. Moore's creature-as-swamp is a vigilante that fights not against criminals threatening humanity but against forces that portend "ecological ruin" (29).

In fact, as Whitted notes in her perceptive essay, Moore's Swamp Thing often finds himself at odds with moral imperatives; rejecting human ethics, the monster sets the protection of nature as paramount to all, even when fighting for it runs counter to conventional notions of morality. For example, in Moore's *Swamp Thing,* we learn that there is a force called "the Green," which is the "home of the life force of all plant life on Earth" (DC Fandom). Less a world than a "dimension," the Green is the "unified mind" where Plant Elementals can communicate with one another. These Elementals "have existed on Earth long before humans. Born when an animal died in flames and merged with the Earth, the Elementals became protectors of plant life throughout history. When they had done their time, they would join the Parliament of Trees, a group mind of former Elementals. These elementals have given up human characteristics like speech and mobility." In Moore's comic, we learn that the Swamp Thing is, in fact, the "final plant elemental" on Earth, and tasked with protecting the planet from threats to the natural world, no matter where they originate.[23]

Moore's reworking of the *Swamp Thing* is not so much a reversal of Wein and Wrightson's creature but an extension of the monster's dirty ecology. If Wein used his creature to explore the magic transformations that occur in the mixing of the nonhuman (plant) and the nonnatural (chemical), Moore moves beyond such meditations into how human consciousness might animate a spirit of ecological protection and conservation. Moore's philosophical run of the comic breaks conventional associations between what a superhero is and for whom he fights. Claire Pikethy marks the pull of antithesis as foundational to the superhero's identity: "Incorporating both sides of an opposition, the superhero embodies a paradox, or in other words, he becomes unsure of what he actually *is*" (28); the paradoxical identity of Moore's Swamp Thing—as both man and not-man, as plant and not-plant or hero and antihero—is the most salient and compelling part of the 1980s run of the comic.

For Pikethy, the incorporation of contradiction into the superhero's identity is tied, inevitably, to his power: "it is the dynamic tension that results from this split that makes him or her *super*human." As an example of this kind of contradiction, Pikethy quotes Moore's Swamp Thing's existential pondering: "Am I a plant that dreams he is a man? Or a man who dreams he is a plant?" The contradictions inherent in the two questions also suggest the contradictions inherent in the two versions of the creature from Wein and Moore—the latter of whom has his monster confront the dirty vigilantism of a plant fighting for the natural world, often against the very humans to whom he ascribes his consciousness. Protecting the planet from threats to Nature repositions Moore's Swamp Thing as a creature that is, at his base, an ecological warrior. Moore's monster talks with Elementals and receives orders directly from the plants that surround him.

As we think about the gaps between the two iterations of the Swamp Thing from 1971 to 1984 and the historical moments in which they were born, I am struck by how the interim marked a time of expanding interest in conservation and protection, especially in connection to swampland. President Jimmy Carter's 1978 Executive Order finally declared wetlands as spaces worthy of preservation and protection, and in the mid-1980s, the swamp itself began to find itself at the center of a new environmentalism.[24] As an ecologically diverse region, Moore's pristine Louisiana swamplands were no longer sites of disease but natural spaces to be celebrated—even transformed into "theme parks" celebrating the exceptionalism of America's ecology by the 1990s.

Anthony Wilson notes that efforts at conservation and preservation also inevitably collided with swamp tourism, which promised "'extreme' encounters with primordial wildlife, appeals to myth and superstition, and carefully constructed claims of cultural authenticity" (176). In his research of various swamp tours, Wilson finds that the majority advertise an ironic rhetoric of conservation and mystery that uses swamp creatures to promote their trips. On one website, Wilson finds an advertisement whose language borders on parodic sendup of the comic swamp of Wein's imagination: "Dare you venture into the night with us deep into the heart of the Manchac Swamp? The very swamp that after being cursed by voodoo queen Julie Brown was totally destroyed by the 1915 hurricane & whose residents are buried in unmarked graves on the property?" (179). The swamp continues to draw us, in part, because of its connection to the abject, even in our contemporary moment.

KATRINA

The draw of the swamp in the twenty-first century inevitably reminds me of not only its symbolic importance in cultural texts but its ecological importance in 2005 when one of the greatest natural disasters in American history occurred in Louisiana. Hurricane Katrina's devastation of the Gulf Coast left a tremendous psychic wound on the very soul of the American South, if not the nation. The force of the storm, the flooding, and the lives lost all are almost without parallel, and much of the ruin was caused by the loss of Louisiana wetlands, which had offered crucial protection from storms forming off the Gulf of Mexico. The importance of the swamp extends beyond its unique ecosystem or the endangered animals and fauna that thrive there; the swamp marks a crucial site between ocean and land that aids in blocking surges often associated with hurricanes and cyclones. A good deal of the devastation caused by Katrina is directly connected to the loss of these wetlands. Because of development and industry, much of the coastal swamplands of Louisiana were depleted throughout the twentieth century. In a 2005 congressional hearing, Beverly Wright, executive director of the Xavier University Deep South Center for Environmental Justice, reported, "Since the 1930s Louisiana has lost more than 1.2 million acres of coastal wetlands. . . . Louisiana is losing about 6600 acres per year, a rate that if unchecked will result in a net loss of 328,000 acres—or an area roughly the size of Rhode Islands—by 2050" (*Hurricane Katrina* 138). That testimony was offered not to bolster ecological conservation activities, but as part of a larger report responding to destruction left in Katrina's wake.

Katrina's impact on the Gulf region—specifically New Orleans and the Mississippi coast—was tremendous. The storm hit Louisiana on 29 August 2005 as a Category 3 hurricane with sustained winds around 125 miles per hour. Though the brunt of the hurricane passed east of the city of New Orleans, the destabilization of the levee system surrounding the city caused a breach of the Industrial Canal in St. Bernard Parish that later ballooned into over fifty more openings, effectively flooding the area as well as 80 percent of the neighboring Parish of New Orleans. Close to twelve hundred people lost their lives from Katrina, and the storm caused over $108 billion in property damage.[25] The loss of the swamps surrounding New Orleans began in the 1970s and 1980s—the same frame in which Wein and Moore achieved success with *Swamp Thing*. In the words of several scientists, "By our calculations, the wetlands lost in the 36 years between [Hurricane] Camille [in 1969] and Katrina [in 2005] would have reduced Katrina's storm surge by approximately 2.0 to 3.3 feet. Given that the peak water levels were estimated to be one to three feet above the tops of floodwalls and levees, it's reasonable to assume that the amount of wetlands lost between Camille and Katrina had a significant effect on the extent of overtopping and subsequent flooding during Katrina" (Huggins et al. 83). Much of the depletion of the wetlands protecting the city can be blamed on industry, specifically drilling for petroleum. Petro companies had argued for decades that they needed a more direct route for their tankers to deliver oil to the Louisiana Gulf. To satisfy their concerns, the Army Corps of Engineers created the Mississippi River–Gulf Outlet (MR-GO), a massive project completed three years before Wein's first issue of *Swamp Thing* in 1968.

The project was, in effect, "a seventy-six-mile-long canal, straight as a gun barrel, running right up from the Gulf of Mexico to the heart of New Orleans" (Palast). Though originally designed to "allow tankers to avoid the Mississippi's twists and turns and shoot right into New Orleans from the Gulf," MR-GO destroyed a "green wreath of cypress and mangrove [that] protected New Orleans" from incoming storms off the Gulf. The canal facilitated the movement and storage of petroleum throughout the Gulf Coast, but it also "allowed the hurricane waves to shoot in as well." Ivor van Heerden of the Louisiana State University Hurricane Center named it a "Hurricane Highway" (qtd. in Palast);[26] Palast called it "Katrina's welcome mat to the city." In the months following the devastation of Katrina, government officials, climate scientists, and city planners recognized that the biggest culprit in the destruction of the city was not, in fact, Katrina, but rather systemic failures and ecological ruin. Katrina's profound reshaping of New Orleans—a unique city—forced Americans to reassess concerns about climate, ecology, and conservation that were inevitably connected to issues of race, poverty, and region.

Addressing at once the failure of the Army Corps levee system, the systematic denuding of the coastal wetlands, the privileging of the petroleum industry over individuals, the lack of imagination of city and state government officials, and the sluggish response by the federal government in rescue and recovery, President Obama famously summed up the legacy of Katrina: "What started out as a natural disaster became a man-made disaster—a failure of government to look out for its own citizens. . . . New Orleans had long been plagued by structural inequality that left too many people, especially poor people, especially people of color, without good jobs or affordable health care or decent housing. . . . Too many kids grew up surrounded by violent crime, cycling through substandard schools where few had a shot to break out of poverty." By connecting race and class inequalities with environment concerns, Obama argued that, in our failure to "look out" for citizens, we likewise failed to imagine their connection to their environment. It was a profound statement finally repudiating the displacement of ecological concerns onto citizens; it refused the rhetoric offered by Keep America Beautiful, that dirty people in communities are responsible for the dirtiness of their environment, that a polluted town or city reflects a dirty ethics.[27]

A decade after one of the worst storms in the history of the region—indeed, the nation—Obama flew to New Orleans to christen a new housing development in the once-flooded Ninth Ward. The structures built, he argued, stood "as a symbol of the extraordinary resilience of this city and its people, of the entire Gulf Coast and of the United States of America" ("Remarks by the

President"). Obama's speech—at least rhetorically—marked perhaps the first time an American president actively shifted an environmental or ecological conversation from an accounting of individuality and into the realm of national, political, and institutional responsibility. Katrina offered a critical pivot point for the nation to redefine how and why narratives about dirt and trash could, in effect, speak back to a history of representing the region as fundamentally polluted (ethically, spiritually, ecologically) and impure.

BEAST IT!

Hurricane Katrina's devastation continues to fascinate America—"Katrina Tours" still offer visitors to New Orleans a private bus ride through areas of the city hit hardest by the storm, especially the flooding in the Lower Ninth Ward caused by a breach of the levees. We are drawn to the destructive potential of nature and its mysterious connection to the people it affects, especially those living in poverty; the appeal is even larger when it is an exploration of the impoverished "folk" of the South and their lives in the swamps, on the margins of recognizable civilization. For that reason, Katrina inspired an outpouring of art and literature. Examining the explosion of narratives of and about Hurricane Katrina from 2005 to 2015 is a useful, if dizzying, exercise in connecting the evolution of a southern ethos of dirty or swampy ethics and ecology into a contemporary moment.

In Benh Zeitlin's 2012 film *Beasts of the Southern Wild,* our hero is six-year-old "Hushpuppy" (Quvenzhané Wallis), who lives with her father, Wink (Dwight Henry), in a couple of broken-down trailers strewn across an open field in a town known simply as "the Bathtub," named because, like New Orleans, it technically lies below sea level, surrounded by water.[28] When a massive storm similar Katrina blows in one night, Hushpuppy and Wink are forced to evacuate to a nearby neighbor's house, where they live until the townsfolk decide what to do next. In an act of rebellion and survival, several of the members of the community travel to a nearby levee and blow it up, thus allowing the water in the town to drain. Once the water recedes, however, very little is left of the town, and the Bathtub—once a vibrant place with nightly celebrations and parties—appears to be destroyed. Days later, helicopters arrive ostensibly to "rescue" the citizens. Officials from an unknown organization (possibly the federal government) take the townspeople to a local shelter, where they learn that Wink is critically ill.[29] Hushpuppy and the others escape and transport Wink home, where he dies peacefully, holding his daughter's hand. At the end of the film, a voice-over by Hushpuppy affirms that, no matter what happens, the citizens of the Bathtub will remain together on their land.

Though the primary plot of the movie is straightforward, *Beasts* has a tertiary mythic narrative. In the alternate or fantastical narrative, science and imagination combine: Hushpuppy learns about an ancient beast in school—the auroch—once a fierce predator that lived on land that is now the present-day home of the Bathtub. Throughout the film, Zeitlin cuts to scenes of the aurochs—first ensconced in ice, floating far from home; then gradually melting and thawing; and, finally, awake, mobile, journeying back across land and sea in a desperate attempt to return to where they once lived. At the climax of the movie, Zeitlin breaks the narrative separation between his mythic and realistic plots: just as Hushpuppy returns to visit her dying father, she senses the aurochs galloping fiercely behind her. Unafraid and unblinking, she stares at her distant father and turns confidently to confront the charging animals. Both beast and child have returned home: the ancient land of the auroch *is* now the current home of the girl; they both share a sense of what it means to return to where one belongs. Perhaps sensing their connection, the animals bow to Hushpuppy, who raises her hand to them in salutation. "You're my friend, sort of," she says quietly. Zeitlin's dual narratives bleed together in spectacular fashion as the mythical quest of the auroch's journey home connects with Hushpuppy's return, Wink's escape from the shelter, and the townspeople's resettlement from the displacement of the storm.

Though the auroch's story might seem like a mythic outlier, Zeitlin connects the ancient beast's journey home to fundamental concerns shared by communities and people displaced by Katrina. In a *New York Times* piece, the author describes *Beasts* as partly born from Zeitlin's desire to "make a film about holdouts—people in Louisiana's bayou country who refused to evacuate from their homes during Hurricanes Katrina, Gustav and Ike" (Brennan). In driving down to the bayou's edge, Zeitlin found a familiar site, the swamp: "the land and water blend together like a spider web. . . . I was so moved by that place," he said, "I knew that I found the story I was trying to tell."[30] Like the inhabitants that live in these swamp towns, the aurochs are bestial "holdouts"; they do not leave of their own free will but are forced to migrate because of disruptions in the natural world. Far from home and frozen, the beasts magically come back to life, possibly from the rise in sea temperatures due to climate change. Zeitlin's subtle reference to the reemergence of the auroch because of a change in climate masterfully suggests that humans' carelessness with the natural world can cause unintended changes, like the thawing of beasts or superstorms like Hurricane Katrina.[31]

Displaced from their home because of natural catastrophe, the aurochs remind the viewer of the displaced residents of New Orleans, many of whom are forced to live far away from home after the storm. In the beasts' fierce animality, the aurochs represent the kind of tenacity and singular commitment that Hushpuppy must adopt to survive. Zeitlin's climactic scene connecting girl and beast "dramatizes the gargantuan challenges faced by children of color" when they are forced to navigate a world that views their humanity with skepticism (Nel 130). Aurochs offer similar lessons to the kind that Wink teaches his daughter throughout the movie: he tells her that, in order to survive in a brutal world, you must become a "beast." Wink urges Hushpuppy to toughen up, and, in one memorable scene, bullies her in front of the townsfolk until she viciously rips open the carcass of a shellfish: his advice could be summed up as "man up," or, in his words, "beast it." Even as he dies, he makes her promise not to cry.

In every interaction with his daughter, Wink urges Hushpuppy to embrace what bell hooks calls "a miniature version of the 'strong black female matriarch,'" which "racist and sexist representations have depicted from slavery on into the present day." hooks's criticism of Zeitlin's film is important, especially for a white director exploring the world of African American characters and in a film that posits that, in order to survive, a young girl of color must bleed out her humanity and become an animal. On the one hand, Zeitlin's movie wants to explore the failure of the nation to recognize "the direct correlation between race, class, and the severity of suffering inflicted by this 'natural' disaster" (Nel 130), but, on the other hand, Zeitlin's movie participates in "the age-old politics of domination . . . insisting that only the strong survive, that disease weeds out the weak (for example, the slaughter of Native Americans), that nature chooses excluding and including" (hooks).

If Zeitlin's movie excavates the disasters left behind by Katrina for mythic aims, it also clearly chooses to investigate the rhetoric of Keep America Beautiful and its presentation of "some people's" dirty ethics. Directly answering a national lack of imagination over issues of poverty and mobility, Zeitlin's film critiques readings of dirty ethics onto communities and people who do not have the ability, time, or resources to participate in cleanup projects, who are forced to live in polluted environments composed of the trash of the waste-making classes: in short, the victims of environmental racism.[32] For Nel, those who live in the Bathtub are "people without the resources to flee a hurricane, the people abandoned by a society that blames the poor for their poverty" (128). And yet, even in their poverty, Yaeger locates an endemic kind of ecological conservation; she describes the dirty ecology of the residents of the fictional swamp lowland as deeply connected to the natural world but also significantly attached to the unbiodegradable trash that ends up on their coast. Rather than reading their use of Styrofoam or aluminum as an environmental sin or a moral fault, Yaeger invites her reader to "dirty" ecology, using the word "as both adjective and verb, a descriptor for the residual, polluting, and valueless, and a practice that destabilizes or erodes boundaries" (Lincoln 218). For Yaeger, this kind of dirty ecology offers transformative potential.

A dirty ecology's transformative potential connects back to the transgressive potential Wein and Moore present in *Swamp Thing*. In the intrusion of the mythic into the ecological, Yaeger finds crucial potential for exploring humanity's relationship to the cosmos through environmental imagination, and her description of the importance of these stories applies as well to the narrative of *Swamp Thing*:

> myths also establish long-term models for guiding behavior. They require, first of all, mystery—awe at the fact of the universe and our place in it; second, a topos—an explication of cosmic shape that can ground us in a felt geography; third, an epistemology—shaping foundations supported by codes or ideas that establish the norms of the social order; and finally an ethic—a set of rules or maxims about how to live within the parameters of the everyday. Beasts bestows a weird movie mythopoeia for reestablishing each of these needs within our present era: the carbon-drunk Anthropocene.

We might easily look to the 1971–86 run of *Swamp Thing* for similar potential: the comic and the character have a clear mystery (the inexplicable transformation of the human into the nonhuman); the same "felt geography" that anchors *Beasts* (indeed, the same state and the same ecological feature); an epistemology that clearly articulates what is worth fighting for (the superhero's code); and an ethics that grounds our hero's values as recognizable and worthy of emulation. Yaeger's description of the film as "an epic comment on our condition of metamorphosis when humans persist in changing Earth's geologic direction" could also be said of Wein's monster.

Beasts is indebted to the swamp just as much as the comic. Because the

Bathtub is below sea level, the world that Hushpuppy lives in is swampy in every sense. Everything in the movie is murky: we follow Hushpuppy through her adventures in the town and the swamp with no clear understanding of what she is doing; moreover, at six years old, Hushpuppy has a muddied understanding of the natural world: normal things appear supernatural or mysterious, and unconventional readings of nature are equally plausible to her, while natural processes seem dizzyingly inchoate. She tries to imagine what animals are saying to one another, and, in one scene, even imagines the voice of her absent mother talking to her while she pretends to cook dinner.

Though she is dimly aware of her father's sickness, Hushpuppy does not understand the difference between chemical (manmade) and spiritual (natural or homeopathic) medicine. When she returns to her father early in the film with a folk remedy, she finds Wink gone. As she runs to find him, Zeitlin writes that she quakes "with fear . . . through a menacing swamp" (Zeitlin and Alibar). As "rising winds swirl the marsh grass all around her," Hushpuppy finds herself dazzled by the mystery of her father's disappearance. She "looks around the swamp, unable to understand," and we hear her voice-over, "Daddy could have turned into a tree, or a bug. There wasn't any way to know." Wink's potential for transformation from human into nonhuman comes critically in the swamp, a space of mystery and fascination, and a profound site for dirty ecology. Hushpuppy's "sense of the world rests upon a creaturely logic in which fantasy and reality converge" (Lloyd 188), and in her childish imagination, we locate dual potential for transgression and transformation. Like *Swamp Thing* before her, Hushpuppy's swampy fantasy of a dirty ecological transformation moves out from the personal and individual ethical reading of humanity's relationship to ecology and instead to "the connection to the historical, the planetary, and beyond" (188). These myths born of dirty ecology do more than just offer transcendence or a fantasies of transformation, they offer the potential "to advance the project of reshaping a planetary epistemology."

Of course, Zeitlin's film is not the only example of a post Katrina-cultural text exploring the transformative and transgressional potential of dirty ecology; his work is one of many that renegotiate conventional conceptions of trash in order to change national conceptions of humanity's relationship to ecology, especially in a world decimated by pollution, climate change, and a rapidly expanding population. One of the more outlandish examples of such dirty transformation and post-Katrina fantasy is comic-book writer Mark Landry's five-issue run at Titan, *Bloodthirsty: One Nation Under Water* (2016). In

Bloodthirsty, our hero is Virgil LaFleur, a former Coast Guard diver from New Orleans who suffers a traumatic experience during Katrina. In the aftermath of the storm, LaFleur rescues several people from flooded houses, but he is crucially unable to rescue his own parents; he almost drowns during the attempt. A decade later, LaFleur suffers from severe post-traumatic stress disorder; when he learns that a new hurricane (Rose) is about to hit the city, he decides not just to evacuate but to leave New Orleans forever. However, his younger brother Trey—a preeminent scientist and biologist—refuses to evacuate because—like Holland—he has almost completed an important experiment.

Trey's chemical enhancer is not the only connection between *Bloodthirsty* and *Swamp Thing:* like Alex Holland, Trey also is involved in a lethal, suspicious explosion in his laboratory. LaFleur suspects that Trey's main investor, Simon Wolfinger—a "disaster capitalist" who takes advantage of depleted post-Katrina power structures to line his pockets—might be behind the murder of his brother.[33] Like Holland, he sets out to get revenge. LaFleur eventually finds Wolfinger did, indeed, use Trey's expertise to create a chemical that synthesizes a genetic mutation, which Landry calls the "hemovore" mutation; this chemical synthesis gives the patient extended life, with one terrible curse: to survive, the patient must continuously feast on fresh blood.

LaFleur's investigation of Wolfinger exposes another kind of corruption: the man plans on taking the chemical synthesis and—like Wein's Nathan Ellery—selling it to whoever can pay him the most money; with the elite and affluent class as chemical vampires, Wolfinger asserts that the impoverished people of the city will supply them with all the blood they need to survive. LaFleur decides to transform himself into a superhero who will fight Wolfinger and uphold the values of the poor folk of New Orleans. He challenges, fights, and eventually defeats Wolfinger—even though, in doing so, he becomes afflicted with the hemovore mutation. No longer human, he stages his own death and continues to operate well after the devastation of Hurricane Rose as a vigilante-vampiric superhero fighting for "justice" for the defenseless residents of New Orleans.

Wolfinger's greed goes beyond economic realities. He does not want to simply aggrandize wealth, he wants to murder poor residents of New Orleans and harvest their blood to prolong the lives of the wealthy. Landry's presentation of Wolfinger's corruption offers a startling critique of the environmental racism of New Orleans and the ease with which the nation grafted a dirty ethics onto the victims of Katrina and not onto the institutions that worked to disempower them.[34] In a climactic scene in which LaFleur finally learns of the villain's evil plans, he overhears Wolfinger's speech to a crowd of affluent and "pure-bred" members of the city. To our hero's horror, he learns that Wolfinger's investment in the chemical enhancer was not to protect and empower all of humanity but instead to be a gift meant for those worthy of it, a worth he defines economically: "The serum you have injected tonight has made you all part of the most significant historical milestone since the taming of fire. . . . you understand that the finest food, the cleanest air, access to the best medicine, and other luxuries are not rights but privileges to be afforded. . . . we are no longer human beings. . . . we are now so much more." The chemical that unlocks the hemovore mutation is, like Holland's bio-restorative formula, something that could benefit all of mankind, but for Wolfinger—like it is for Nathan Ellery and the Conclave—it is merely a commodity to be bought by those rich (and therefore, worthy) enough to buy it.

In *Bloodthirsty,* Landry critiques the capitalist view of disasters like Katrina as potential investments to seize poor people's capital and transform them into spaces only for white, affluent non-natives. Like any good villain, Wolfinger does not believe in justice, only a skewed system of economic Darwinism; he believes that the ability to buy the hemovore chemical is an assertion of "our genetically appointed dominance." Wolfinger views the new culture that will come from the rise of the wealthy hemovores as "one based on the fairness of natural law, not the artificial 'same-ness' that . . . [believes] all humans are created equal and somehow remain equal regardless of their contribution." In the final act of the comic, LaFleur must rescue the common folk of the city who cannot escape the hurricane (just as he did in the Coast Guard during Katrina), but this time, they are locked in the Superdome, famous during Katrina as the site of last resort for thousands who could not leave before the hurricane hit.[35] In Landry's comic, though, the structure is not there to safely house the poor victims of a storm but to trap them in a central place where their blood can be harvested. The connection is clear enough by this point: in *Bloodthirsty,* the rich are literally feeding off the poor. The truest villainy in the comic is Landry's literalization of the metaphorical damage done to poor residents of color by those in positions of power after Katrina.

Perhaps frustrated by the inability to bring justice to post-Katrina New Orleans, Landry shows "no mercy" for the villains of his story; they are viciously dealt with by LaFleur and, in one memorable instance, nature itself: the corrupt mayor of New Orleans is decapitated when one of his campaign signs is

MARK LANDRY | ASHLEY WITTER | RICHARD PACE

Blood ⚜ thirsty™
ONE NATION UNDER WATER

The cover art for Mark Landry's *Bloodthirsty: One Nation Under Water* shows Virgil LaFleur after his transformation to hemovore standing in front of the Superdome, the shelter of last resort during Katrina and the prison for thousands of poor New Orleans citizens during the fictional storm of Landry's comic book. Simon Wolfinger plans on harvesting the blood of those taking refuge inside the dome so that he may feed the hundreds of wealthy hemovores whom he has injected with a life-extending serum.

weaponized by the hurricane's winds, while Wolfinger has his throat ripped open from a vampiric bite by LaFleur. Landry's message in *Bloodthirsty* seems to echo that of the authors of other texts: to beat the dirty monsters of this swampy town, you must become a beast—even if a benevolent one, a beast for the good of humanity. Similar to Hushpuppy's transformation in *Beasts,* LaFleur realizes that he must become a monster in order to survive and protect those who look to him for leadership.

Crucially, all three of these cultural texts—the comic runs of *Swamp Thing,* Zeitlin's Technicolor odyssey of *Beasts of the Southern Wild,* and Landry's *Bloodthirsty*—offer swampy ecology as the only cure for dirty ethics; this muddied ecology offers potential for transformations that allow human heroes to become superhuman. To achieve such a transformation, each author returns to the fetid Louisiana swampland as the ultimate site of metamorphosis. Only there—in the bayou, in the "Bathtub," on the swampy outskirts of New Orleans—can these artists locate a setting that offers possibilities for transformation. The swamp in these texts suggest simultaneously the muddiness of an enterprise of ecology in the dirty South as well as the transformative and transcendent power of the swamp.

The corruption and disenfranchisement LaFleur exposes mirror the anxieties that paralyzed the nation after Katrina, as displaced residents of New Orleans (especially poor residents of color) found themselves suddenly unable to return because of venture capitalists rebuilding and gentrifying destroyed neighborhoods. But unlike politically powerful officials of New Orleans, Simon Wolfinger is more than just a corporate monster: he is an *actual* monster. To defeat him, LaFleur must become a bloodthirsty beast. LaFleur's transformation from everyday hero to superhero vigilante mirrors Holland's metamorphosis into the Swamp Thing: like Holland, LaFleur works to better humankind; he is a Coast Guard member who rescues victims. When confronted with the dirty ethics of those who seek power to manipulate those below them, LaFleur finds that he must become a monster to win his epic fight, his own version of a swamp "thing." And, just as Hushpuppy learns to "beast it" if she wants to survive, so, too, does LaFleur find his survival tied to living as an animal feeding off the blood of others.

It is a troubling idea that one must become a beast, a monster, a vigilante, or a superhuman (which each one of these cultural texts offers as a solution) to protect the ecological or human world. In his opening to the collected edition, Landry makes clear the ideals of his comic are not regional or national but universal and should be part of a collective ethical imperative: "We have no tolerance for the greedy that prey upon the weak, no sympathy for corrupt government officials, and scarce mercy for this who would stand in the way of freedom and justice" (introduction). But this kind of absolutism is troubling and quasi-fascist in its self-righteousness, its not very veiled acceptance of righteous violence: no tolerance, sympathy, or mercy. I am suspicious of this kind of violence and its potential connections to Dickey's praising of (white) vigilante "justice."

Even though LaFleur supposedly fights on behalf of the downtrodden, his ethics are, likewise, muddied. After all, every superhero is, at heart, a vigilante. Comics deal all the time with the superhero who must take matters into his own hands because the conventional forces of justice are either corrupt or, if well-intentioned, not up to getting the job done. Thus our dirty superhero is also pure: the true servant of justice even though using extralegal means to secure it. That kind of vigilante dirty ethics is different from the straightforward dirty ethics of selfish gain, but nevertheless it must be subject to the same skepticism. Further, to transform into a comic-book vigilante superhero, one must, in a sense, reject one's humanity, become superhuman—the fascist appeal to the strong man, to the Übermensch; the transformation into the inhuman, bestial in its overcoming the human body's frailties—and, perhaps, overcome human pity. The problem becomes how to imagine achieving justice within the limits of the human, without requiring a fantasized escape from the human into something else. And I am troubled that the space reserved for such escapism is the American South, which regrettably reminds me of President Trump's boast that you can only threaten to murder immigrants in the Florida Panhandle. Regardless of which values one fights for, a southern valorization of bestial violence and vigilantism must always be regarded with the most rigorous skepticism.

Swamp Thing, Beasts of the Southern Wild, and *Bloodthirsty* all tell us that justice cannot be secured by the normal legal channels (either they are corrupt or weak); their heroes must take matters into their own hands. These vigilante ethics are dirty (outside the law) but in the name of higher "justice." The rejection of humanity, however, is concerning inasmuch as it connects (inevitably) to an embrace of the inhuman, either the bestial or the superhuman (or some combination of both), in order to overcome human limits. That's how the "dirty" transforms into a recurrent fantasy. In *Deliverance,* Dickey wants a dose of primitivist southern violence to restore his suburban men's manliness—an easy fantasy to repudiate. However, the dirty ethics of vigilantes are not overtly criminal (like the psychopaths of *Chain Saw*) and are more recognizably tied to what looks like a clear-eyed view of systemic environmental racism. But, critically, their proposed solutions to that injustice and racism are relatable: both because the solution is a fantasy of escaping the human and because it (as much as *Deliverance*) sees violence as purifying.

Regardless of how it operates in connection to these fantasies, the swamp continues to work as a mediator between the natural (ecological) world and the unnatural (supernatural) world, and these mediated fantasies often have wildly contradictory consequences—they are not just narratives in isolation but stories that have political, social, and environmental effects. Swamp water's murkiness invites us to imagine what lies beneath, what has been repressed or buried in its waters—or indeed what those waters might obscure. Even in the twenty-first century, the swamp compels us with its mystery. We might also consider the inarguable popularity of other swampy settings: the vibrant and brutal city of New Orleans explored in the HBO series *Treme* (2010–13); the doomed and sunken "Pit" of Jesmyn Ward's Bois Sauvage in *Salvage the Bones* (2011); and the theme-park-ified scrap of land just off the Florida coast in Karen Russell's *Swamplandia!* (2011), to name a few.[36]

Finally, what value remains in things dirtied or expelled as trash? Using the recycle bin as a model for scholarship, I believe that thinking through the American South and the cultural texts that describe or seek to animate it participates in a kind of endless recycling or resignification that is always connected to declarations or contestations of value. These competing conversations feel to me like the true voices of dirty southern artists and scholars in the shifting terrain of literature and cultural texts of or about the American South after 2020.

RECYCLING THE SOUTH

Rubbish is transformed into new rubbish, only slightly increased in quantity. . . . this isn't a mere technical problem because the spirit of dead things rises over the earth and over the waters, and its breath forebodes evil.

  —Ivan Klima, *Love And Garbage*

The Old South may be your American Downton Abbey but it is our American Horror Story, even under the best circumstances it represents the extraction of labor, talent and life we can never get back. . . . 2020 and 1619 have just been linked together in an ignoble chain.

  —Michael Twitty, *The Shadow of the Bin*

D uring the several years it took to write *The Dirty South,* there have been numerous works of art that share my title—from the Crystal Bridges Museum of American Art's 2022 exhibition "The Dirty South: Contemporary Art, Material Culture, and the Sonic Impulse," which "examines the aesthetic and musical traditions of southern Black culture in the past century, influences now common throughout the American South and contemporary American art and culture," to L. H. Stallings's 2019 *A Dirty South Manifesto: Sexual Resistance and Imagination in the New South.* It seems as though the notion of a "dirty South" is more rooted than ever in American consciousness, especially how dirt might be transformative to those on the margins. In rooting through southern trash, artists and authors have uncovered productive ways to re-imagine what "dirt" means as a point of resistance and contestation to celebrate, for example, "the roots of radical sexual resistance in the New South—a movement that is antiracist, decolonial, and transnational" (Stallings back cover). Even as my book claims to end its exploration of the dirty South in 2020, the contemporary moment continues to find itself crawling around inside the trash bin.

The ubiquitous trash bin draws me back to processes by which trash gets re-signified or returns in endless cycles of valuation, radically altering meaning and context—the way, for example, dung can be used as fertilizer. Although waste leaves our body, it is not gone forever: and it can be valuable. Even if we repress its existence and our relationship to it, waste reminds us of cultural values—what a person or a society wants to render invisible, even nonexistent. The bin also offers a way to think of the temporality of trash: something we once thought valuable or useful or worth possessing, but now discard; in this way, the bin can be linked to self-revision, to changing self-images, and the sense of one's identity. Our ambivalence to the trash bin mirrors our own ambivalence to self—there can be shame about past values and tastes but also pride, an affirmation of change. The dynamics of pride and shame form relationships and communities that can—and often do—resist colonial, homophobic, or racist ideologies frequently tethered to southern identity. Dirt is a powerful rhetorical marker that more and more is being claimed as a symbol of radical political resistance by those on the margins.

I find this current obsession with the dirty South fascinating, and not just as a scholar: for why study the South at all—except to find useful ways to resignify it, to create something worthwhile out of the history and narratives produced about it? The ethos of this new turn to the dirty South might account for ambivalences, the shifting re-signification of the region, and make the work we do more valuable, not just as scholars, but as individuals, as southerners. What we get from dirty South artists and authors might not look like clean and bordered work: there are no simple answers or policed line between what is clean and what is dirty, what is disposable and what is valuable. And the goal of such work is not to do a neat reversal of what the "Old South" might have represented, of making dirty what was once clean and arguing for the value in what was considered trash; this new obsessions with a dirty South by necessity will be complex, messy. The kind of work I imagine will be contained inside the trash bin, a symbol of the complicated work of sorting, mixing, revaluing, and recycling our trash endlessly, of rummaging through waste to find narrative debris that might be bricolaged into something meaningful. Moreover, the subjects artists investigate needn't be the prestige genres of literature, art, and history, but can be pieces drawn from whatever trash heaps, flickering screens, or throwaway websites offer valuable narratives. It can be as simple as the food on our plate.

TOWARD AFROCULINARIA

Michael W. Twitty's concept of *Afroculinaria* is an exciting corollary in foodways to what I hope a dirty southern studies might be in scholarship.[1] Described on his blog as "a food writer, independent scholar, culinary historian, and historical interpreter personally charged with preparing, preserving and promoting African American foodways and its parent traditions in Africa and her Diaspora and its legacy in the food culture of the American South," Twitty seeks to reclaim southern foodways from the white celebrity chefs and scholars who have wholesale stolen traditions and techniques directly from enslaved Africans while recycling their recipes as a marker of regional authenticity.

In an open letter to one such celebrity chef, Paula Deen, Twitty starts by noting their similarities: "we are both Southern. Sweet tea runs in our blood, in fact is our blood," but he is quick to point out that Deen's matriarchal character on the Food Network actually works on behalf of a racist system that continues to segregate Black chefs and diners from white prestige foodways: "Systemic racism in the world of Southern food and public discourse . . . are [sic] what really piss me off. There is so much press and so much activity around Southern food and yet the diversity of people of color engaged in this art form and telling and teaching its history and giving it a future are [sic] often passed up or disregarded." Twitty labels Deen's tremendous popularity a "culinary injustice," a specific type of fracturing of foodways in which "some Southerners take credit for things that enslaved Africans and their descendants played key roles in innovating." For Twitty, the "Southern food you have been crowned the queen of was made into an art largely in the hands of enslaved cooks, some like the ones who prepared food on your ancestor's Georgia plantation," and yet the debt that Deen owes to the nameless Black cooks and histories of cooking is never acknowledged, nor can it ever be adequately repaid.

Because of the continued displacement of chefs of color from southern cuisine, Twitty despairs of a future where "Barbecue, in my lifetime, may go the way of the Blues and the banjo. . . . a relic of our culture that whisps away. That tragedy rooted in the unwillingness to give African American barbecue masters and other cooks an equal chance at the platform is . . . galling." By the end of his open letter, it is clear that Twitty hopes to start a conversation about the way in which Deen's fame laid bare how southern foodways actively disenfranchise Black voices and labor: "Culinary injustice is the annihilation of our food voices—past, present and foreseeable future—and nobody will talk about that like they are talking about you. . . . For shame."

Twitty's open letter to Deen was reposted and reblogged thousands of times on social media. It was one of the first public reckonings of southern foodways and its dirty secrets—not only its segregationist and racist tendencies but also its wholesale whitewashing of a cuisine and a culture that was imagined, produced, and perfected by people of color throughout the world. "Your barbecue is my West African babbake," he tells Deen, "your fried chicken, your red rice, your hoecake, your watermelon, your black eyed peas, your crowder peas, your muskmelon, your tomatoes, your peanuts, your hot peppers, your Brunswick stew and okra soup, benne, jambalaya, hoppin' john, gumbo, stewed greens and fat meat—have inextricable ties to the plantation South and its often Black Majority coming from strong roots in West and Central Africa." By calling out southern cooking's intrinsic ties to the African diaspora, Twitty created a space through which Black southern chefs can be at the center of recycling and mediating southern food, not those whose consumption of it guided capitalist investments in corporations like Cracker Barrel Old Country Store or Paula Deen Enterprises. Twitty's blog serves as a constant critique of white folksy celebrations of foodways that actively disenfranchise African Americans. In talking about the burgeoning Charleston food scene, Twitty finds a similar lack of respect for the Gullah culture that originated the cuisine that now identifies itself as "low country."[2] He says, "You have to respect the tenets of the culture from which you borrow. Respect the people. I don't always see that in the Charleston food scene. I see this acknowledgement of the people, acknowledgement of the story, but I think that the story is often used to upsell the food, upsell the product. That's not quite the same as respecting the people" (qtd. in Dixler).

Twitty's critique of Deen and the Charleston food scene feels appropriate for the machine of southern foodways scholarship and the fetishization of southern cooking: Twitty ties the corporatization of southern foodways to appropriation of African cultures at the expense of the very descendants of those responsible for the recipes. It is a double-edged cut that both denies the space of African diaspora chefs from a position of power as the originators of a cultural product but also limits their potential economic mobility, keeping them as laborers as opposed to investors. The denial of participation in the economic enterprise of southern cooking does more than just disenfranchise southern chefs, it perpetuates the deprivileging of impoverished African Americans throughout the region.

In an open letter to another famous southern white chef—Sean Brock—Twitty again implores the southern food scene to think beyond their myopic celebration of regional exceptionalism, if for no other reason than the descendants of these Africans are dying. We are dying of stress and chronic health ailments rooted in diet and quality of food and access. We are in need of economic opportunity and food is such an important gateway for that. We are dying of police bullets and terrorist bullets and many don't really give a fuck. We are joining our Ancestors faster than we should and as our Rome burns other people's Rome rises. This is why I'm hot. This is why I cook. This is why I insist on my right of return as the descendant of Charleston's enslaved and of the rice growers that gave the Lowcountry a story to sell. The South shall rise again, but will we? We need economic development, food justice—and most of all we refuse to be put at the periphery of our narrative when we should remain at its center. (Twitty, "Dear Sean")[3]

Twitty's urgent appeal to the luminaries of southern foodways feels more prescient now than ever; in the wake of violence against unarmed Black men and women throughout the nation, systemic racism in all forms is being exposed in the roots of some of the most venerated cultural traditions of the region, and, indeed, the nation. But instead of offering communities of color a lifeline, southern foodways instead reject them.

The very phrase "southern cooking" is a violence to communities of color, for whom food could provide, in the words of Twitty, "a better life in the new economy, a way out of the health and chronic illness crisis, and a way to reduce the vast food deserts that plague many of our communities" ("About Afroculinaria"). Though we are over fifty years removed from founder Dan Evins's white fantasy of a Cracker Barrel, we still reckon with the consequences of institutions, individuals, corporations, and alliances like the Southern Foodways Alliance celebrating the exceptionalism of southern cuisine. Founded in 1999, at a time when Cracker Barrel was facing its first legal challenge from the NAACP and when Paula Deen first appeared on the Food Network, the Southern Foodways Alliance continues to be another voice in service to the endless praise of southern cuisine.

Although the organization is inarguably an important resource in documenting the shifting dynamics of southern cooking, it too often bleeds beyond its original scope to suggest that one can tell a kind of history through food. That claim is not just tenuous, it performs its own kind of eroding of history. The production, labor, consumption, and enjoyment of food are deeply personal and often undeniably subjective, and the position of authority and authorship has too often belonged to white, heterosexual men. The ongoing debates over what constitutes "authentic" southern food or the region's connection to mythic hospitality are not rigorous academic arguments but rather essentialist claims whose rhetoric is impossibly bound to white cultural monoliths and histories of disenfranchisement, exclusion, and segregation. What we need more than a good recipe for collard greens or a braided elegy on the sweet potato is a commitment first to the lived lives of impoverished communities and people of color for whom food is not an academic discourse or opportunity for prosody but a necessity for survival and economic mobility. If we can start by addressing the critiques of Michael Twitty, then perhaps we can begin to untangle the long and complicated connections to what constitutes "southern cooking" in the second decade of the twenty-first century and begin to own up to the dirt that's been accumulating underneath the veneer of "southern cooking" over the last fifty years.

Thankfully, a new kind of backlash seems to be growing among the ranks of new southern studies scholars, those who, like Twitty, despair over "the idolization of ingredients and materials over meaning, over morals, over human lives" (Dixler). As an example, Twitty comments on one of the most celebrated foods of Low Country cuisine, Carolina gold rice, long a staple of the region.[4] "You mean to tell me that there's Carolina gold rice that's $12, $15 a bag, [which means] the average black child who lives in North Charleston can't afford to eat Carolina gold rice? It's the same rice their ancestors were brought to Charleston to grow" (qtd. in Dixler), he tells one reporter. Echoing Twitty's critique of the economic consequences of romanticizing Carolina gold rice, Scott Romine tells *the New York Times,* "Think about the bodies that died in those South Carolina rice fields. . . . You don't want to pay $12.99 for heirloom Carolina Gold rice if that's the image you have behind it" (qtd. in Severson). Together with Twitty, southern scholars are beginning to expose the dirt behind southern foodways writing, the latent rhetoric of southern exceptionalism linked with white supremacy that lurks within a celebration of the region.

The work of reframing southern cooking is, as one scholar notes, "not just a cute story or a conventional trope in some cookbooks. It is a discourse in the public sphere, and the comments and commentary demonstrate how fragile—and yet how vitally important—are these claims to southern authenticity" (Tippen 146). Pushback in the academy has come from a mighty minority who are set to publish the collection *Against Cornbread Nationalism: How Foodways Partisans Misrepresent the South,* which critiques the SFA for "relying on outdated scholarship (essentialism, agrarianism), myths (the 'southern welcome table'), and feel-good celebrations of 'authenticity' and 'southern identity' that tend to flatter (largely white and upper-class) southern readers, students, and donors rather than inviting the public to engage with the exciting but challenging ideas that presently animate southern studies" (Peacock).

DIRTY SOUTHERN STUDIES

On 23 February 2020, a young Black man, Ahmaud Arbery, was lynched by Gregory McMichael and his son Travis McMichael; the men stalked Arbery while he jogged in the Satilla Shores neighborhood just outside Brunswick, Georgia. The two men followed Arbery in a pickup truck and later told police that they believed he was a suspect in several robberies in the neighborhood. Travis, armed with a shotgun, confronted the unarmed Arbery, and the two scuffled for almost a full minute before three blasts rang out. Ahmaud Arbery died at the scene before police or paramedics could arrive. Three months after Arbery's murder, Minneapolis policeman Derek Chauvin responded to a call about an African American man who had allegedly been caught trying to use a counterfeit twenty-dollar bill at a local grocery store. Chauvin and fellow officers J. Alexander Kueng, Tou Thao, and Thomas Lane approached George Floyd and attempted to place him under arrest. Although Floyd never attacked any officers, Chauvin threw him—still handcuffed—to the ground and knelt on his neck. With one hand casually in his pocket, Chauvin continued kneeling on Floyd's neck for over eight minutes as Floyd gasped for air and told him more than fifteen times that he could not breathe. When he became unresponsive, the officers called in an ambulance. George Floyd was pronounced dead an hour later at the Hennepin County Medical Center.

Both Arbery and Floyd had been murdered in the space of three months— one by white vigilantes and one by deputized police officers, but the cases were, essentially, the same. Even though murders of Black men and women at the hands of white officers and vigilantes have taken place across the country for centuries,[5] the deaths of these two men sparked mass outrage across the nation for one clear reason: they could be *seen* in graphic detail. Floyd's murder was recorded on neighbors' smartphones; the video was horrific not just for the casual violence of a white man kneeling on a Black man's neck but for the voices imploring officers to stop. William "Roddie" Bryan, a neighbor of Travis McMichael, filmed the confrontation and murder of Arbery. Bryan's video was not released to the public until 5 May, twenty days before Floyd's murder. Because both videos came out around roughly the same time, it was almost impossible to ignore their connections. Even though one took place in the "South," deep in Georgia, and the other far North, in Minneapolis, both videos depicted systematic and cold-blooded murders of two Black men by (largely white) men who felt safe enough to do so in broad daylight. Cloaked by their commitment to uphold "law" and "order," these men felt they could act without fear of conviction or imprisonment. Though one murder was decidedly an act of vigilantism, Floyd's death came at the hands of police officers who, ostensibly, were tasked with protecting Floyd.

Like Emmett Till, Trayvon Martin, and countless other African Americans before him, Arbery had been lynched by white vigilantes who, in the tradition of the Ku Klux Klan, targeted a Black man simply for existing in a space and engaging in practices reserved for white people. On the other hand, Floyd's death came at the hands of the very institution set up to eliminate a need for vigilantism. The connection was clear: vigilantism and policing were both examples of how white power asserted and protected its value, and even though the former might be discursively dirty, it was tacitly tolerated, even encouraged by white property owners. Whatever the difference between policing and vigilantism might have been before 2020, the deaths of Ahmaud Arbery and George Floyd made it painfully obvious that the gap between them was razor thin, arbitrary, a rhetorical millimeter. In 2020 America, men and women of color were threats to white power structures, and their murders could be rhetorically spun by multiple forms of discourses that obfuscated the fundamental truth of systems of power in the country: they were built first and foremost by white people and continue (and will continue, if unchallenged) to operate to entrench white power. White Americans began to recognize and own their complicity in systems of power that facilitated the murder of people of color, denied the persistence of white vigilantism even as it nostalgically praised its immediacy, and operated with complete impunity, with no fear of reprisals from politicians and judges.

The videos of both murders were instrumental in galvanizing protests of both the Minneapolis Police Department and the Glynn County Police Department, the latter of which had been ordered by the Brunswick District Attorney's Office not to issue arrest warrants for either of the McMichaels. Evidence in Arbery's case later revealed that Gregory McMichael was, in fact, a former GCPD officer (1982–89) who had retired a year earlier from the Brunswick Judicial Circuit District Attorney's Office. According to the *Atlanta Journal-Constitution,* Commissioner Allen Booker stated, "The police at the scene went to [District Attorney Jackie Johnson], saying they were ready to arrest both of them. These were the police at the scene who had done the investigation. . . . She shut them down to protect her friend" (Melendez). Without the video of Arbery's murder surfacing, it is doubtful that the men responsible for his death would have faced justice. Just like Emmett Till's mutilated face on the cover of newspapers, the gruesome videos of both horrific murders were responsible for the indictment of the police officers and the McMicheals. Though he tried to argue for a plea deal, Chauvin was arrested for third-degree murder (now second-degree murder) four days after the video of him with his knee on Floyd's neck surfaced, and, after being arrested in early May, a grand jury indicted Greg and Travis McMichael and William Bryan on nine charges on 24 June.

During the summer of 2020, white allies came to terms with what had long been obvious to people of color throughout America, and the nation responded with revolution, protest, and revolt. Protestors marched all over America and inspired similar demonstrations across the world. Murals of George Floyd appeared on street corners from Alabama to Paris. "Black Lives Matter" was etched onto major streets, including in the nation's capital and outside the Trump Tower in New York City.[6] Though white America surely knew of the epidemic of deaths of people of color at the hands of the police, they did not truly believe it until they were forced to *watch* the murders. The country grappled with difficult questions about what justice meant and how it might be achieved in a world in which unequal rights fractured concepts of morality and ethics. What would "justice" for George Floyd or Ahmaud Arbery look like? Was there justice for Breonna Taylor? Tony McDade? Dion Johnson? Rayshard Brooks? The only justice for these murdered Americans would be that they could be alive, living safely with their families. Absent that, what does it mean to seek justice in a system whose primary aim is to justify itself, not to right wrongs? How do you find solace in an institution with dirty affiliations to vigilantism and corrupt networks that entrench whiteness?

I end this book with more questions. When I first began this project over two years ago, I was reasonably sure that I was going to be working on a book about "the South" and how it had remained a fixed imaginary for about fifty years. I settled on experiments in how different kinds of dirty tropes began in the post–civil rights movement of the 1970s and then persisted in contemporary cultural and literary texts. But I found my hypothesis tested, and in some ways, strained. I concluded that whatever kind of dirty or contested idea that found prominence in the 1970s—be it vigilantism, wounds or trauma, pollution, or outlaw music—really spoke to white anxieties over the threatening (and, at the time, newly emergent) wave of enfranchisement and visibility for people of color throughout the nation. I assumed the reason such dirty imaginaries persisted was largely because they were so entrenched in that moment—a time in which America was forced to face its fights over segregation, political crises, and global entanglements, so that southern identity became crystallized for decades. These dirty southern tropes still persist because white anxieties over enfranchisement of communities of color never disappeared (and never will); they are still with us, white zombie fears with a rising body count.

For much of its existence as a popular idiom, "the South" has conjured imaginaries of a region in which white powers, values, and institutions have remained relatively unchallenged; even in deriding the static whiteness of the region, the South offered national discourses a way to disown racist tendencies while simultaneously presenting the region as a space of exceptionalism. However southern culture, foodways, music, or folk might be conceived of as "dirty," that dirt was valuable: it was something worth owning—a feature, not a bug. Moreover, southern exceptionalism's dirty rhetoric was a varnish that could be layered onto existing conceptions of the region that did not threaten the inherent whiteness of institutions of power.

Southern vigilantism was a nightmare for African Americans throughout the twentieth century, but its supposed "vanishing" in the "postracial" twenty-first century morphed into nostalgia for its immediacy as well as a useful way to mask cryptic white vigilantism inherent in policing across the nation. The traumas of the civil rights movement—including the bombing of four little girls in a Birmingham church—were a national tragedy that easily rejected the culpability of the nation by scapegoating the dirtiness of Alabama, all the while never owning the complicity of judicial and political institutions facilitating such acts.[7] Ecological devastation throughout the South was presented as a symptom of the intellectual poverty of its people—eliding, as a matter of course, the economic poverty of the communities of color who were the true victims. Southern foodways were a dirty but delicious decadence, and their prominence through corporate chains and white celebrities erased chefs of color from any affiliation with a region in which they were born. Country music felt like an authentic music of the people, but its emphasis on lawlessness and dirty men romanticized an unequal judicial system in which white men could dress in black with six shooters but Black men could not even buy Skittles without being murdered.

In every dirty trope I investigated, these imaginaries were consistently entrenched in southern exceptionalism, even—or *especially*—in their seeming contestation of value. The contemporary instances of dirty southern imaginaries were still articulating the importance of southern exceptionalism, even in an age of globalization and deregionalized identity. The centrality of whiteness to the articulation and celebration of a dirty South was profound. And yet, in each instance, I found other voices in other rooms, other regions, other histories, proudly speaking back and asking the nation to own up. I heard voices in Minneapolis and Atlanta showing the world the connections between American policing and vigilantism; in *Get Out,* Jordan Peele eviscerated the myth of a postracial America by exposing it as a swampland of horrors for Black people; I saw the contemporary fight for environmental justice by activists in Flint, Michigan,[8] and across North Carolina; I took a deep dive into the soul of Atlanta music with the rise of Goodie Mob and OutKast as they actively contested their displacement from hip-hop and the city they loved; and I read the blog of Michael Twitty and his battles exposing the "culinary injustices" that rob African Americans of their role in southern culture. Each pushback was a reframing of dirt—not a reclamation, but a transformation; it was a way of seeing, of speaking: it was a vernacular I desperately needed to learn.

I want to urge scholars and artists alike to think about kaleidoscopic potentials in dirty imaginaries, especially as they get imposed on regions, peoples, communities, and identities. I envision a dirty southern studies that finds other iterations of dirt that I have not even considered and explores them to blow past the exhausting virulence of whiteness in the region, the nation, the culture, the academy. As a white scholar, I want to be thoughtful about what it means to be a good ally to those whose voices have been systematically eroded from the region and the discipline. I want to learn to shut up and listen to those stories, and I want to be a better ally by hearing them, sharing them, amplifying them. I want to do better. Because, in truth, I inherited a field from a bunch of bros who were largely sharing fantasies of white masculinity with each other—some kind of horrific neo-Confederacy fanboy book group—and I have to own the consequences: that southern studies' origin story is built around an infatuation with an imaginary that still animates the worst tendencies of a nation, frames them in nostalgic terms that refuse the real consequences of their history. As Michael Twitty writes to a white visitor to a plantation who was upset by the presentations of stories of the enslaved forced to work there, "The Old South may be your American Downton Abbey but it is our American Horror Story, even under the best circumstances it represents the extraction of labor, talent and life we can never get back" ("Dear Disgruntled").

The meaningful work of a contemporary dirty southern studies scholar or artist must be to consistently and tirelessly clap back at the lie of that fantasy and to expose the dirt of that imaginary. And to do that work humbly, abandoning desire for prestige and love of voice. Dirty southern studies work should be done in multiple venues and by diverse scholars and artists from all different communities. With whatever privilege has been afforded me, I want to be visible in public spheres, speaking out, talking back, unrelenting in community building. Above all, I strive to be kind and self-reflexive about my work. The dirty southern studies I envision is not just monographs and articles; it does not solely exist it in the library: it's on Twitter; it's graffiti; it's a podcast; it's in the classroom; it's around our kitchen tables; it's a zine. With whatever voice I have and whatever time I am gifted inside and outside of this profession, I want to amplify the multivocal song of those whose voices have long been ignored as they declare, "The South got something to say."

NOTES

Prologue: A Dirty Book

1. "New southern studies" was first defined by Houston Baker and Dana Nelson in their special issue of *American Literature* titled "Violence, the Body, and 'The South.'" The editors begin their essay by explaining how, "Slowly the idea took hold that we needed to collaborate on a project that would contribute to a new Southern studies, an emerging collective already producing a robust body of work in current American Studies scholarship. By a new Southern studies, we have in mind efforts such as Patricia Yaeger's *Dirt and Desire: Reconstructing Southern Women's Writing, 1930–1990;* Ann Goodwyn Jones and Susan Donaldson's collection *Haunted Bodies: Gender and Southern Texts;* Richard Gray's *Southern Aberrations: Writers of the American South and the Problems of Regionalism;* and other monographs, essays, histories, and films that reconfigure our familiar notions of Good (or desperately bad) Old Southern White Men telling stories on the porch, protecting white women, and being friends to the Negro. We thus resolved to edit a special issue of *American Literature* investigating regions, national formations, speculations, intuitions, and assertions adumbrated in our extended telephone conversation. The plans for our special issue were in place when we hung up telephones north and south" (231–32). Since that 2001 issue, "new southern studies" has become an expansive field that, at this point, describes much of the contemporary work of scholars in southern studies.

2. Though excerpts of Zimmerman's call to police can be found in multiple news stories about the incident, the full text I quote from throughout the prologue comes from archive.org/stream/326700-full-transcript-zimmerman/326700-full-transcript-zimmerman_djvu.txt.

3. According to blacklivesmatter.com/about/herstory/, "In 2013, three radical Black organizers—Alicia Garza, Patrisse Cullors, and Opal Tometi—created a Black-centered political will and movement building project called #BlackLivesMatter. It was in response to the acquittal of Trayvon Martin's murderer, George Zimmerman." Since 2013, "The project is now a member-led global network of more than 40 chapters. Our members organize and build local power to intervene in violence inflicted on Black communities by the state and vigilantes. Black Lives Matter is an ideological and political intervention in a world where Black lives are systematically and intentionally targeted for demise. It is an affirmation of Black folks' humanity, our contributions to this society, and our resilience in the face of deadly oppression."

4. Title XLVI , Chapter 776, or 776.013 of Florida statue is titled: "Home protection; use or threatened use of deadly force; presumption of fear of death or great bodily harm." The larger index for the law falls under Florida statues for "Justifiable Use of Force." For the entirety of

the language of the law, see www.leg.state.fl.us/statutes/index.cfm?App_mode=Display_Statute&URL=0700-0799/0776/Sections/0776.013.html.

5. See Kreyling, *Inventing Southern Literature*.

6. For a useful text that explores all the complexity surrounding property and ownership of or for African Americans in the American South from the nineteenth through the twentieth century, see King, *Race, Theft, and Ethics: Property Matters in African American Literature*.

7. See Douglas, *Purity and Danger*. Douglas claims that the articulation of dirt as "a matter out of place" initially comes from Lord Chesterfield, but, as Richard Fardon, Douglas's literary executor, claims in *Anthropology Today*, "the authorship of something close to this phrase was more likely Lord Palmerston's, and it arose in the context of policy concerns over urban sewage and rural fertilizer. The phrase was picked up immediately, made more abstract, and applied in a variety of contexts that drew together moral judgements with considerations of hygiene. Hence the phrase had a complex authorship and usage that had already prepared it for the uses to which Douglas would put it, and its history shows how the aphoristic formulation of a widely held notion can provoke thought by, in twenty-first century terms, going viral" (25, abstract).

8. See www.smh.com.au/entertainment/tv-and-radio/new-podcast-from-serial-makers-stown-breaks-download-records-20170403-gvc412.html.

9. Direct quotations from the podcast come from the show's website and their transcriptions; see stownpodcast.org/chapter/1.

10. For a more detailed description of the "tragic mulatto" figure and its history and evolution, see Sollors, *Neither Black Nor White Yet Both*.

11. According to Romano, McLemore's "estate is suing the podcast for profiting off his identity without his consent. More specifically, the estate—which includes McLemore's mother—is claiming that *S-Town* did not have its subject's permission to use his identity in marketing the podcast, or to explore many aspects of his personal life."

12. Trump's inaugural address reads, in part, "January 20th, 2017 will be remembered as the day the people became the rulers of this nation again. The forgotten men and women of our country, will be forgotten no longer. Everyone is listening to you now. You came by the tens of millions to become part of a historic movement, the likes of which the world has never seen before. At the center of this movement is a crucial conviction, that a nation exists to serve its citizens. Americans want great schools for their children, safe neighborhoods for their families, and good jobs for themselves. These are just and reasonable demands of righteous people and a righteous public, but for too many of our citizens a different reality exists." For the full text of his speech, see www.politico.com/story/2017/01/full-text-donald-trump-inauguration-speech-transcript-233907.

13. I take this quotation from the transcript captured by *Vox*: www.vox.com/2017/8/15/16154028/trump-press-conference-transcript-charlottesville.

Introduction: The Dirty South

1. I don't claim any of these versions of southern identity or of regional association as being in any way an essentialist descriptor of any "real" or "authentic" South, but rather, as Scott Romine argues in *The Real South: Southern Narrative in the Age of Cultural Reproduction* as "conceptual tools that individuals and groups use to test their worlds, to orient scenarios, and to project themselves imaginatively into social spaces" (10). "The dirty South" I investigate is less a kind of "metaphysical or psychoanalytic" category and more akin to an exploration of the term in the way

Romine examines authenticity, as a study seeking to understand "how individuals and groups *use* these concepts."

2. The reference here to Foucault's *The History of Sexuality* (1976) is intentional, for I want to be clear about the evolution of trash both as a concept and as a practical thing. Just as Foucault traces a history of cultural understandings of what constitutes a sexual act as well as a history of the representation of those acts, I want to think broadly about the shifting definitions of how we conceive of and describe trash over the course of the twentieth and twenty-first centuries. Strasser emphasizes the latter throughout her book, but the former interests me as well.

3. Writing of Kristeva in her essay "Linguistic Leakiness or Really Dirty? Dirt in Social Theory," Carol Wolkowitz connects the notion of the abject with the borders of the body (interiority/exteriority) but also between the individual and collective: "The abject provokes fear and disgust because it exposes the fragility of the border between self and others, threatening to dissolve the self" (Campkin and Cox 18).

4. Wolkowitz asserts as much about the abject's potential as a conduit for desire: "The abject is also a source of fascination, and hence a source of pleasure" (Campkin and Cox 18).

5. I don't use such a loaded word—"community"—lightly, and I take my cue from Scott Romine's groundbreaking work on southern communities. In *The Narrative Forms of Southern Community,* Romine uses the language of systemic order to define a model of community: "The first two conditions of community, a boundary and a structure, are essentially structural (if not perfectly stable); that is to say, they maintain what integrity they have through opposition and difference. The third, an image, is not" (7). Romine finds in the image a "mimetic orientation in which the positive attributes of community (cohesiveness, order, stability, interdependence, and so on) are lent a kind of iconic integrity, or, to put the matter another way, are displaced into things" (8). In the American South, we have, obviously, a notion of a border, and in the conception of the region, there are certainly recognizable structures. It is in "the image" that I want to place the concept of "dirtiness." The dirty imaginary acts, in Romine's terms, as a "community's icon [which] permits a way of thinking about community that effaces its status *as* thinking, since the community appears in this configuration as an object there to be perceived rather than as the product of collective or quasi-collective projection" (8). "Dirty southern communities," then, might provide a model for Romine's community model that actually works to resist or contest the "iconic integrity" of the system it is supposed to mimetically perform. If Romine finds the community iconography to be both "highly selective" and also a way for white southerners to "claim to be judged on the basis of its best icons," we can define a dirty southern community as a purposeful space of play and reversal that challenges dominant discourses of order and stability by redefining southern community altogether. Even so, any talk of "community" must acknowledge the disparateness of identity that distorts similarity between southern whites and southern Blacks, not to mention queer southerners, and women southerners—the multiple and different "communities" that Yaeger invokes. Using dirt to "create community" is done in radically different ways than the model of the segregation.

6. I mean here both Yaeger's conception of desire as a "matter of attraction" (*Dirt and Desire* 87) in concert with Jon Smith's articulation of it in *Finding Purple America:* "Everybody feels desire because of some kind of narcissistic lack." Smith uses desire as a critical tool investigating the melancholic (especially in the melancholic confusion over what is lacking), while Yaeger presents desire as foundational to recognizing our attraction to dirt as a site of revision and play.

7. I want to be clear that the three theorists grounding my monograph, while similar in their articulations of the potential of dirt or impurity to bring pleasure, define that pleasure or fascina-

tion in radically different ways. Kristeva and Yaeger are far more interested in "pleasure" or "desire" as a feminist interpretation of Freud's concept of pleasure, while Douglas describes a kind of cultural pleasure principal that is more aligned with the desire for social structures to adhere to an order. For this study, I collapse much of the differences through an emphasis on "desire," not "pleasure." Desire seems to encompass all kinds of fantasies and the attendant binaries those fantasies suggest, including, but not limited to, interiority/exteriority, self/other, region/nation, and individual/community.

8. For further reading on the South's relationship to impurity and anxieties over disease and hygiene, see Savitt and Young, *Disease and Distinctiveness in the American South;* McCandless, *Slavery, Disease, and Suffering in the Southern Lowcountry;* and Weiner and Hough, *Sex, Sickness, and Slavery: Illness in the Antebellum South.*

9. Douglas's study investigating the divide between primitive and European (or we might say "Western" or even "modern") culture is a useful place to begin with how anxiety over dirt (even symbolically) leads to fears over contamination and impurity that become part of the colonial enterprise of empire building. For how such a rhetoric works in other sites, see especially Warwick Anderson, *Colonial Pathologies: American Tropical Medicine, Race, and Hygiene in the Philippines;* Steinbock-Pratt, *Educating the Empire: American Teachers and Contested Colonization in the Philippines;* Briggs, *Reproducing Empire: Race, Sex, Science, and U.S. Imperialism in Puerto Rico;* and McNeill, *Mosquito Empires: Ecology and War in the Greater Caribbean, 1620–1914.*

10. For further reading on anxieties over miscegenation in American popular and political culture, see Lemire, *"Miscegenation": Making Race in America;* Pascoe, *What Comes Naturally: Miscegenation Law and the Making of Race in America;* and Hiraldo, *Segregated Miscegenation: On the Treatment of Racial Hybridity in the US and Latin American Literary Traditions.*

11. I'm also interested in the way that this guilt becomes symptomized as one iteration of white melancholy. In its most fundamental definition, melancholy manifests largely through a few symptoms: the lack of pleasure, disruptions in patterns of cognition, and excessive guilt. For white southerners who lived in the generation after the Civil War or in the generation following the civil rights movement, such internalized guilt connects in interesting ways to a psychoanalytic diagnosis. No study does a better job connecting white southern melancholy and guilt than Jon Smith's *Finding Purple America,* which argues for a reappraisal of "old southern studies" (which we might define as the prolific number of books investigating and celebrating southern literature and culture from roughly 1921 to 2001) as melancholic, "not as a lament over the loss of white male privilege but more fundamentally as a free-floating Lacanian drive" (31). See Smith, *Finding Purple America,* especially 32–49.

12. Beyond Duck's book, which I explore extensively in the introduction, see Blum, *Reforging the White Republic: Race, Religion, and American Nationalism, 1865–1898,* and McMillen, *Remaking Dixie: The Impact of World War II on the American South.*

13. See Hale, *Making Whiteness: The Culture of Segregation in the South, 1890–1940;* Reynolds, *Maintaining Segregation: Children and Racial Instruction in the South, 1920–1955;* and Cole and Ring, eds., *The Folly of Jim Crow: Rethinking the Segregated South.* As a counter-text, see Purnell, Theoharis, and Woodard, *The Strange Careers of the Jim Crow North: Segregation and Struggle Outside of the South.*

14. The long history of representing the South as a land of poverty and immorality hardly began with H. L. Mencken, but his 1919 essay "Sahara of the Bozart" popularized the region as the site of a different kind of poverty, intellectual and aesthetic: "But consider the condition of his late

empire today. The picture gives one the creeps. It is as if the Civil War stamped out every last bearer of the torch, and left only a mob of peasants on the field. One thinks of Asia Minor, resigned to Armenians, Greeks and wild swine, of Poland abandoned to the Poles. In all that gargantuan paradise of the fourth-rate there is not a single picture gallery worth going into, or a single orchestra capable of playing the nine symphonies of Beethoven, or a single opera-house, or a single theater devoted to decent plays, or a single public monument that is worth looking at, or a single workshop devoted to the making of beautiful things" (185).

15. See 12 Southerners, *I'll Take My Stand: The South and Agrarian Tradition,* especially Donald Davidson's essay, "A Mirror for Artists," in which he sarcastically chides Mencken for his criticism of the South's lack of symphonies by imagining an artistic mobilization of aesthetic aid: "Much as the Red Cross mobilizes against disease, the guardians of public taste can mobilize against bad art or lack of art; one visualizes caravans of art, manned by regiments of lecturers, rushed hastily to future epidemic centers of barbarism when some new Mencken discovers a Sahara of the Bozart" (32–33).

16. For readings involving a history of racial violence throughout America, especially in sites not connected to the South, see Amy Wood, *Lynching and Spectacle: Witnessing Racial Violence in America, 1890–1940;* Phillips, *Blood at the Root: A Racial Cleansing in America;* Tuttle, *Race Riot: Chicago in the Red Summer of 1919;* Hirsch, *Riot and Remembrance: The Tulsa Race War and Its Legacy.*

17. See especially Isenberg, *White Trash: The 400-Year Untold History of Class in America.*

18. The kinds of models of abjection and horror that I explore cross a number of lines of narrative forms, including genre (horror, comic), cultural texts (films, music), and historical events (civil rights marches, Hurricane Katrina).

19. Quotations in this paragraph come from a transcript of the campaign event. See factba.se/transcript/donald-trump-speech-maga-rally-panama-city-beach-florida-may-8-2019.

20. Though I hesitate to give much attention to the murderer and his abhorrent philosophy, the full text of Cruisus's manifesto can be found online easily, as late as the fall of 2019. See louis-proyect.org/2019/08/04/the-manifesto-of-the-el-paso-white-supremacist-killer/.

21. The original magazine article published in January of 1956 is also available online, where these quotations come from. See law2.umkc.edu/faculty/projects/ftrials/till/confession.html.

22. In his *Freedom Riders: 1961 and the Struggle for Racial Justice,* Raymond Arsenault notes that, even though Reverend Shuttlesworth arrived on the scene just after the attack, "It took nearly an hour to locate an ambulance company willing to have anything to do with the Freedom Rides" (159). Some of the injuries to the activists were so serious, the reverend was not entirely sure that they "would even make it to the hospital" (160).

23. Reports on the incidents of the Freedom Riders—especially the violent attacks they endured—were so widespread that, according to Ann Curthoys, they reached all the way to Australia: "The attacks in Anniston and Montgomery, Alabama and the violence and goaling [*sic*] of Freedom Riders in Jackson were well covered. Newspaper reports emphasizes [*sic*] the hostility of the whites" (31). To be sure, Anniston was not the first example of such intimidation; violent retribution against African Americans in the South was commonplace and well documented in literary and cultural texts throughout the late nineteenth and into the mid-twentieth century. There are many monographs devoted to documenting the use of violence to disenfranchise and threaten African Americans in the South; for the period between 1865 and 1955, see especially Kidada Williams, *They Left Great Marks on Me: African American Testimonies of Racial Violence from Emancipation to World War I;* Krugler, *1919, The Year of Racial Violence: How African Americans Fought Back;*

Evans, *Cultures of Violence: Lynching and Racial Killing in South Africa and the American South;* Ortiz, *Emancipation Betrayed: The Hidden History of Black Organizing and White Violence in Florida from Reconstruction to the Bloody Election of 1920;* and Amy Wood, *Lynching and Spectacle: Witnessing Racial Violence in America, 1890–1940.*

24. Much of the collapsing of class identity into organizations advocating white supremacy was purposefully done to check working-class and poor whites from identifying too strongly with the working-poor African Americans or Native Americans whose economic conditions closely mirrored their own. By maintaining a discourse of plainness and offering fantasies of mobility to poor and working-class whites, organizations like the Ku Klux Klan created an aesthetic of whiteness that appealed to the impoverished but was, in fact, a means to convert poor and working-class whites into accepting dominant economic conditions. David A. Chang argues in *The Color of the Land: Race, Nation, and the Politics of Landownership in Oklahoma, 1832–1929,* that the Klan in Oklahoma certainly "promulgated a form of whiteness" that effectively operated as a way "to replace rural whites' class-conscious whiteness with one that would . . . [help them] to learn to see wealthy whites as their racial brothers rather than their class enemies" (194). According to Michael Newton's *White Robes and Burning Crosses: A History of the Ku Klux Klan from 1866,* the Klan's commitment to appearing to be for or about the poor whites even made it onto their applications, where they rhetorically appealed to potential members that they were the only ones who might stand up for "those of our brothers and sisters that many of the politicians call 'poor white trash'"(91).

25. First published in 1937 as a collaboration between photographer Margaret Bourke-White and fiction writer Erskine Caldwell, *You Have Seen Their Faces* contained photographs of many men and women throughout the rural South—however, photographs of poor white southerners, Caldwell's central fictional subject, were the predominant focus.

26. Just as the rise of photojournalism was critical in popular obsession with poor whites throughout the nation in the 1930s, the centrality of television—specifically the intimacy of moving images and words broadcast directly into the home—cannot be underestimated in the civil rights era. For more on how television facilitated the civil rights movement, see Bodroghkozy, *Equal Time: Television and the Civil Rights Movement,* which argues that television "encouraged audiences to engage self-reflexively with 'Northern' and 'Southern' categories of regional identity, as well as categories of 'Blackness and whiteness.' For many Americans, television became a key site on which they grappled with the changes fomented by the civil rights movement" (3).

27. I use the term "hillbilly" throughout this and the following chapter, but I am aware that the word has an evolving history and competing connotations that mutate over the course of the century following its first documented use in 1899. Anthony Harkins traces the evolution for the popular idiom of the "hillbilly" in *Hillbilly: A Cultural History of an American Icon;* he finds a shift in the depiction of the hillbilly starting around the time of the murder of Emmett Till in the mid-1950s when "fears of hillbilly 'invasions' of midwestern cities prompted press accounts of backward and degenerate men and women who despite their 'superior' racial heritage threatened the comity of the industrial heartland" (49, 174). By the 1960s, however, "at a time when the Civil Rights movement was exposing the ugliness of southern white racism," images of the violent hillbilly proliferated in the national imaginary and exposed "the racial battle lines of the day." While there were certainly many other derogatory invectives that were used in this and other decades to describe poor, white southerners, I choose the term for this chapter both because of the specific vicious "mountain men" that appear in Dickey's *Deliverance* (1970) but also because, unlike "white trash," "redneck," or "cracker," "hillbilly" is a remarkably flexible term that crosses boundaries between

value and race. Harkins's summary of the myriad discursive possibilities in the word explicates why and how the word works best for this study: "As representatives of mountain, country life, hillbillies can thus reflect either heroism-bravery and loyalty to traditional ways or a deviance, sadism and primitivism that is said to fly in the face of modern progress. In other words, the hillbilly served the dual and seemingly contradictory purposes of allowing the 'mainstream,' or generally non-rural, middle-class white, American audience to imagine a romanticized past, while simultaneously enabling the same audience to recommit itself to modernity by caricaturing the negative aspects of pre-modern, uncivilized society. And of course, since modernity and 'civilization' are racialized as Western and white, the dual function of the hillbilly is as much a matter of race as it is a marker of primitivism and poverty—and as much a matter of race as of gender and sexual transgression" (14).

28. American commitments to freedom and democracy were two of the more resilient forces animating notions of "American exceptionalism," and yet, tying exceptionalism to systematic disenfranchisement of African Americans, first through enslavement and later through Jim Crow laws "made America exceptional among liberal democratic states" in a different way, argues Michael Ignatieff (19). The disconnection between an American concept of commitment to democracy for all and the southern commitment to segregation and resistance became nothing less than an existential threat to the nation's progressive ideals.

29. Kristen M. Lavelle's *Whitewashing the South: White Memories of Segregation and Civil Rights* makes it clear that the word "mob" or "rioters" was often language purposefully disconnected from attacking white southerners to protestors themselves in order to rhetorically position the activists as the criminal aggressors: "several participants [of the study] used loaded terms like 'mob' and 'riot' to describe nonviolent protestors—dehumanizing terms that also imply disorganization, unruliness, and intent to cause harm. This language situates protestors as attackers" (116).

30. But it wasn't just a collection of brutal beatings that galvanized the national imagination; hillbilly vigilantism in the 1960s went national. It had its dirty fingerprints on the spate of assassinations during the decade, first of the president, John F. Kennedy, in the southern state of Dallas in 1963; later that year of activist Medgar Evers in Jackson, Mississippi; and five years later of civil rights leader Martin Luther King in Tennessee, in 1968. As an act of vigilante justice, assassinations remain a dominant part of the history of the 1960s. It is undeniable that the political assassinations that shook the nation mostly occurred in southern states and largely against figures who were notable for their commitment to advocating desegregation and enfranchisement of African Americans.

31. President Lyndon Johnson first articulated his idea of a "War on Poverty" on Wednesday, 8 January 1964, in his State of the Union address; he was anxious about the sharp rise in poverty across the United States, specifically in urban areas. Though the process of passing legislation was tricky, Johnson eventually got through the Economic Opportunity Act, which freed federal funds to be administered to states and localities by the Office of Economic Opportunity (OEO). Though much of the target of funds was urban sites, rural spaces throughout the South, including Appalachia, benefited from Johnson's legislation. The "War on Poverty" put the hillbilly's poverty back in the center of the political and cultural consciousness of America. In the fall of that year, Johnson visited Kentucky to reframe the issue: "poverty was a problem facing the entire nation and not just inner city minorities" (Harkins 185). Soon after Johnson's visit, Harkins notes, "nearly every major general circulation magazine and newspaper featured articles on 'the plight of the hill people,' punctuated by the faces of dirty, ill-clothed, and malnourished men, women, and children living in tarpaper shacks" (185–86).

32. It was not the first time Americans became introspective about southern hillbillies: an obsession with white poor people—especially southern white poor people—was a hallmark of the Depression era, when public and political sentiment found itself tied up with anxieties about documenting, understanding, and helping poor white southerners. And yet, what makes the decade of the 1960s so different from the 1930s is a shifting interpretation of what poor, white southerners represented. If hillbillies or rednecks or sharecroppers stood as an identity that might expose systemic corruption and exploitation of decent, marginalized families trying to survive in the 1930s, those same figures morphed in the thirty years after into a far different symbol, one with almost nothing in common with their Depression-era kin. No longer the victims of a dynamic of power that economically disenfranchised them, hillbillies were the enactors of their own economic and political isolation. For more information about the photo-texts of the 1930s, see my prologue, above, especially note 25.

33. For more on the American prism-like perspective on the hillbilly, see Harkins: "Despite their poverty, ignorance, primitiveness, and isolation, 'hillbillies' were 'one hundred percent' Protestant Americans of supposedly pure Anglo-Saxon or at least Scotch-Irish lineage, which countless commentators of the late-nineteenth- and early-twentieth centuries, greatly concerned by waves of Southern and Eastern European immigrants, took pains to prove. Thus, middle-class white Americans could see these people as a fascinating and exotic 'other' akin to Native Americans or Blacks, while at the same time sympathize with them as poorer and less modern versions of themselves" (7).

34. In *Black, White, and in Color: Television and Black Civil Rights,* Sasha Torres compares the brutality of white vigilante mobs and police brutality against activists with the civil rights workers' nonviolence, which afforded the movement "the moral authority" both of Christian doctrine and "the rhetoric of American democracy to make a new national culture" (15).

1. The South's Got Something to Play: Of Glitter and Gangsters

1. Television critic David Bianculli notes that, "despite three successful seasons on CBS from 1967 to 1969 and an announced renewal for a fourth," the network fired the Smothers Brothers and pulled the show from its time slot. Under increasing pressure from the Nixon administration for its challenge to their political rhetoric, CBS pulled what was, in the words of David Steinberg, "the most innovative variety show on television" (x). The decision by CBS set a dangerous precedent for celebrities and personalities openly critical of Nixon and his administration.

2. During this "rural purge," shows with themes and settings that emphasized the country life of the South or were comprised of hillbilly stereotypes were dumped in favor of more urban settings and a grittier, more realistic style. Television shows like *The Real McCoys, The Andy Griffith Show, Green Acres,* and *Petticoat Junction* that were immensely popular in the 1960s no longer felt financial viable to networks, and CBS president Fred Silverman's open hostility toward the redneck material did not help matters. According to Eskridge, "In his eyes, rural comedies were a waste of airtime and appealed only to people whose opinions and tastes did not matter anyway" (174). Regular character actor Pat Buttram would later remember, "It was the year they cancelled everything with a tree—including *Lassie*" (Harkins 203).

3. *Billboard* proclaimed *Hee Haw* "the veteran haybales show . . . [and] the champ for longevity" (17 October 1981) and argued that its success spawned more "country tune producers" to go "the route of syndication" to turn a profit (Oerman 24).

4. For more on the connection between country music and western aesthetics, see especially Cusic, *The Cowboy in Country Music: An Historical Survey with Artist Profiles.*

5. Though Owens moved away from Bakersfield to become a country music star, he always returned. "The people here in Bakersfield are my kind of folks," he tells Nicholas Dawidoff, "Nashville used to call Bakersfield Nashville West. I called Nashville Bakersfield East. I know everybody else left and went away and that nobody ever comes back here. I stayed here because these are my kind of people. The kind of people who come over to offer help because they see help's needed before you have to ask" (246). Country music star Merle Haggard also hailed from the city of Bakersfield.

6. For more on the history of the *Opry* and its rise to mass popularity, see Wolfe, *A Good-Natured Riot: The Birth of the Grand Ole Opry,* and Havighurst, *Air Castle of the South: WSM and the Making of Music City.*

7. Pecknold finds in the firing of the Smothers Brothers and the promotion of *Hee Haw* "a profitable form of political pandering. Contrasting the heartland humor of *Hee Haw* with the critical satire of *The Smother Brothers Comedy Hour,*" he finds a "shift . . . driven only incidentally by political cowardice; far more important . . . was the desire to capture middle-American conservatives as a lucrative audience" (*Selling Sound* 223).

8. Perhaps sincerity is the quality most admired in a musician like Hank Williams, who once claimed that his appeal comes from his believability: "You ask what makes our kind of music successful, I'll tell you. It can be explained in just one word: sincerity. When a hillbilly sings a crazy song, he feels crazy. When he sings, 'I Laid My Mother Away,' he sees her a-laying right there in the coffin. He sings more sincere than most entertainers because the hillbilly was raised rougher than most entertainers. You got to know a lot about hard work. You got to have smelled a lot of mule manure before you can sing like a hillbilly." For more on Williams and sincerity, see Goodson and Anderson, eds., *The Hank Williams Reader.*

9. Television critic Murray Forman asserts, "Popular music and television are inextricably entwined" (17). For a complete history of how the evolution of television changed how popular recording artists saw and marketed themselves, see his *One Night on TV Is Worth Weeks at the Paramount: Popular Music on Early Television.*

10. For more on "hard country," see Ching's perceptive and exhaustive study, *Wrong's What I Do Best: Hard Country Music and Contemporary Culture,* which attempts to analyze the performativity of Wagoner's aesthetic as art that is "self-consciously low, and self-consciously hard, a deliberate display of burlesque abjection" (4).

11. For an excellent accounting of Elvis's increasing popularity throughout the 1960s and beyond, see Guralnick, *Last Train to Memphis: The Rise of Elvis Presley.*

12. Dubbed the "Singing Cowboy," Autry was an early frontrunner of western crossover performers. Like Roy Rogers, Autry was only one of several Hollywood cowboys who appeared in movies as singer-actors. In addition to Cusic's *The Cowboy in Country Music,* see Green, *Singing in the Saddle: The History of the Singing Cowboy,* and Stanfield, *Horse Opera: The Strange History of the 1930s Singing Cowboy.*

13. For an overview of how fashion connected with country music during the 1960s–70s, see Beard, *100 Years of Western Wear.* For some analysis of Nudie Cohen's legacy as well as a chance to see photographs of some of his suits, see Nudie and Cabrall, *Nudie the Rodeo Tailor: The Life and Times of the Original Rhinestone Cowboy,* and MacKenzie, *Dream Suits: The Wonderful World of Nudie Cohn.*

14. Wagoner's show was one of the most popular variety shows on television during what is

arguably the variety show's golden age. Though there is some accounting for why his show was so popular in Eng's slight biography, *A Satisfied Mind: The Country Music Life of Porter Wagoner,* see especially chapter 7 of Morris's *The Persistence of Sentiment: Display and Feeling in Popular Music of the 1970s:* "Crossing Over with Dolly Parton."

15. Possibly the best academic study of Parton's gender performativity, especially in connection with class performance, is Edwards, *Dolly Parton, Gender, and Country Music,* especially chapter 2, "My Tennessee Home," which parses Parton's aesthetic with her multiple appeals to authenticity.

16. Though widely disputed, the term "Nashville Sound" has come to represent a specific period of dominance in country music where major studios, especially RCA, attempted to broaden the genre's appeal to popular audience by borrowing instrumentation, phrasing, structures, and techniques that were more palatable to mass consumption. The shift toward a smoother sound and a more general, universal instrumentation caused many of the studios to borrow the same session musicians and emphasize a softer, more mellow vocality that made a figure like Eddy Arnold famous. For more on the rise of this "Nashville Sound" and the consequences it had on the performers, see Jensen, *The Nashville Sound: Authenticity, Commercialization, and Country Music,* and Hemphill, *The Nashville Sound: Bright Lights and Country Music.*

17. For a good biography that also discusses the big-studio push toward a "Nashville Sound," see especially Streissguth, *Eddy Arnold: Pioneer of the Nashville Sound.*

18. For a broad history aimed at a beginner audience, see Perone, *Music of the Counterculture Era,* but for more academic studies about the counterculture's connection to music in the 1960s and 1970s, see Whiteley and Sklower, *Countercultures and Popular Music,* and Doyle, *Imagine Nation: The American Counterculture of the 1960's and 70's.*

19. There is a pretty great book-length study that provides some historical context for Haggard's song and its ensuing popularity: La Chapelle, *Proud to Be an Okie: Cultural Politics, Country Music, and Migration to Southern California* (especially chapter 6). Equally illuminating is Rubin, *Merle Haggard's Okie from Muskogee.*

20. Nixon's invitation for Haggard to perform at the White House came largely from the success of "Okie from Muskogee," but the president clearly didn't know any of the performer's other songs. According to Willman, "Nixon was known to be such a fan of 'Okie from Muskogee' that he asked Johnny Cash to perform it during a visit to the White House; Cash turned him down, though that have had less to do with disavowing its politics than feeling insulted by a royal request to impersonate a rival." Though Haggard performed the song for Nixon, he eventually regretted his connection to the president, saying later, "If they took a poll of the top three assholes of all time, who would they be. . . . It'd have to be Hitler and Nixon, and the G.W. [Bush] would be in there right under 'em. . . . I'd just like one chance to get my songs back" (258)

21. For a history of how country music engaged with conservative political ideology (and how certain artists resisted and contested those overtures), see especially Willman, *Rednecks & Bluenecks: The Politics of Country Music.*

22. *The WSM Barn Dance,* as it was first called, officially began broadcasting in November of 1925. Two years later, it would change its name to *The Grand Old Opry.* At that time, the show was recorded at the downtown Nashville National Life building. The program's popularity skyrocketed, and soon, it needed a venue big enough to hold a live audience. It moved from various locations—the Hillsboro Theatre, the Dixie Tabernacle, and the War Memorial—always trying to find space for larger and larger audiences. In June of 1943, the *Grand Old Opry* premiered at the Ryman Auditorium, and it remained at that location for thirty-one years. On 15 March 1974,

the program bid the Ryman farewell and moved to the Grand Ole Opry House at the newly built theme park Opryland.

23. Much has been written about Douglas's *Purity and Danger: An Analysis of Concepts of Pollution and Taboo,* especially in regards to "dirt," "purity," and "taboo," but precious little criticism and analysis have focused on her conception of "danger." Douglas writes of the connections between marginalization and danger, "To have been in the margins is to have been in contact with danger, to have been at a source of power." This notion of a "source of power" that is inextricably connected with the danger of the marginalized is exactly the kind of "luminosity" that I find in the outlaw country movement.

24. *Billboard* notes that "the rise of the RCA Nashville studios closely parallel the rise of the 'Nashville sound.' The label became the first major record firm with its own Nashville studio in 1964 when it opened a studio with the Methodist and Radio Television Foundations" ("Bradley Sees" 53).

25. Artists who are or who have been associated with "outlaw country" in the 1970s also include Townes Van Zandt, Kris Kristofferson, Steve Earle, Merle Haggard, David Allan Coe, Billy Joe Shaver, and Johnny Paycheck, among others.

26. Cash's ownership over the persona of "the Man in Black" was more than just an aesthetic choice, though his black outfits were as recognizable as the cartoon Nudie suits that Porter Wagoner wore on his show. Though Cash often wore black suits when performing, he used his choice of clothing to make a statement when he recorded the song "Man in Black" in 1971. As his biographer Robert Hilburn notes, the song was introduced "in a show aimed at young people and featuring guests James Taylor, Neil Young, and Joni Mitchell. In a sequence taped at Vanderbilt University, he met informally with students to answer questions on subjects ranging from drugs to Vietnam." Hilburn admits that "some critics accused him of being a fraud because the black clothing dated back to the Sun days and had nothing to do, really, with any social causes" (390).

27. For an informative and enjoyable history of how Nashville transformed its image into that of "Music City," see Kosser, *How Nashville Became Music City, U.S.A.: 50 Years of Music Row.*

28. Michael Streissguth describes the offices of Hillbilly Central in his book *Outlaw:* "Its doors propped open to let in the young breezes sweeping through the West End, the so-called Hillbilly Central offices became an outlaw safe haven. Former employees recalled Willie Nelson lazing on the front lawn, and Waylon haunting the offices at three in the morning. The studio hosted a fraternity of singers, songwriters and Nashville dropouts living the verse of a strumming and bumming honky-tonk song. Sessions burned into the small hours" (138).

29. Unlike *Hee Haw, Austin City Limits* presented a single performer playing his or her music for the entirety of the sixty-minute run time—no sketches or humor. The pilot episode was recorded in 1974, and the program is still broadcast weekly by Public Broadcasting Service stations throughout the nation. For a history of how the program evolved from a small television show on a public access station to an international phenomenon, see Laird, *Austin City Limits: A History.*

30. Writing about the political beliefs of Hank Williams Jr. and country performer Charlie Daniels, *Rolling Stone* reporter Jon Freeman notes, "Neither Daniels nor Williams were [sic] big fans of President Barack Obama because they perceived his policies as a weakening of the military—whether through cuts in defense spending or drawing down troops in Iraq. . . . At the 2012 Iowa State Fair, [Williams Jr.] unleashed an anti-Obama rant from the stage, unprovoked, saying: 'We've got a Muslim president who hates farming, hates the military, hates the U.S. and we hate him!' This shouldn't have been surprising to anyone who was paying attention: Williams was doubling down after an incident on *Fox & Friends* where he said that Obama playing golf with

John Boehner was like Hitler playing golf with Benjamin Netanyahu. Shortly after, ESPN dropped Williams—and his 'Are You Ready for Some Football?' tagline—as the musical face of its Monday Night Football broadcasts."

31. On the official website of the SiriusXM "Outlaw Country" station, under the tab for "What You'll Hear" is the description, "Renegades, rebels, rabble rousers and rogues."

32. Indeed, much of the evolution of what was called "Outlaw country" in the 1970s has shifted in the contemporary vernacular of music criticism. "Americana" music, with its emphasis on traditional forms and craft songwriting certainly connects to the ethos of outlaw, but "alt-country" and its anti-establishment country ethos also feels purposefully connected to many of the foundational ideals behind outlaw musicians in the 1970s. For more information about alt-country, see the run of the magazine *No Depression* as well as Fox and Ching, *Old Roots, New Routes: The Cultural Politics of Alt.country Music.*

33. Beyond shout-outs to LaFace and Organized Noize, OutKast points out the suburbs of Decatur, East Point, and College Park, predominantly Black neighborhoods that were known for being targeted by police for their involvement in the drug trade. According to Steve Visser and Marcus K. Garner, the red dog crew, which "is said to stand for Run Every Drug Dealer Out Of Georgia—came into being during the crack-cocaine epidemic in the 1980s when Atlanta, like other cities had open-air drug markets and almost weekly drive-by shootings."

34. Rapper and artist Cool Breeze first penned the phrase "Dirty South" and came up with a hook for a song that would later cause some confusion over the ownership of it: "Dungeon Family affiliates Goodie Mob get the lion's share of the credit, since the song only appears on the group's 1995 debut *Soul Food.* What doesn't help is how streaming services credit Frederick Bell as a 'Dirty South' songwriter but don't list Cool Breeze as a featured artist" (Lee).

35. *Stankonia* is another space like "The Dungeon" or "Hillbilly Central" that celebrates its marginalization and reconfigures its contested value into something worthy of praise. In fact, *Stankonia* was OutKast's most popular record when it was released in 2000, and the very title offers the dirty as something to be cherished: both in the literal stink and in its translation through country slang to "stank."

36. As the recent controversy surrounding Lil Nas X's presence at the Country Music Awards shows, the genre of country music has not always been welcoming to performers of color, nor as open to introducing new musical artists from inside the world of hip-hop to collaborate with their artists. For more on country music's muddy relationship with issues of race, see Hughes, *Country Soul: Making Music and Making Race in the American South,* and Pecknold, *Hidden in the Mix: The African American Presence in Country Music.*

37. Jennings's 1978 song "Don't You Think This Outlaw Bit's Done Got Out of Hand" was one of the more popular tracks from his album *I've Always Been Crazy* and referenced the true story of his arrest for possession of narcotics when DEA agents raided the studio he was recording in the year prior. Though he was successful in getting rid of all the drugs in the studio, the agents still arrested him. Eventually, all charges were dropped, but the song effectively narrates Jennings's loss of interest in living an outlaw lifestyle.

2. Let Us Now Praise Hillbilly Justice: *Deliverance* and Dirty Elegies

1. First envisioned as a mass demonstration by King and the Southern Christian Leadership Conference (SCLC), the campaign sought to connect those communities who were economically

disenfranchised and oppressed and promote visibility of their shared concerns. Their vision was bold because, for the first time, a group protesting the conditions of oppression would include African American and white workers throughout every region of America, including white coal miners in Kentucky and mill workers in North Carolina marching alongside African American sanitation workers from Tennessee. In part a reaction to the violence they encountered during the Freedom Rides, the Poor People's Campaign and its subsequent march on Washington were founded on King's allegiance to nonviolence. The protest would meet the fury of the white hillbilly with King's trademark laconic and dispassionate calm.

2. In interviews Dickey was always careful to position *Deliverance* as better than the novels to which they were compared. When one reviewer compares the themes of *Deliverance* to Faulkner's "The Bear" and Conrad's *Heart of Darkness,* the author replies curtly, "it's a lot better than either one of them, easily" (Anthony 110). Similarly, he shrugs off a compliment from another reviewer about how *Deliverance* reminds him of Golding's *Lord of the Flies* with this: "*Deliverance* is a better novel than *Lord of the Flies . . .* [which] is too contrived. This could happen" (Baughman 78).

3. In a conversation shortly after the 1971 Logue interview, Dickey summarized his novel: "It seemed to me that in a situation of this sort, which really just does come down to gut survival, characteristics in these people over whom the veneer of civilization has placed a kind of patina would then link up with the age-old preoccupation of men to preserve themselves—that they would feel that linkup with human-necessity situations that goes all the way back to the caves" (Baughman 72). In still another interview, he claims the novel is concerned with "whether you ought to be extremely vigorous in your notions as to what constitutes abstract justice and the law" (Anthony 109) And, in another interview, he offers this backhand summary of the setting: "The Southern setting of *Deliverance* was more or less accidental; it's just the landscape, the riverscape. It's not really particular Southern. What I was after was a more abstract projection of what seems to me the most salient condition of our time—the thing we're most concerned about . . . being set upon by malicious strangers. Whether its [sic] those two criminals in *Deliverance,* who were just degenerates, just mean, vicious, and perverted, real monsters, or some guy who sticks a gun in your ribs in New York City—it's the same thing" (Baughman 163).

4. Buoyed by Dickey's musings on his novel's universal truths, early critics saw in *Deliverance* an engagement with litanies of ancient stories; reviewers found connections to "the Bible, the Orpheus myth, the 'night journey,' and the quest of the archetypal hero in American literature" (Otten 192). One scholar claims that "mythological and archetypal readings, even Jungian interpretations, suggest that Dickey . . . caught in his novel something far more than the average adventure story" (Calhoun and Hill 118). Another early review offers that *Deliverance* presents an archetypal and violent male quest story. A 1975 critic finds the universal theme of "othering" as the concept critical to Dickey's novel: "man becomes fully human, or at least comes fully into a possession of such opportunities as are afforded him to be human, only to the degree that he is willing to acknowledge the 'other' and then respond to it. . . . Dickey has shown [how such an opportunity] can shock us out of the boredom and complacency of the daily round, out of the grim banalities of everydayness, and thus retrieve for us some comprehension of . . . *Importance*" (Gunn 197). A few years later, in 1979, another critic likewise analyzes *Deliverance* as a meditation on the universal importance of art as "a necessary mediator between nature . . . and modern urbanized 'civilized' life" (Doughtie 167). While these reviews are indicative of early responses to the novel, it's safe to say that most critical analyses of *Deliverance* focus substantially more on universal themes and symbols; very few analyze the novel's connection to history or place.

5. In a letter to his editor in 1969, Dickey writes cryptically, "If anything happened to me between now and the time I was able to revise [*Deliverance*], I hope you would go ahead and print it just as it stands in this draft that we have now" (Hart 441). A few months later, he again expressed his anxiety that, soon, he might well "vanish without a trace—or maybe [more] to the point—without a trace of the manuscript" (442).

6. The one notable exception to a novel almost devoid of African Americans characters is the "Negro ambulance driver" (Dickey, *Deliverance* 238), who is the first to find Ed after the men escape the river's rapids. Dickey presents the character as an almost angelic presence who rescues his main character and treats Ed with empathy and kindness. He is the opposite of the corrupt deputies, backwoods hillbillies, and deformed white townsfolk the characters encounter during their trip. Ed says of him, "He not only felt good to me, but he felt like a good person, and I needed one bad; just that contact was what I needed most" (239). Though Dickey changed his novel's title to *Deliverance,* his initial title, "The Deliverer," seems a fitting description of the function of Dickey's magical ambulance driver.

7. In *Summer of Deliverance,* a memoir by Christopher Dickey detailing his complicated relationship with his father, he writes of Atlanta, "Mayor [William B.] Hartsfield's creed, in the midst of the integration wars, that Atlanta was the city 'too busy to hate' [was] part wishful thinking, part willful blindness." However, the rhetoric of it was enough "to keep Atlantans feeling civilized while the attack dogs raged through [Commissioner of Public Safety] Bull Connor's Birmingham, and crosses of the Klan burned in the dark night of the cotton fields" (83).

8. Dickey spent a lot of time in the early 1970s talking about *Deliverance,* and the author's description of his process composing the novel exposes a lack of engagement with American culture or history. As an example, though he often changed his story about his inspiration, Dickey intimated that the initial idea for the plot of the book came from an image burned into his mind during a trip with his family to Positano, a coastal village just south of Naples in Italy. One afternoon, while relaxing on a boat, Dickey watched a young man climbing the rocky cliff surrounding the city. The man's body clinging to the slippery rocks of the craggy coastline so impressed the author that he was able to compose his story almost instantaneously. But his descriptions of the inspiration for the novel shifted constantly. According to one interview, Dickey claimed that the entire novel sprung into his mind from that image of a man climbing a rocky cliff: "I mean I knew the whole story in five minutes. The whole thing! And where it would take place and who the people would be. And the general outline of the action I knew in five minutes or less, or maybe even one minute" (Van Ness 325). But, in another venue, Dickey admits that, while the germ of the image and the story it suggested was apparent to him, the novel was a laborious process that was by no means straightforward, for there were always "the small changes, the alterations, the shifts, the colorings, the birth and death—and sometimes rebirth—of details, the balancements of form that took place during the speculation about the story and the writing of it" (325).

9. There are, in fact, some pretty obvious reasons why James Dickey might have wanted to distance himself from *Deliverance*'s connection to the brutal atrocities of the South in the 1960s. As a white author, any attempt to speak for or about Black experience, especially violent oppression of Black men and women by white southerners, was tricky at best and controversial at worst. Dickey had only to look at the uproar surrounding southern novelist (and friend) William Styron when his work of historical fiction, *The Confessions of Nat Turner,* won the Pulitzer Prize in 1967 to see the difficulties inherent in such a task.

10. Some reviewers find niggling connections not to the 1960s and the civil rights movement

but to the later years of the 1970s, when threats to the white southern male are more philosophical than political. As an example, one critic writes,

> For many white Americans after John F. Kennedy's assassination, much seemed amiss in the world. . . . The ability of *Deliverance*'s suburban-soft Ed to confront inexplicable brutality and overcome the enemy in the woods likely was a welcome relief for readers concerned about the threat posed by the primitive but wily Viet Cong. Perhaps it comforted white Americans to believe that if they steeled themselves, they could "man up" and prevail in the face of violence that they associated with racial Others—not only Vietnamese but blacks, with whom they associated rioting, a street crime epidemic, a skyrocketing homicide rate, and bombings by radical antiracist organizations. White southerners furious over the civil rights movement but gung ho for corralling the threat of the Viet Cong may have identified with the hillbillies' attempts to discipline interlopers just as strongly as they did with the city protagonists' attempts to eradicate predatory hillbillies" (Satterwhite 135)

Reading *Deliverance* as a revenge epic on behalf of "predatory hillbillies" and their "attempts to discipline interlopers" marks a compelling reading of the novel, one that I believe accounts for much of its success.

11. Dickey's exploration of the value of masculinity also leads some critics to connect the novel to the civil rights era, if only because of the threat such a movement had toward white southern masculinity. Many reviewers note that Dickey is intent on solving a "crisis of masculinity," and "the civil rights movement, the women's movement, and the gay and lesbian movement had a decided impact on this crisis, for they challenged the standard assumption that white, heterosexual men were entitled to all of the power and privilege that they possessed" (Kimmel and Kaufman 17–18). The men of *Deliverance* respond to their threatened and fragile masculinity by doing something "manly," going out into the wilderness. In rafting, fishing, hunting, and surviving the woods, men attempted to exorcise the demons of their imagined disenfranchisement from rapidly changing systems of power. In (re)colonizing the unspoiled wilderness of North Georgia, the suburban men of *Deliverance* enact an imaginary kind of revenge on the forces that they perceive to be threatening their position of dominance, including newly enfranchised minorities and women. The violence of the hillbillies is met with a counterviolence from the men, and such a metric of violent responses manifests how "American men prove their competence through violence when necessary—and it is often necessary, against whatever comes along to threaten the status quo" (Williamson 155). According to the author of *Hillbillyland,* the civil rights movement destabilized men's place within an economic structure that was rapidly shifting: "Another clear forerunner for obsessive male anxiety was the birth and growth of the American economic system. Industrialization reduced men to cogs in wheels and also brought women into the work force. Ironically, once there, women began to get dangerous ideas about their own economic freedom, bolstered by paychecks that allowed them to taste it. Responding to that threat . . . men intensified their traditional gender-distinctive pursuits—hunting, fighting, risking death, 'the manly arts.' These activities expressed a willful belief in dominance over chaos, over nature, and this assumption of dominance became a hallmark of American male self-esteem" (115).

12. For more on the two epigraphs and their connection to the philosophy of the novel, see Tschachler.

13. "Black Draught" is the name of a popular laxative of the time, though it was often substituted as a remedy for a number of different ailments. Clabber Girl would have been known at the time of *Deliverance* as a baking-powder company.

14. Little has been written about O'Connor's connection to Dickey, but both her fiction and *Deliverance* offer the potential for spiritual fulfilment through a violent (even disfiguring) act.

15. Dickey's editor at the time, Jacques de Spoelberch, wrote him that "The sexual molestation of Bobby should be made slightly less graphic . . . and the many references to sexual parts should be deleted" (Hart 441). Dickey refused.

16. In his *Masculinity: Bodies, Movies, Culture,* Peter Lehman notes, "Across the South, mobs castrated or cut off the penis of one in three lynching victims, reserving this practice for the very worst crimes and assaults." The castration was part of the power of the murder itself: "But to perform the lynching was to dehumanize [the victim], to gut him like a hunted animal. The 'Black beast rapist' was thus both inhuman brute ('beast') and hypersexual man ('rapist'). To transform him into an animal was to deflate the sexual threat he represented, while at the same time inflating the white man's human masculinity. Genital dismemberment was and remains such a powerful symbol of lynching for these reasons" (204). Writing of Baldwin's short story "Going to Meet the Man," Dora Apel notes, "Not surprisingly, the fascination with and fetishization of the black penis made it the most highly prized lynching souvenir. The sexualized power of the castration ritual and its lifelong effects is [sic] movingly imagined" in the story (136). The hillbilly's repeated references to Ed as an "ape," as well as his directive for Bobby to squeal like a pig remind us of Lehman's lynching aesthetic of dehumanizing the victim.

17. Ed's connection with the closed bowels of the redneck southerner (through his reading of the advertisements on barns) connects brutally with the contracting and closing of his own rectum here. It is Ed's biological reaction to the threatening of Bobby that closes him physically even as it opens him spiritually to the kind of dirty and violent revelation that the men of this Georgia wilderness are not just characters in a movie or people of no consequence; for Ed, at this moment, they are men of the utmost consequence who are forcing him into a situation that will fundamentally alter his entire identity.

18. If Dickey is being precocious by playing on his narrator's sarcastic dismissal of the closed bowels of the rural southerner through the forced sodomization (opening) of Bobby, the second part of the stereotype he finds—of southerners binging gospel music and going to church—gets reconfigured when the men attempt to rape Ed. "Fall down on your knees and pray, boy," the tall man tells Ed as he prepares to violate him. However, the reversal of penetration comes not from Ed's rape but from Lewis's arrow as it strikes the man directly in the heart. "It was there so suddenly," Ed notes, "it seemed to have come from within him" (123).

19. One critic finds in the hillbillies of *Deliverance* an articulation of absolute undifferentiated and terrifyingly free masculine id: they can be "seen as elements of the libido, an unchecked and undifferentiated sexual energy which is frightening and destructive until brought under control by the psyche" (Butterworth 75).

20. Ed's stalking of the hillbilly is an act that, for one critic, connects to "elemental libidinous forces that galvanize him into action" (Otten 200); his desperate need to think like his prey is "a form of psychological intercourse" (201) that makes the murder "a paradoxical act of murder love . . . [wherein] he kills his brother-lover." In the end, Ed and the hillbilly "become 'one flesh'—but not in the manner Gentry has fantasized" (209). For Otten, "The climax of the hunt (and the novel) is a kind of liebestod. It displays a union of the primal tensions of human existence" (212).

21. Written when Dickey was thirty-six, "Notes on the Decline of Outrage" is a useful resource for understanding *Deliverance* and its connection to the values and challenges of being a white southerner in a time of racial progress, but, more importantly, it gives us a rubric for reading

(white) anxiety over issues of racial progress in *Deliverance*. In fact, "Notes" could be annotations for Dickey's central characters in *the novel* as well as their hillbilly counterparts. Writing of "Notes" to Ernest Suarez, Dickey proclaimed his alliance with the ideals of the civil rights movement far before many of his contemporaries in the South. Though the essay is less than an outright endorsement of policies and legislations and more of an ambivalent interpretation of the white southerner's perspective after *Brown v. Board of Education,* Dickey claimed that "Martin Luther King quoted from the end of that essay in his speeches—that for white southerners 'it can be a greater thing than the South has ever done' to discover that Blacks are our 'unknown brothers.'" Further, Dickey congratulates himself on his progressivism in the 1950s, "which, as far as the Civil Rights Movement was concerned was practically prehistory" (Hart 326). And, in a final boast about his visionary ethos in the essay, he concludes, "I took an awful lot of flak for that. I didn't get a job I wanted with an advertising agency in Atlanta because the people were so rabidly pro-Southern and antiblack." It's important to note that, in his 1959 piece, eventually published in 1961, Dickey's revisionary history of its importance is its connection to the rhetorical agency of Martin Luther King and the loss of an advertising job in Atlanta (the occupation of the main character, Ed Gentry, in *Deliverance*).

22. The ethics of provisional laws and vigilante justice certainly divide critics. William Stephenson writes, "I think Dickey was the victim of his own trap, which ultimately is his secret belief that men are free when they are straying and breaking away" ("Deliverance from What?" 117); in that analysis, Stephenson finds that Dickey perpetuates a myth of "the brotherhood of good outlaws" (118) that is a damaging fantasy. For Eric Wilson, *Deliverance* is a critique of fantasies of vigilantism: "Dickey's novel is a dual meditation on the inherent limitations of social contract theory, both geographical and existential" (122); he finds that Ed and Lewis "must establish their own zone of private sovereignty within the frontier" (153), but "the problem of the crime is solved through the formation of a 'private contract' which is itself a mimetic copy of the original or 'model' contract and that serves as the foundational act." Finally, Wilson argues that *Deliverance* proves "that the outermost boundary of the law is nothing other than the extreme limit of mimetic rivalry that gives bloody birth to the 'field-of-force'" (160). Another critics writes: "a more serious problem . . . has to do with the general purport of the novel, which suggests not only Lewis' reduction of real philosophical complexities to simple physical solutions, but a positive infatuation with violence, an easy acceptance and justification of killing" (Patrick 192).

23. When Ed tries to rescue the wounded body of Drew in the river, the connections to Kennedy are obvious: "I went after him, stepped in a hole under him, finally wrestled and floated him back to the rock nearest the canoe and laid him over it on his stomach. I looked at his head. Something had hit him awfully hard there, all right. But whether it was a gunshot wound I didn't know; I had never seen a gunshot wound. The only comparison I had to go by were the descriptions of President Kennedy's assassination, the details afforded by eyewitnesses, doctors and autopsy reports which I had read in newspapers and magazines like most other Americans had, at the time. I remembered that part of Kennedy's head had been blown away. There was nothing like that here, though. There was a long raw place under the hair just over his left ear, and the head there seemed oddly pushed in, dented. But there was no brain matter showing, nothing blown away."

24. In meditating on the connections between *Deliverance* and the Kennedy assassination, it's significant to note that the hillbilly assassin in the hills might not be the best stand-in for Lee Harvey Oswald; Oswald might, in fact, be Ed himself. In *Night Hurdling*, Dickey claims that it's the security of middle-class suburbia that creates "the Lee Harvey Oswalds of the world . . . [who] would rather be murderers than the nothings that they are" (95–96).

25. To address why *Deliverance* might not feel like a straightforward elegy, I'd offer that Dickey's structure in the novel works to obscure some of his rhetoric. Moreover, as John B. Vickery argues, for the modern prose elegy, the work of mourning is far less of a straightforward rhetoric than that employed by the elegiac work of the pastoral poets: "lamentation found in the modern prose elegy is of a . . . subdued order. Neither individual characters nor their public worlds appear to register any formal expression of grief at all over the losses suffered. Diffidence, detachment, irony, and doubt or uncertainty all conspire to mute the protracted lamentations celebrated in traditional elegies" (4). Dickey's prose is nothing if not "detached," and Ed is almost the font of the doubting and ironic skeptic throughout much of the novel. But *Deliverance* finds something to mourn in the vanishing potential value of the hillbilly.

26. In "Notes On the Decline of Outrage," Dickey presents a southerner caught between two worlds, one of heritage for a past he has no actual relationship to and one of a progressive future for which he has no vision. The reactionary impulse of the white southerner stems not from a perversion of desire or depravity but, Dickey claims, because of his anxiety over displacement and potential extinction: "he does not want the *sense* of this place, the continuity of time as it has been lived, the capacity of the past to influence and if possible to assist him in thought and action, to disappear entirely" (267). An anxiety over the vanishing southern landscape or sense of values is at the very heart of *Deliverance.* The space of redemption for Ed and Lewis is the wilderness of the Georgia forests, a mythical landscape for Lewis because of its imminent destruction. While showing the others the spot where he'd like to camp, Lewis notes, "This whole valley will be under water. But right now it's wild. And I *mean* wild; it looks like something up in Alaska. We really ought to go up there before the real estate people get hold of it and make it over into one of their heavens" (*Deliverance* 14). For Lewis, the wildness of the spot is predicated by the fact that it soon will be vanquished, flooded over by the river when the dam is finished in the nearby town of Aintry; his desire to see the natural wilderness in its perfected state echoes a nostalgia for the agrarian and pastoral odes to southern landscape that proliferated after the Civil War. But what is important for Lewis is the rhetoric of why this space is so important: the spot of Georgia wilderness that he wants to see is vital because it is threatened. At some point in the not too distant future, it will cease to look like it was, and it will be transformed into a space that looks like anywhere else, a dream of real estate developers who wish to turn it into more suburbs. Lewis's romantic obsession with the vanishing pastoral South directly connects with Dickey's view of the southerner (obviously masculine) in the mid-twentieth century that he writes about in "Notes." It is not too far to claim that Lewis represents the man Dickey writes about in that essay, for the central figure of "Notes" is a man who "does not want the *sense* of this place . . . to disappear entirely."

27. Because Trump ended up winning long-held Democratic states by a scant few thousand of votes in the Rust Belt in the 2016 election, a major theme emerging in the winter of that year through the spring of 2017 was the perils of ignoring the mind of the white working-class voter. For many political pundits, Hilary Clinton's decision not to visit Michigan and Ohio in the final days of her campaign was evidence of her lack of interest in the working-class white voters of the region, hillbillies, and rednecks; for a special point of emphasis, these same political pundits criticized her gaffe of referring to some of Trump's base as a "basket of deplorables."

28. See *What You Are Getting Wrong about Appalachia* by Elizabeth Catte; *Ramp Hollow: The Ordeal of Appalachia* by Steven Stoll; *White Trash* by Nancy Isenberg; *White Rage* by Carol Anderson; *The New Minority* by Justin Gest; *Politics of Resentment* by Katherine Cramer, and *Strangers in Their Own Land* by Arlie Hochschild.

29. Responding to questions about what a victory by Trump would mean, Vance writes, "On the Democratic side, it's 'Look at those racist rednecks, they nominated their candidate and now he's going down in flames, and we're going to spend the next four years moralizing.' If that's the direction, then I think the white working class is going to become more isolated and all of the problems we've talked about just become bigger." On how Democrats can better understand the hillbilly, he answers, "Just being sympathetic and cognizant of that fear is very powerful and has been a big part of Trump's appeal. [And if Hillary Clinton wins], instead of castigating half of Trump supporters as a 'basket of deplorables,' a better strategy is to recognize that most people have offensive views about one topic or another, and that folks are a lot more complicated than deplorable or not deplorable" (Berenson).

30. See Dina Smith, 369–88.

31. For an example of this type of genre, see Goad, *The Redneck Manifesto*.

32. For more on how a trope of the "undead" operates in southern literary and cultural texts, see Anderson, Hagood, and Turner, eds., *Undead Souths: The Gothic and Beyond in Southern Literature and Culture*.

3. GTFO: The Violation of Sunken Places

1. According to commentary on the DVD version of *Carrie*, Boorman's final scene in *Deliverance* was the influence for the final scene in Brian De Palma's 1976 film. Though the films are separated by subject matter (Carrie is not about rural horror but rather religiosity existing on the margins of the suburbs), they both investigate revenge, especially the consequences of reenacting monstrosity on those who have wronged you. Both films are also adaptations of wildly successful novels, and both are read as horror films where the terror lurks below the surface. One critic notes that the poster for *Deliverance* plays with another set of submerged hands: "the tag line, 'What did happen on the Cahulawassee River?' appears over an image of the mountain man's shotgun, which two disembodied hands aim at a distant canoe, emerging ominously from the river—an image not present in the film."

2. For more on connections between fear and repression—especially in relation to horror films of the 1970s—see Robin Wood's *Hollywood from Vietnam to Reagan . . . and Beyond* (1986), especially the chapter "The American Nightmare: Horror in the 1970s," which differentiates instances of repression. Borrowing heavily from Gad Horowitz's *Repression—Basic and Surplus Repression in Psychoanalytic Theory* (1977) as well as the concept of the "other," Wood argues that horror films in the 1970s expose the repression of the other in American culture (what Horowitz labels "surplus repression").

3. Though *The Texas Chain Saw Massacre* was very loosely based on the crimes of Ed Gein, the movie begins by claiming the story to be absolutely true—"The film which you are about to see is an account of the tragedy which befell a group of five youths, in particular Sally Hardesty and her invalid brother, Franklin. It is all the more tragic in that they were young. But, had they lived very, very long lives, they could not have expected nor would they have wished to see as much of the mad and macabre as they were to see that day. For them an idyllic summer afternoon drive became a nightmare. The events of that day were to lead to the discovery of one of the most bizarre crimes in the annals of American history, The Texas Chain Saw Massacre." Similarly, *Deliverance*'s appeals to authenticity (which came both from Dickey's assertion that the events that take place in the novel were based on his own experiences) led many viewers to believe that what they were

watching was a reenactment. In her *Dear Appalachia,* Emily Satterwhite quotes a fan letter to Dickey saying, "You must tell me which of the characters around the gas station where the banjo was played were authentic hill people? . . . Were any of the scenes shot without the locals knowing they were on camera?" (157).

4. Hart's 2000 biography of Dickey chronicles much of the author's interaction with Boorman and the studio, but for an in-depth (though somewhat biased and comical) view of Dickey's engagement with the filming of *Deliverance,* see his son Christopher's 1998 memoir *Summer of Deliverance.*

5. The most recognizable movie star in the film is, obviously, Burt Reynolds, and the sudden interruption of Lewis's asking for men to drive the car is more than just a red herring. He appears at precisely that moment because, as one critic says, "Whereas the 'where you goin' city boy?' rapists represent the violent hillbilly southerner we must leave behind, Reynolds embodies the type of southerner who will carry the region and the nation forward: a fairly forward looking professional-managerial class type with roots in a different soil" (Long 39).

6. Boorman's collaborator, Rospo Pallenberg, had found a local boy, Billy Redden, to play the banjo boy; Boorman loved his "strange, degenerate look," even though the teenager could not play the banjo at all.

7. In his script, Dickey writes, "these are the first notes of a piece called Duelling Banjos [*sic*] as recorded by Mike Russo and Ross Brentano in Portland, Oregon, in 1964" (14); according to Hoyle, Boorman convinced the head of Warner Brothers to "release the piece as a single. As there was at the time no known composer to pay, the profits went to the studio and recouped the entire budget of the film" (82). Creadick reports that "'Dueling Banjos' sold 10 million copies as a single, and was a crossover hit, going to No. 2 for four weeks on the 1973 Hot 100 list (all four weeks, ironically enough, behind Roberta Flack's 'Killing Me Softly With His Song'), topped the adult contemporary chart for two weeks the same year, and reached No. 5 on the Hot Country Singles chart as well."

8. Creadick sums up how the banjo acts as an implement of violent retribution in this dual: "in a drama of domination and submission, the banjo boy scene is actually the first time the city slickers are dominated by the mountaineers. The rape is the second. . . . the banjo is the violence, and the violence has a banjo soundtrack, not only here, but intertextually, in future films and popular culture iterations. While the rape scene is actually filmed in haunting quiet, the bent notes of the banjo song established in the beginning of *Deliverance* trail along like a refrain as the horrors of the film continue."

9. The reliance on inbreeding to describe the hill people of the movie is not coincidental; the stereotype of the hillbilly's insistence on "'choosing' one's ancestors" through the intermarriage with family is, according to one critic, a way of signaling just how removed they are from civilized society: "Incest and in-breeding, both cultural and "biological," recur in many images of Appalachian otherness" (Portelli 37).

10. Creadick notes that Billy Redden could not shake his connection to the rape scene: "After *Deliverance,* Redden describes how relieved he was to get 'back to [his] normal self again' but that he was teased about his role by kids in his school, and ever since, especially about 'that one part in the woods' that 'shouldn't have been in there': 'everybody will joke around with me about it, you know. "It wasn't you, was it?" I said, "'No!' Cause once I did my part I was gone, I was back in school! I made good grades. I did. I did well" (68).

11. The casting of a local boy, Redden, as the banjo savant was one of the crucial appeals to authenticity that Boorman used, and yet, as Creadick notes, Redden's experience with the movie

is less than ideal: "'I'd like to have all the money I thought I'd make from this movie,' he said in a recent interview. 'I wouldn't be working at Walmart right now. And I'm struggling really hard to make ends meet.' Pulled out of his fourth-grade classroom to play the 'banjo boy,' Redden said they told him to 'act natural' but then made him 'shave his head' and 'wear makeup.' Though he asked to wear his 'regular clothes' of 'blue jeans and a shirt,' he was told, 'We want the movie to look like a movie.' He was paid $500. Boorman gave him the banjo he played on set to keep, but his mother, a custodial worker, later sold it to pay bills" (73).

12. The banjo boy's reappearance in the script before the rape in the clearing makes no narrative sense, but it does make thematic sense. One critic notes, "The banjo boy and the rapist (in the text, often simply referred to as "the man") are linked because of the narrative's suggestion that their monstrosities stem from the same root" (Creadick 73). Moreover, "The banjo boy and the hillbilly rapists symbolize extreme versions of the masculinities that are both desired and feared by our urban protagonists: Drew desires the banjo boy's abilities; Lewis desires to 'go native'; Ed desires Lewis's strength; and Bobby desires dominance. As part of a scared-straight narrative in which they are all fucked by the river, each of these fantasies is called out, then snuffed out: Drew is killed, Lewis handicapped, Bobby brutally raped, and Ed not so much saved as scarred, a marked man" (74).

13. The phrase "wrong turn" turns into the title of a horror movie franchise that begins in 2003; the plots of each one of the films (currently at six) involve a feral and cannibalistic family in West Virginia who stalk, murder, and eat unwitting city folks who accidentally trespass on their homeland.

14. Earlier in the film, the language of violation (especially sexual) is articulated by Lewis, who sees the progress of damming the river as an act of rape: "Just about the last wild, untamed, unpolluted, unfuckedup river in the south. Don't you understand what I'm sayin'? They gonna stop the river up. There ain't gonna be no more river. It's just gonna be a big dead. [. . .] That ain't progress, that's shit! [. . .] You just push a little more power into Atlanta, little more air conditionings, for your smug little suburb and you know what's gonna happen? We gonna rape this whole goddamn landscape. We're gon' rape it!" Echoing a sense of the already violated space of the natural world responding with its own violation. Entzminger writes, "The novel links these hillbillies to their natural setting; they are, in a sense, violated nature responding with violation" (98).

15. One critic writes of the banjo and rape connection: "The hillbillies in the "rhododendron hell" of the rape scene are deranged not because they sodomize Bobby (Ed clearly and consensually engages in anal intercourse with his wife in an opening scene), but because the act is forced. . . . As the "paddle faster" of the bumper sticker reminds us, it is the river that links the banjo to the rape. If the logic of the novel/film is man versus nature, the 'hillbillies' are aligned with nature, and nature, or too much nature, has mutated boys and men into something Other" (Creadick 73).

16. Regarding the fixation on the rectum, one critic offers a fine analysis: "the film's anal fixation is firmly established by the rape scene, by the repeated references to 'shit' that populate the screenplay, and by the depiction of phallic arrows piercing the bodies of three different men throughout the narrative. After Bobby is sodomized, Lewis shoots the first mountain man from behind and the camera lingers on the arrow that has penetrated his body, which bends lifelessly over a branch, an echo of Bobby's body which had been bent forcefully over a log during the rape. In the novel, Ed's 'intestines contract' as he watches Bobby's assault, and the men then dig the grave for the mountain man with an old latrine shovel. The novel offers this depiction of a wasted landscape: 'The ground came up easily, or what was on the ground. There was no earth; it was all

leaves and rotten stuff. It had the smell of generations of mold. They might as well let the water in on it, I thought; this stuff is no good to anybody'" (Narine 460).

17. Hooper's use of the true crime story of Ed Gein has been well documented; though Gein's grisly murders took place in Wisconsin, Hooper decided to shoot and set his film in Texas. Most of the inspiration from Gein's case involved grave robbing and decorative pieces that Gein made from corpses. For more about Gein, see Robert H. Gollmar, *Edward Gein: America's Most Bizarre Murderer*, and Harold Schechter, *Deviant: The Shocking True Story of Ed Gein, the Original Psycho.*

18. Carol Clover in her *Men, Women, and Chain Saws* offers a similar reading of horror movies as an extension of the dramatic genre of the frontier, the western: "there is, indeed . . . a remarkable fit between horror and the western. . . . The case could also be made that westerns are really horrors 'underneath,' for the terms of violation and revenge in the western seem often to slide beyond an economic analysis into a psychosexual register" (165).

19. These terms—"urbanoia," "rape-revenge" and "slasher"—need some unpacking. Clover's discussion of "urbanoia" involves horror films that mark those outside the city as a "threatening rural other" (124) that always traffic in the language of class differences. The rape-revenge film, such as *I Spit on Your Grave,* has a plot in which those victimized by a profound violation (such as rape or other perversions of violence) enact a methodical (and graphically violent) revenge on those who attacked them. These rape-revenge plots can be done by proxy (revenge done not by the victims but on their behalf) or can be a part of a larger narrative, such as *Deliverance*'s urbanoia and survivalism. "Slasher" is more straightforward in that it has several categories that make up its plot, including, "killer," "terrible place," "weapons," "victims," and Clover's most famous term, "final girl." For Clover, *Deliverance* shares a bit from both the urbanoia and rape-revenge genre, while *Chain Saw* is more of a cross between a slasher and urbanoia drama.

20. I believe there is dynamic potential in investigating how place operates in horror movies, for so many of these films privilege setting over plot and advertise the terror of place in their title: TEXAS *Chain Saw,* AMYTIVLLE *Horror, A Haunting in* CONNECTICUT.

21. I am not alone in finding *Chain Saw* an indictment of the historical events of the 1960s and 1970s. Critics have seen in the film both "a 'prophetic accident' in which its director foresees a Gothic future controlled by an oil-hoarding patriarchy" and "a horrific parody of American values"; indeed, "the film's theme of 'cannibalistic capitalism' plays out the tensions borne of the historical and political circumstances of the period of the film's production. The far-from-triumphant end of the Vietnam War, the loss of confidence in political authority and integrity following the Watergate scandal, the oil crisis (which disrupted the lives of ordinary car-driving Americans) leading into a major stock market crash and recession" (Merritt 202–3) all are present in *Chain Saw.*

22. Our protagonists' ignorance or naivete about what conditions are like for small-town poor people clearly mark them as hapless victims but also, in a sense, as somehow a dirty indictment of the ignorance of the privileged. Part of the pleasure we might experience in the movie comes from what one critic calls "sadistic pleasure from the initial terrorizing of the well-off" (Hutchings 123).

23. Though not identified as the Sawyers in the first movie, in the sequels we learn the last name of our monsters.

24. I am referring here to the marriage of the experiments of Gregor Mendel to understand the way DNA works to bind species together with the eugenics movement in America in the early twentieth century. The result of this specious alliance was to look for specific traits in people that might mark them as "unfit" for procreation, thus using the exterior body to map moral or ethical

deficiencies. A "Mendelizing characteristic" offered an easy way to tell about someone's interior by reading their exterior body, and traits such as albinism, color blindness, mutations, deafness, and mental retardation" were examples of ways to understand someone's potential for negative social interactions. The banjo boy's albinism as well as the hitchhiker's red mark could easily represent such a characteristic that was usually used to mark poor whites as unfit for procreation.

25. In her essay "Monster Mishmash: Iconicity and Intertextuality in Tobe Hooper's 'The Texas Chain Saw Massacre,'" Dudenhoeffer connects Hooper's film with the history of Universal studio's monster movies: "The Texas Chain Saw Massacre suggests that Dracula and Frankenstein now reside within our own territories, and thus within us. The Universal monster icons, in remaking us, enable The Texas Chain Saw Massacre to remake these films, with Europe transliterating into Texas, a state notorious for insisting on its independence from the rest of the nation and the outsider forces of counterculture—as Rock Hudson's character in Giant says, Texas is 'almost its own country.' The Texas Chain Saw Massacre, much like the Universal films of the 1930s, visualizes America's anxieties over change, invasion, and colonization and inflicts on its audience a sense of its own monstrousness in the form of America's fear, mistreatment, and marginalization of those outside the mainstream" (53).

26. The Old Man's assertion that the people of the country don't like outsiders and "don't mind letting you know with a little buckshot" (32) reminds me of Lewis's warning that hillbillies don't think much of murdering people.

27. Hooper's ability to get the audience to feel sympathy for the murders and annoyance with the victims is a hallmark of the movie. I am reminded, of course, of Robin Wood's description of watching a showing of Chain Saw with a group of twenty-somethings; despite the fact that the victims in the movie mirrored the same ethnic, class, and racial makeup of the crowd, he confessed, "Watching it recently with a *large, half-stoned* youth audience, who cheered and applauded every one of Leatherface's outrages against their representatives on the screen, was a terrifying experience" (84).

28. Leatherface's intensity is clearly one of the reasons why we are drawn to him as a monstrous character. Humphries claims, "one is both impressed and horrified by the character's eruption from nowhere and his implacable pursuit of his victims" (123).

29. Sally is forced to witness the bizarre and brutal dynamics of a family that she has no context for or history with. That the family is in despair is even more compelling, for, as Tony Williams offers in his book, the villain responsible for the demise of the institution was never external: "The antagonist was no external *force such as the Frankenstein monster,* Count Dracula, or Cat Woman; instead the threat came from within" (13).

30. One of the more disturbing death scenes in the movie is the murder of Franklin as he attempts to escape in his wheelchair from a determined Leatherface. I find eerie similarities between the character of Franklin and that of Bobby in *Deliverance,* both of whom are portrayed as sarcastic and whiny and both of whom are violated in part because of their repeated detachments from the real violences that surround them. I am also interested in the connections that Franklin has to the albino boy and Leatherface, both as figures of ejection and paralysis.

31. The main character in *Just Above My Head* (1979) claims, "Look at a map, and scare yourself half to death. On the northern edge of Virginia, on the Washington border, catty-corner to Maryland, is Richmond, Virginia. Two-thirds across the map is Birmingham, Alabama, surrounded by Mississippi, Tennessee, and Georgia" (400).

32. The second chapter in Clover's *Men, Women, and Chain Saws* discusses possession films; Clover asserts that possession can only take place on a subject who is either physically or symbolically "opened" to it. See especially 65–113.

4. Dirty Ethics and Swampy Ecology

1. Though "environmentalists found a friend in President Lyndon Johnson" in the 1960s, Nixon was a slow convert. His reluctance came, in part, from the belief throughout his administration that those clamoring for environmental laws were largely left-leaning enemies of the president still antagonistic to progressive agendas. Instead, Nixon found his focus split over the war in Vietnam and domestic issues. And yet the groundswell of support for conservation laws, coupled with a petroleum spill in the Pacific Ocean, forced Nixon to act.

2. The 1969 oil spill in the Santa Barbara Channel was a huge story that year. At the time of the catastrophe, it was the largest spill of its kind, and is third only to the Deepwater Horizon (2010) and Exxon Valdez (1999) today. The event happened on 28 January 1969 on "Platform A," approximately six miles off the coast, when drillers experienced a "blow out" while finalizing their preparation of several wells. After ten days, close to 100,000 barrels of oil spilled into the ocean. The resulting pollution and its effect on dolphins, sea birds, and other marine life quickly became the major story of the year and one of the major factors that inspired activists and conservationists who became the driving force behind the nation's first "Earth Day" the next year.

3. Much of the success of the first Earth Day owes a debt to student activism. When the idea of Earth Day was first announced in 1969, organizers took advantage of the year's prolific number of marches and protests across college campuses to gain traction for their new event. Just three weeks after Earth Day's announcement, on 15 October 1969, thousands of students were galvanized by marches in opposition to the war. Protests inevitably connected with the environmental activism as students opposed to the war turned their ire toward the corporations and businesses that partnered with the government.

4. Environmental historian Philip Shabecoff suggests that the principles of American conservation and protection might have their roots in "the beginning of the nineteenth century," when "doubt was beginning to spread that the conquest of nature was the proper goal of mankind. People slowly became aware that in industrialized countries, civilization had reached a point that demanded a new relationship between humans and the natural world. . . . The balance had shifted so far that humans would have to protect and conserve other living things" (161).

5. Originally formed in 1953 by a combination of American businessmen, government agencies, and nonprofits, "Keep America Beautiful" was primarily focused on combatting litter. Early commercials and advertisements for the organization were not as memorable as the ones culminating in "The Crying Indian." In fact, Keep America Beautiful's campaign against littering in 1971 was organized to coincide with the first Earth Day, including their slogan "People start pollution. People can stop it."

6. The commercial's appeal to indigenous culture as part of its dirty ethical rhetoric is, of course, outrageous. Questions surrounded the ethnicity of the actor who portrayed the indigenous man in the commercial: Cody, "actually born Espera De Corti," did not have a connection to American Indian ancestry but was, in fact, "an Italian-American who literally played Indian in both his life and onscreen" (Dunaway 80). Cody "would play Native American roles in more than one hundred film and television roles throughout his career," starting in 1926 and lasting through

until 1990. Though he "insisted that he was Native American (claiming to have Cherokee-Cree roots)," in 1996 "his half-sister revealed that Cody had Italian ancestry, not Native American roots." The public service announcement participates in a willful and tone-deaf appeal to Americans to respect and protect Native lands in a country that exploited those same descendants. The ad projects a version of a nation virtually erased of the memories of the wholesale murder and removal of indigenous people, not to mention one in which the colonizing project depleted and exploited the natural resources of their lands (Berumen 26–27). Moreover, the commercial's mantra of "individual responsibility" deliberately obscures responsibility for whites' genocidal relation to Native Americans.

7. And yet, as Krech points out, "the Crying Indian is an effective image and advocate because its assumptions are not new" (16). Keep America Beautiful only borrowed from the traditional "noble savage" stereotype of Native Americans, suggesting they were a symbol of ultimate purity: "From the moment they encountered the native people of North America and represented them in texts, prints, paintings, sculptures, performances—in all conceivable media—Europeans classified them in order to make them sensible. They made unfamiliar American Indians familiar by using customary taxonomic categories, but in the process often reduced them simplistically to . . . stereotypes" (Krech 16).

According to Berkhofer, one of the reasons that the American Indian's connection to stereotypes of the "noble savage" were so compelling was the trope's connection to competing, if not antithetical, conceptions of primitivity and aspirationalism: "The primitivist tradition influenced the Renaissance explorers' perceptions of the native peoples they encountered," while the American Indian's spiritual potential offered a key "to the future coming of utopia" (72). Krech calls this new symbolic rhetoric of the "Crying Indian" a cross between the tradition of the ecologically pure indigenous man—whose relationship to the land is unspoiled—with the stereotype of the "savage"—a figure who stands uncorrupted by modernity and automation, the "Ecological Indian: the Native North American as ecologist and conservationist" (16). As a symbol of a progressive (ecological movement) and primitive (nostalgia for natural purity), the "Crying Indian" did double work on behalf of a decade in which "progress" and "primitivity" were not antithetical, but inextricably linked. By offering the Native American as "an emblem of protest, a phantomlike figure whose untainted ways allow him to embody native ecological wisdom and to critique the destructive forces of progress," Keep America Beautiful managed to coopt much of the fervor over environmentalism and ecological preservation and reframe these movements as a paean for American responsibility and nation-building discourses of colonialism and expansion (Dunaway 89). Moreover, the ad "trivializes the complicated relations between both Indian people and the nonhuman 'persons' in the form of animals and plants that make their lives possible, as well as with the different kinds of groups in the dominant society" (Nesper and Schlender 302).

8. As one example of how the South's ethical history relates to its ecological one, historian Donna Haraway offers that "the slave plantation system was the model and motor for the carbon-greedy machine-based factory system that is often cited as an inflection point for the Anthropocene" (160). In their essay "South to the Plantationocene," Aikens, Clukey, King, and Wagner affirm that these theories like Haraway's "place plantation not only at the heart of Western modernity, but also conceive of it as a central engine of capitalism, empire, industrialization, ecological destruction, geological change, and climate change" and yet reposition the plantation not as a southern capitalist system but as a national imaginary that gets configured as a regional fantasy: "plantation isn't just a material institution that has led to the planetary catastrophes of the Plantationocene;

it's also a set of ideas, archives, ideologies, and, most important for our purposes as literary and cultural critics, narratives. Ideologies of the plantation fundamentally shape history, economics, and ecologies on a planetary scale, and they also fundamentally shape how human beings relate to each other and to the natural world. Put another way, the Plantationocene depends upon the cognitive, psychological, and epistemological affects of plantation colonialism, which makes the plantation imaginary crucial to its success."

9. Ellen Griffith Spears notes that, "until midcentury, pollution control was largely left to states and localities," which allowed southern states to act as they pleased in regard to what they labeled as pollution. In Alabama, this meant the law "explicitly exempted from regulation industrial discharges in existence when the law was enacted in 1949. State enforcement was spotty, uncoordinated, and limited to the more egregious, visible, and well-publicized 'accidents,' such as large fish kills" (131). The lack of enforcement of environmental laws throughout the region made it a favorable site for industry in much of the second half of the twentieth century.

10. According to historian Robert D. Bullard, "environmental racism is racial discrimination in environmental policymaking. It is racial discrimination in the enforcement of regulations and laws. It is racial discrimination in the deliberate targeting of communities of color for toxic waste disposal and the siting of polluting industries. It is racial discrimination in the official sanctioning of the life-threatening presence of poisons and pollutants in communities of color. And, it is racial discrimination in the history of excluding people of color from the mainstream environmental groups, decision-making boards, commissions, and regulatory bodies" (3). Bullard notes that "the term 'environmental racism' was coined" as a response to a protest in which the poor and largely African American Warren County in North Carolina "was selected for a PCB landfill not because it was an environmentally sound choice, but because it seemed powerless to resist." When hundreds of residents protested, "the behavior of county authorities was seen as an extension of the institutional racism many of them had encountered in the past—including discrimination in housing, employment, education, municipal services, and law enforcement" (3).

11. Though Yaeger's conception of "dirty ecology" is a national imaginary that offers potential for transformation, the phrase itself has a significance in biological studies of the environment in which "pollution effects" become part of the scientific study of "environmental ecology" ("Beasts"). The seeming contradiction in including pollution as a part of the environment and its place in biological studies of ecology has led some scientists, most notably Vorobeichik, to label pollution studies as the "ecology of impacted areas . . . or even 'dirty ecology'" (Zvereva et al. 2).

12. The word "swamp" is already a contested term. According to the *Oxford English Dictionary,* a swamp can be "A tract of low-lying ground in which water collects; a piece of wet spongy ground; a marsh or bog," or "a tract of rich soil having a growth of trees and other vegetation, but too moist for cultivation." The word "swamp" inspired countless nineteenth-century American writers, including Stowe and Thoreau, the latter of whom saw the swamp as "a place for play as well as a place to undertake the imaginative work of remaking oneself" (Petersheim and Jones 120).

13. The court's verdict was a landmark in the classification of what was "navigable waters," and therefore a "stream." Swamp waters were partially deemed "land" that affected the navigation of streams and therefore were impediments to be removed, not protected.

14. Though the groundswell of legislation during the 1970s focused attention on wetland conservation, as recently as 1994, federal protections of wetlands have eroded. According to environmental historians Ronald Keither Gaddie and James L. Regens, in 1994, "virtually the entire framework of environmental legislation enacted since the 1970s as well as the federal agencies

responsible for environmental management came under scrutiny. One focal point for efforts to limit federal authority in environmental regulation was in the area of wetland protection" (1–2). By placing wetland protection under Section 404 of the Water Pollution Act, the federal government essentially "encouraged states to assume authority for" such conservation and protection. The resulting shifting of responsibility has been hugely controversial and a microcosm of arguments of federal authority versus states' rights. Regulations and legislation that would have protected many acres of wetlands have been tied up in political fights.

15. Long thought of as a region with not just a favorable climate for agriculture, the American South has temperate winters and abundant sunshine, making it the region of the United States most agreeable for leisure and recreation. Of course, climate conditions that made the South an important economic region also had the deleterious effect of aggravating the very systems of inequality and disenfranchisement that marked the political and economic realities of being poor and Black in the region.

16. The contradictory ecological features of the swamp directly relate to its diversity. See the textbook *Ecosystem Ecology:* "Swamps are important for the diversity of habitat conditions that they provide. At the large scale, swamps comprise part of the mosaic of land types, yielding wet, vegetative conditions among uplands. At smaller scales, within a swamp, there are a multitude of habitat conditions that are largely dictated by elevation relative to the mean high water level" (Jorgensen 416).

17. In a 1978 executive order, Carter directed "federal agencies to improve their implementation of the National Environmental Policy Act under new regulations . . . [in order to] examine the environmental effects of federal actions abroad [and] preserve and restore natural values of wetlands and floodplains" (Carter, vol 2: 1354).

18. The change in terminology matters, for the word "'wetland' itself projects a certain respectability otherwise lacking for the mere swamp, marsh, or bog" (Gardner 7).

19. Though this film about mosquitos was among a mere handful of films produced by the Walt Disney Corporation for propaganda, Jack Cutting, the head of Disney's foreign office, "wrote Walt early in 1945 that *The Winged Scourge* . . . created a greater sensation than 'Gone with the Wind' in a small Cuban village where mosquito infestation was rampant" (Gabler 412).

20. Initially founded as National Allied Publications in 1934, the comic-book publisher changed its name to DC, short for its anthology series "Detective Comics," which premiered in 1937. The series would gain fame for introducing the iconic superhero Batman just a couple of years later.

21. Perhaps the most famous comic-book plant-human monster to predate the Swamp Thing, "the Heap" first appeared in an issue of Air Fighters Comics in 1942. Born as Baron Eric von Emmelman, the German air fighter was shot down during World War I. His plane crashed into a swamp in Poland. Though his body decayed in the muck, Emmelman's mind continued to struggle for life, and eventually he arose a few decades later as a creature known as "the Heap." Other human-plant monster hybrids in comics include those that predate Swamp Thing ("It," Theodore Sturgeon, Unknown Comics, 1940); those concurrent with the Wein release ("The Man-Thing," Stan Lee, Roy Thomas, and Gerry Conway, Marvel Comics, 1971); and those that were inspired by the Swamp Thing ("Bog Swamp Demon" and "Muckman" of the Teenage Mutant Ninja Turtles, 1980s–90s).

22. See especially Vertigo's run of "Brightest Day," in which Swamp Thing's decision to protect Earth leads him to decide that he must end all human life. He is eventually stopped by a string of major DC heroes, including Hawkman, the Martian Manhunter, and Aquaman. In the aftermath

of that series, other major comic figures, such as John Constantine, Batman, and Superman try to locate the creature.

23. Moore's transformation of Swamp Thing into a "Plant Elemental" not only ties his creature into a new relationship with the environment but also dramatically expands the monster's superpowers. As an Elemental, the Swamp Thing has the power of limitless regeneration as well as the ability to travel throughout the planet. In what is perhaps a callback to Wein's original story, Moore's Swamp Thing can communicate with and also control all plant matter throughout the universe.

24. Following Carter's 1978 Executive Order, the public perception of wetland protection began to shift. The order effectively put an end to all federal projects whose sole purpose was to drain and fill wetlands so that they could be transformed into land suitable for business or agriculture. Carter's order changed the term "wetland" from a source of national anxiety over waste and disease into something worthy of being protected: "Wetlands means those areas that are inundated by surface or ground water with a frequency sufficient to support and under normal circumstances does or would support a prevalence of vegetative or aquatic life that requires saturated or seasonally saturated soil conditions for growth and reproduction. Wetlands generally include swamps, marshes, bogs, and similar areas such as sloughs, potholes, wet meadows, river overflows, mud flats, and natural ponds" (*Code of Federal Regulations* 135).

25. Though Katrina was not the deadliest storm in the nation's history, it was one of the worst natural disasters in almost half a century. With the technological improvement in the tracking of storms as well as advances in mass communication and mobilization, much of the profound disillusionment associated with Katrina came not from its numbers—loss of lives, property damage—but from the realization that such wholesale devastation could affect so many during an age with so many advantages over the storms of 1900 and 1915.

26. Even before Katrina, "for years, coastal experts had been calling on the federal government to close down this underused and fragile seventy-six-mile waterway that the Army Corps had so arrogantly built forty years earlier to save ships from the twists and turns of the Mississippi" (Rivlin 38).

27. Only recently have social and economic historians tried to fight back against what Martinez-Alier labels "the cult of wilderness" and "eco-efficiency" by emphasizing the "Environmentalism of the poor," or "environmental justice," which focuses attention on the deleterious affects of both environmentalists and economic interests by pointing "out that economic growth unfortunately means increased impacts" such as "geographical displacement of sources and sinks" (10). The impacts of growth affect "social groups that often complain and resist (even though such groups do not necessarily describe themselves as environmentalists)" (11).

28. Often described as existing at the bottom of a bowl or in a cup, New Orleans is surrounded by water. The city's protection system—the levees—keep the water out of the metropolitan area, but, as was the case with Katrina, when one of the levees is breached, the water from around "the below-sea-level basin" will begin "to fill up like a bathtub" (Wolanski et al. 648).

29. Though Wink's illness is never identified in the movie, we do get some critical clues from the dialogue as well as Wink's obvious symptoms—collapsing, wheezing, and so on. He cryptically tells his daughter at one point in the movie, "My blood is eating itself."

30. Though Zeitlin is careful not to talk in interviews about the debt his movie owes to Katrina, many critics see obvious connections. One writer notes that Zeitlin was inspired to make a movie "while following the devastating path of Hurricane Katrina on his cellphone": the director

has "a Eureka moment: He would tie the story to the storm. So he and his cohort of producers and designer (united under the name "Court 13") made their way to New Orleans." Zeitlin also cast two native New Orleans residence who survived the storm. Dwight Henry, who plays Wink, assures one interviewer, "everything you see is real. Benh could have gone to California, to New York, maybe gone and got an actor to play my part. But what he wanted was somebody who actually, in real life, went through what we go through in the movie, with storms and the like. I'm from New Orleans, and this is something we go through every year. We have to deal with the possibility of a storm coming in, evacuating—family goin' all different places—so having someone that has gone through this brings a realness. I was caught in hurricane Katrina. . . . when things like that happen, vandals come to your business, they loot it. And I refused to let that happen. So when Katrina came, I stayed down there, and I had to get out of neck-high water to save my life! That was a real thing that I brought to the movie. Versus getting someone from Hollywood who's never been through these things" (Lidz).

31. The legacy of Katrina's impact drew the focus of environmentalists back to the conception of human-made climate change, especially how cities like New Orleans are often "the terrain where the catastrophes of climate change are felt most intensely." According to Dawson, "Hurricane Katrina generated some of the most powerful representations of what the sociologist Ulrich Beck calls 'the world at risk,' as the media was saturated with images of New Orleans's poor and predominantly African-American residents, abandoned by their country, standing on rooftops begging for help, huddled in unsanitary conditions in the SuperDome, lying face down in the toxic floodwaters."

32. Like the residents of the "Bathtub," those who lived in the Lower Ninth Ward of New Orleans were economically depressed and without the means or ability to retreat as the storm advanced. New Orleans historian Douglas Brinkley notes, "New Orleans had a higher proportion of people living below the poverty line (27.9 percent in 1999) that similar-sized cities." "Intertwined with the city's poverty rate was its racial composition. African Americans constituted 67.3 percent of the population. . . . in the face of a natural disaster, the world of the poor in New Orleans, particularly that of the poor black . . . could not be romanticized" (33).

33. Landry's critique of Wolfinger has some obvious connections to the "imposition of the New Orleans disaster capitalist agenda," which as the privately run Road Home program, which was set in place "to ostensibly help private homeowners rebuild [even though] the privatized reconstruction model paradoxically reinforced the government failure of ideology" (Powelson 178).

34. Landry's emphasis on Wolfinger's corruption connects to real corruption after the storm. Post-Katrina, we have "one of the largest, if not the largest, instances of contractor fraud." Harvey finds that such fraud occurs because of the disaster-capitalist logic in which "neoliberal polices are pushed through by a small group of wealthy and powerful in the aftermath of disasters" that end up reinscribing power dynamics: "Who profits and how they profit furthers the marginalization" (Harvey 300).

35. Though it was never designed to be a shelter, the Superdome was declared a shelter of last resort should the city experience a catastrophic weather event. Because of the extensive flooding throughout the city, thousands of residents flocked to the structure, which became ground zero for television news reports about the devastation. During its first night as a shelter, part of the roof was ripped off the dome, and rain pelted those inside. The stadium's inability to house, feed, shelter, and provide hygienic conditions for so many eventually became a huge point of contention for a national public outraged by the lack of preparation for the hurricane.

36. Just as an example of the staggering amount of narratives that come from Katrina, see movies like *Bad Lieutenant: Port of Call New Orleans* and *When the Levees Broke;* books like *The Tin Roof Blowdown: A Dave Robicheaux Novel* and *Zeitoun;* and comics such as *A.D.: New Orleans After the Deluge* and *The Parish: An AmeriCorps Story.*

Coda: Recycling the South

1. Twitty's frequently updated blog is a multifaceted series of articles on everything from "culinary justice" to his work on kosher food preparation and Judaic identity. He often writes open letters to celebrity chefs as well as addressing cultural issues of interest to the southern, African American, or Jewish chefs of America.

2. Broadly defined as belonging to African Americans who live in the Low Country of Georgia, Florida, and South Carolina, the Gullah culture is renowned for Geechee, its creolized mixture of African and English language. For more on Gullah culture and its connection to American and indigenous cultures, see Pollitzer, *The Gullah People and Their African Heritage,* and Cooper, *Making Gullah: A History of Sapelo Islanders, Race, and the American Imagination.*

3. Author of several cookbooks as well as head chef of the famous restaurant chain Husk, Sean Brock was criticized by Twitty on his blog for his negative reaction to Twitty's commentary on the whitewashing of Charleston's food scene.

4. The recent resurgence of Carolina gold rice's popularity is a corollary to the celebration of southern foodways. Initially one of the established grains of the Low Country of South Carolina, Carolina gold rice was hugely profitable to the early colony and the local economy of the region for more than two centuries. Unfortunately, the conditions under which it had to be grown as well as the intense labor required to produce and manufacture it eventually made the farming of it unprofitable following the Emancipation Proclamation. Now, the grain is again a trendy dish that supposedly celebrates the rich history of a region, but its association with brutal conditions of production as well as the history of death, disease, and injury in its farming is virtually obscured.

5. For more on the history of police violence aimed at Black men and women—especially as a means to control behavior through fear and terror, see Cazenave, *Killing African Americans: Police and Vigilante Violence as a Racial Control Mechanism.*

6. Though "Black Lives Matter" was etched in large yellow letters in front of Trump Tower on 9 July 2020, the lettering has been defaced at least four times as of the writing of these notes (31 July 2020).

7. I'm referring here to the bombing of the African American 16th Street Baptist Church in Birmingham, Alabama, on Sunday, 15 September 1963. The attack was planned and carried out by a group of white-supremacist men, Thomas Edwin Blanton Jr., Herman Frank Cash, Robert Edward Chambliss, and Bobby Frank Cherry. Though the men were initially not charged in the deaths of Addie Mae Collins, Cynthia Wesley, Carole Robertson, and Carol Denise McNair, Robert Chambliss was later tried and convicted in 1977. From 2001 to 2002, the state prosecuted Blanton and Cherry, who were also convicted of four counts of murder. They were sentenced to life in prison.

8. Flint, Michigan's water crisis of 2016 highlighted the inequities of resources for Black communities. The mostly Black city found itself dealing with a situation in which they had "been exposed to lead in their drinking water. And the long-term health effects of that poisoning may not be fully understood for years." Even now, in 2020, as Peggy Shepard of WE ACT for Environmental

Justice, argued, "The disproportionate rates of [Covid-19] infection, hospitalization and deaths are linked to lingering and persistent health, social, economic and environmental inequities facing Black Americans, conditions which are rooted in oppression, discrimination, medical apartheid and structural racism . . . and which today have created a perfect storm" (National Black Environmental Justice Network).

WORKS CITED

Acheson, Hugh, and Rinne Allen. *A New Turn in the South: Southern Flavors Reinvented for Your Kitchen.* Potter, 2011.

Agee, James, and Walker Evans. *Let Us Now Praise Famous Men.* Ballantine: 1966, 1941.

Aikens, Natalie, Amy Clukey, Amy K. King, and Isadora Wagner. "South to the Plantationocene." *ASAP Journal.* asapjournal.com/south-to-the-plantationocene-natalie-aikens-amy-clukey-amy-k-king-and-isadora-wagner/.

Alexie, Sherman. "The Texas Chainsaw Massacre." *Kenyon Review* 14.3 (Summer 1992): 45–46.

Anderson, Carol. *White Rage: The Unspoken Truth of Our Racial Divide.* Bloomsbury, 2016.

Anderson, Eric Gary, Taylor Hagood, and Daniel Cross Turner, eds. *Undead Souths: The Gothic and Beyond in Southern Literature and Culture.* Louisiana State UP, 2015.

Anderson, Warwick. *Colonial Pathologies: American Tropical Medicine, Race, and Hygiene in the Philippines.* Duke UP, 2006.

Anthony, Frank. "After 'Deliverance': An Exchange with James Dickey." *New England Review* 18.4 (Fall 1997): 108–10.

Apel, Dora. *Imagery of Lynching: Black Men, White Women, and the Mob.* Rutgers UP, 2004.

Appy, Christian G. *American Reckoning: The Vietnam War and Our National Identity.* Penguin, 2015.

Arsenault, Raymond. *Freedom Riders: 1961 and the Struggle for Racial Justice.* Oxford UP, 2006.

Bad Lieutenant: Port of Call New Orleans. Directed by Werner Herzog. First Look, 2009.

Badgett, M. V. Lee. "A Win at Cracker Barrel." *The Nation* 276.5 (January 23, 2003): 7.

Baker, Houston A., Jr., and Dana Nelson. "Preface: Violence, the Body, and 'The South.'" *American Literature* 73.2 (June 2011): 231–44.

Bakare, Lanre. "Get Out." [Review.] *The Guardian,* 28 February 2017. theguardian.com/film/2017/feb/28/get-out-box-office-jordan-peele.

Baldwin, James. *Just Above My Head.* Random House, 1979.

Bane, Michael. "The Outlaws: Revolution in Country Music." In Travis D Stimeling, ed., *The Oxford Handbook of Country Music.* Oxford UP, 2017. 208–22.

Baughman, Ronald, ed. *The Voiced Connections of James Dickey: Interviews and Conversations.* U of Michigan P, 1984.

Bauman, Zygmunt. *Wasted Lives: Modernity and Its Outcasts. Wiley,* 2003.

Beard, Tyler. *100 Years of Western Wear.* Gibbs-Smith, 1993.

Belcher, Christina. "S-Town, Shit World." *Society + Space,* 6 June 2017. societyandspace .org/2017/06/06/s-town-shit-world/

Berenson, Tessa. "J. D. Vance on Why Life Might Get Worse for the White Working Class." *Time,* 3 November 2016. time.com/4556065/jd-vance-white-working-class/.

Berkhofer, Robert F. *The White Man's Indian: Images of the American Indian, from Columbus to the Present.* Knopf, 1979.

Bertoia, Rich. *Country Store Advertising, Medicines, and More.* Schiffer Military History, 2001.

Berumen, Frank Javier Garcia. *American Indian Image Makers of Hollywood.* McFarland, 2019.

Bevck, Laura. "Read Paula Deen's Depo: She Loves the Look & Professionalism of Slaves." *Jezebel,* 19 June 2013. jezebel.com/happily-i-no-longer-live-in-the-south-and-if-people-w-516843363#!.

Bianculli, David. *Dangerously Funny: The Uncensored Story of "The Smothers Brothers Comedy Hour."* Touchstone, 2009.

Bibler, Michael. "The Podcast and the Police: STown and the Narrative Form of Southern Queerness." *Southern Spaces,* 24 March 2020. southernspaces.org/2020/podcast-and- police-s-town-and-narrative-form-southern-queerness/.

Blake, Linnie. *The Wounds of Nations: Horror Cinema, Historical Trauma and National Identity.* Manchester UP, 2013.

Blum, Edward J. *Reforging the White Republic: Race, Religion, and American Nationalism, 1865–1898.* Louisiana State UP, 2005.

Bodroghkozy, Aniko. *Equal Time: Television and the Civil Rights Movement.* U of Illinois P, 2012.

Bone, Martyn. *The Postsouthern Sense of Place in Contemporary Fiction.* Louisiana State UP, 2005.

———,William A. Link, and Brian Ward. *Creating and Consuming the American South.* UP of Florida, 2015.

Boorman, John. "How We Made *Deliverance." The Guardian,* 29 May 2017. www.theguardian.com/film/2017/may/29/how-we-made-deliverance-johnboorman-jon-voight.

Bouie, Jamelle. "'Watchmen' Dares to Imagine a Righteous Black Vigilante." *New York Times,* 25 November 2019. www.nytimes.com/2019/11/25/opinion/watchmen-hbo.html.

Bowles, David. "Cummins' Non-Mexican Crap." *Medium,* 18 January 2020. medium .com/@davidbowles/non-mexican-crap-ff3b48a873b5.

Boyagoda, Randy. "The American Dirt Controversy Is Painfully Intramural." *The Atlantic,*

30 January 2020. www.theatlantic.com/ideas/archive/2020/01/american-dirt-controversy/605725/.

Boxcar, Ruby Ann. *Ruby Ann's Down Home Trailer Park Cookbook.* Citadel, 2015.

Bradley, Regina. *Chronicling Stankonia: The Rise of the Hip-Hop South.* U of North Carolina P, 2021.

"Bradley Sees a Bright Future." *Billboard* 89.4 (9 April 1977): 53.

Braxton, Greg. "Frank Peppiatt Dies at 85; Co-creator of 'Hee Haw.'" *Los Angeles Times,* 9 November 2012. www.latimes.com/local/obituaries/la-xpm-2012-nov-09-la-me-frank-peppiatt-20121109-story.html.

Brennan, Emily. "Q&A: A Filmmaker's Impressions of the Bayou." *New York Times,* 16 August 2012. www.nytimes.com/2012/08/19/travel/the-filmmaker-benh-zeitlins-impressions-of-the-bayou.html.

Briggs, Laura. *Reproducing Empire: Race, Sex, Science, and U.S. Imperialism in Puerto Rico.* U of California P, 2002.

Brimner, Larry Dane. *Twelve Days in May: Freedom Ride 1961.* Highlights, 2017.

Brinkley, Douglas. *The Great Deluge: Hurricane Katrina, New Orleans, and the Mississippi Gulf Coast.* HarperCollins, 2009, 2006.

Brod, Harry, and Michael Kaufman, eds. *Theorizing Masculinities.* Sage, 1994.

Brooks, Garth. "Friends in Low Places." Capitol Nashville, 1990.

Bruccoli, Matthew J., ed. *Crux: The Letters of James Dickey.* U of Michigan P, 1999.

Brundage, W. Fitzhugh. "From Appalachian Folk to Southern Foodways: Why Americans Look to the South for Authentic Culture." In Bone et al., eds., *Creating and Consuming the American South.* 27–48.

Bullard, Robert D. *Confronting Environmental Racism: Voices from the Grassroots.* South End, 1993.

Burke, James Lee. *The Tin Roof Blowdown.* Pocket, 2008.

Butterworth, Keen. "The Savage Mind: James Dickey's 'Deliverance.'" *Southern Literary Journal* 28.2 (Spring 1996): 69–78.

Caldwell, Erskine, and Margaret Bourke-White. *You Have Seen Their Faces.* U of Georgia P, 1995, 1937.

Calhoun, Richard J., and Robert W. Hill. *James Dickey.* Twayne, 1983.

Campkin, Ben, and Rosie Cox, eds. *Dirt: New Geographies of Cleanliness and Contamination.* I. B. Tauris, 2007.

Carrie. Directed by Brian De Palma. United Artists, 1976.

Carson, Clayborne. *A Call to Conscience: The Landmark Speeches of Dr. Martin Luther King, Jr.* Grand Central, 2001.

Carter, Jimmy. *Public Papers of the Presidents of the United States.* U of California P, 1980.

Cash, Johnny. *Man in Black.* Columbia, 1971.

Catte, Elizabeth. *What You Are Getting Wrong about Appalachia.* Belt, 2018.

Cazenave, Noel A. *Killing African Americans: Police and Vigilante Violence as a Racial Control Mechanism.* Taylor and Francis, 2018.

Chang, David A. *The Color of the Land: Race, Nation, and the Politics of Landownership in Oklahoma, 1832–1929.* U of North Carolina P, 2010.

Charles, Dora, and Fran McCullough. *A Real Southern Cook In Her Savannah Kitchen.* Houghton Mifflin Harcourt, 2015.

Ching, Barbara. *Wrong's What I Do Best: Hard Country Music and Contemporary Culture.* Oxford UP, 2001.

Clover, Carol J. *Men, Women, and Chain Saws: Gender in the Modern Horror Film.* Princeton UP, 2015, 1992.

Code of Federal Regulations Containing a Codification of Documents of General Applicability and Future Effect as of December 31, 1948, with Ancillaries and Index. Division of the Federal Register, National Archives, 1996.

Cole, Stephanie, and Natalie J. Ring, eds. *The Folly of Jim Crow: Rethinking the Segregated South.* Texas A&M UP, 2012.

Cook, Eden. *Tobe Hooper's 'The Texas Chainsaw Massacre' as Social Commentary: The Breakdown of Classicism in Form and Content.* Verlag, 2016.

Cooley, Angela Jill. *To Live and Dine in Dixie: The Evolution of Urban Food Culture in the Jim Crow South.* U of Georgia P, 2015.

Cooper, Melissa L. *Making Gullah: A History of Sapelo Islanders, Race, and the American Imagination.* U of North Carolina P, 2017.

Corcoran, Michael. *All Over the Map: True Heroes of Texas Music.* U of North Texas P, 2005.

"Cracker Barrel Founder Dan Evins." *Cracker Barrel Old Country Store.* crackerbarrel.com/about/dan-evins.

Cramer, Katherine J. *The Politics of Resentment: Rural Consciousness in Wisconsin and the Rise of Scott Walker.* U of Chicago P, 2016.

Crank, James A. "Down N' Dirty." *south: an interdisciplinary journal* 48.2 (Spring 2016): 157–69.

———. "Remembering Patsy Yaeger: A Written Roundtable." *Mississippi Quarterly* 67.1 (Winter 2014): 4–30.

Creadick, Anna. "Banjo Boy: Masculinity, Disability, and Difference in *Deliverance.*" *Southern Cultures* 23.1 (Spring 2017): 63–78.

Cremins, Brian. "Bumbazine, Blackness, and the Myth of the Redemptive South in Walt Kelly's Pogo." In Whitted and Costello, eds., *Comics and the U.S. South.* 29–61.

Crocker, Brittany. "Cracker Barrel CEO Sandra Cochran Leads Charge for Chain's Racial, LGBTQ Inclusivity." *Knox News,* 21 June 2019. www.knoxnews.com/story/news/2019/06/21/grayston-fitts-controversy-highlights-cracker-barrel-advances-on-diversity-inclusivity/1498513001/.

———. "Tennessee Detective's Church Sermon Calls for Execution of LGBTQ People." *Knox News,* 12 June 2019. www.knoxnews.com/story/news/nation/2019/06/12/knox-county-detective-lgbtq-execution-grayson-fritts/1433604001/.

Cummins, Jeanine. *American Dirt.* Macmillan, 2020.

———. "Murder Isn't Black or White." *New York Times,* 31 December 2015. www.nytimes .com/2016/01/03/opinion/sunday/murder-isnt-black-or-white.html.

Curthoys, Ann. *Freedom Ride: A Freedom Rider Remembers.* Allen and Unwin, 2002.

Cusic, Don. *The Cowboy in Country Music: An Historical Survey with Artist Profiles.* Mc-Farland, 2011.

———. *Discovering Country Music.* Praeger, 2008.

Daft, Richard K. *New Era of Management.* Thompson/South-Western, 2008.

Dawson, Ashley. *Extreme Cities: The Peril and Promise of Urban Life in the Age of Climate Change.* Verso, 2017.

Davison, Peter. "The Burden of James Dickey." *Atlantic Monthly* 282.2 (August 1998): 106–8.

Dawidoff, Nicholas. *In the Country of Country: A Journey to the Roots of American Music.* Knopf Doubleday, 1997.

DC Fandom. "Parliament of Trees." dc.fandom.com/wiki/Parliament_of_Trees.

Deen, Paula, and Sherry Suib Cohen. *It Ain't All About the Cookin'.* Simon & Schuster, 2006.

Dees, Diane E. "Cracker Barrel Sued for Discrimination—Again." *Mother Jones,* 13 February 2006. www.motherjones.com/politics/2006/02/cracker-barrel-sued-discrimination-again/.

Deliverance. Directed by John Boorman, Warner Brothers, 1972.

Desty, Robert, and U.S. *Supreme Court. The Supreme Court Reporter, vol. 26.* West Publishing Co., 1906.

Di Placido, Dani. "HBO's 'Watchmen' Has Never Felt More Timely." *Forbes,* 12 June 2020. www.forbes.com/sites/danidiplacido/2020/06/12/hbos-watchmen-has-never-felt-more-timely/#4fbeea9702fd.

Dickey, Christopher. *Summer of Deliverance: A Memoir of Father and Son.* Simon and Schuster, 1998.

Dickey, James. *Deliverance.* Houghton Mifflin, 1970.

———. *Night Hurdling: Poems, Essays, Conversations, Commencements, and Afterwords.* Bruccoli–Clark Layman, 1983.

———. "Notes on the Decline of Outrage." In *Babel to Byzantium: Poets & Poetry.* Farrar Straus & Giroux, 1981. 257–75.

———. *Self-Interviews.* Louisiana State UP, 1984.

———, and John Boorman. *Deliverance Screenplay.* Warner Brothers, 1971.

Dixler, Hillary. "How Gullah Cuisine Has Transformed Charleston Dining." *Eater,* 22 March 2016. www.eater.com/2016/3/22/11264104/gullah-food-charleston.

Doggett, Peter. *Are You Ready for the Country.* Penguin, 2001.

Doughtie, Edward. "Art and Nature in 'Deliverance.'" *Southwest Review* 64.2 (Spring 1979): 167–80.

Douglas, Mary. *Purity and Danger: An Analysis of Concepts of Pollution and Taboo.* Praeger, 1966, 1969.

Doyle, Michael William. *Imagine Nation: The American Counterculture of the 1960's and 70's,* ed. Peter Braunstein. Routledge, 2001.

Duck, Leigh Anne. *The Nation's Region: Southern Modernism, Segregation, and U.S. Nationalism.* U of Georgia P, 2006.

Dudenhoeffer, Larrie. "Monster Mishmash: Iconicity and Intertextuality in Tobe Hooper's *The Texas Chain Saw Massacre.*" *Journal of the Fantastic Arts* 19.1 (2008): 51–69.

Dunaway, Finis. *Seeing Green: The Use and Abuse of American Environmental Images.* U of Chicago P, 2015.

Dyer, C. E. "Surprising 'Difference' Predicts Which Candidate Will Win in Each State." *Federalist Papers,* 12 April 2017. thefederalistpapers.org/us/surprising-difference-predicts-which-candidate-will-win-in-each-state.

Edge, John T. *The Potlikker Papers: A Food History of the Modern South.* Penguin, 2017.

Edwards, Leigh H. "'Backwoods Barbie': Dolly Parton's Gender Performance." In Diane Pecknold and Kristine M. McCusker, eds., *Country Boys and Redneck Women: New Essays in Gender and Country Music.* UP of Mississippi, 2016. 189–210.

———. *Dolly Parton, Gender, and Country Music.* Indiana UP, 2018.

Egerton, John T. *Southern Food: At Home, on the Road, in History.* U of North Carolina P, 1987.

Eggers, Save. *Zeitoun.* Knopf, 2010.

Eggertsson, Gunnar Theodor, and Charles Forceville. "Multimodal Expressions of the Human Victim Is Animal Metaphor in Horror Films." In Charles J. Forceville and Eduardo Urios-Aparisi, eds., Applications of Cognitive Linguistics: Multimodal Metaphor. Mouton de Gruyter, 2009. 429–50.

Ellsworth, Scott. *Death in a Promised Land: The Tulsa Race Riot of 1921.* Louisiana State UP, 1992.

Eng, Steve. *A Satisfied Mind: The Country Music Life of Porter Wagoner.* Rutledge, 1992.

Entzminger, Betina. *Contemporary Reconfigurations of American Literary Classics: The Origin and Evolution of American Stories.* Taylor and Francis, 2013.

Epstein, Reid J. "Liberals Eat Here. Conservatives Eat There." *Wall Street Journal,* 2 May 2014. blogs.wsj.com/washwire/2014/05/02/liberals-eat-here-conservatives-eat-there/.

Eskridge, Sara K. *Rube Tube: CBS and Rural Comedy in the Sixties.* U of Missouri P, 2018.

Evans, Ivan Thomas. *Cultures of Violence: Lynching and Racial Killing in South Africa and the American South.* Manchester UP, 2009.

The Evil Dead. Directed by Sam Raimi. New Line, 1981.

Eyster, Warren. "Two Regional Novels." *Sewanee Review* 79.3 (Summer 1971): 469–74.

Fardon, Richard. "Citations out of Place." *Anthropology Today* 29.1 (February 2013): 25–27.

Farmer, Angela. "The Worst Fate: Male Rape as Masculinity Epideixis in James Dickey's Deliverance and the American Prison Narrative." *Atenea* 28.1 (2008): 103–15.

Faulkner, William. *Absalom, Absalom!* Vintage, 1990, 1936.

Flippen, J. Brooks. *Nixon and the Environment.* U of New Mexico P, 2000.

Forman, Murray. *One Night on TV Is Worth Weeks at the Paramount: Popular Music on Early Television.* Duke UP, 2012.

Foster, Gwendolyn Audrey. *Hoarders, Doomsday Preppers, and the Culture of Apocalypse.* Palgrave, 2014.

Foucault, Michel. *The History of Sexuality, vol. 1: An Introduction.* Trans. Robert Hurley. Vintage, 1990, 1976.

Fox, Pamela, and Barbara Ching. *Old Roots, New Routes: The Cultural Politics of Alt.country Music.* U of Michigan P, 2008.

Freeland, Cynthia. *The Naked and the Undead: Evil and the Appeal of Horror.* Taylor and Francis, 2018.

Freeman, Jon. "Hank Williams Jr. and Charlie Daniels: Inside Their Defiant Politics." *Rolling Stone,* 23 June 2017. www.rollingstone.com/music/music-country/hank-williams-jr-and-charlie-daniels-inside-their-defiant-politics-198585/.

Frum, David. *Trumpocracy: The Corruption of the American Republic.* HarperCollins, 2018.

Gabler, Neal. *Walt Disney: The Triumph of the American Imagination.* Vintage, 2006.

Gaddie, Ronald Keith, and James L. Regens. *Regulating Wetlands Protection: Environmental Federalism and the States.* State U of New York P, 1999.

Gardner, Royal C. *Lawyers, Swamps, and Money: U.S. Wetland Law, Policy, and Politics.* Island P, 2011.

Garner, Dwight. "'Deliverance': A Dark Heart Still Beating." *New York Times,* August 25, 2010, C1.

Gest, Justin. *The New Minority: White Working Class Politics in an Age of Immigration and Inequality.* Oxford UP, 2106.

Goad, Jim. *The Redneck Manifesto: How Hillbillies, Hicks, and White Trash Became America's Scapegoats.* Simon and Schuster, 1997.

Goldstein, Richard. "My Country Music Problem—and Yours." *Mademoiselle* 77.2 (June 1973): 114.

Gollmar, Robert H. *Edward Gein: America's Most Bizarre Murderer.* Hallberg, 1981.

Goodie Mob. "Dirty South," LaFace, 1995.

Goodson, Steve, and David Anderson, eds. *The Hank Williams Reader.* Oxford UP, 2014.

Graham, Allison. *Framing the South: Hollywood, Television, and Race during the Civil Rights Struggle.* Johns Hopkins UP, 2001.

———. "The South in Popular Culture." In Richard Gray and Owen Robinson, eds., *A Companion to the Literature and Culture of the American South.* Wiley, 2004. 335–52.

Gray, Richard. *Southern Aberrations: Writers of the American South and the Problems of Regionalism.* Louisiana State UP, 2000.

Green, Douglas B. *Singing in the Saddle: The History of the Singing Cowboy.* Vanderbilt UP, 2005.

Greene, Doyle. *Rock, Counterculture and the Avant-Garde, 1966–1970: How the Beatles, Frank Zappa and the Velvet Underground Defined an Era.* McFarland, 2016.

Greever, Carl J., Rachel Ward, and Christian L. Williams. "The Growing Problem of Diabetes in Appalachia." In Wendy Welch, ed., *Public Health in Appalachia: Essays from the Clinic and the Field. McFarland,* 2014.

Griffith, Jean. *Earth Day: America at the Environmental Crossroads.* Page, 2019.

Grofman, Bernard. *Legacies of the 1964 Civil Rights Act.* U of Virginia P, 2000.

Grunwald, Michael. *The Swamp: The Everglades, Florida, and the Politics of Paradise.* Simon & Schuster, 2007.

Gunn, Giles. "American Literature and the Imagination of Otherness." *Journal of Religious Ethics* 3.2 (Fall 1975): 193–215.

Guralnick, Peter. *Last Train to Memphis: The Rise of Elvis Presley.* Little, 2002.

Gurba, Myriam. "Pendeja, You Ain't Steinbeck: My Bronca with Fake-Ass Social Justice Literature." *Tropics of Meta,* 12 December 2019. tropicsofmeta.com/2019/12/12/pendeja-you-aint-steinbeck-my-bronca-with-fake-ass-social-justice-literature/.

Haggard, Merle. "Okie from Muskogee." Composed by Roy Edward Burris and Merle Haggard. Capitol Records, 1969.

Hale, Grace Elizabeth. *Making Whiteness: The Culture of Segregation in the South, 1890–1940.* Knopf Doubleday, 2010.

Hansen, Gunnar. *Chain Saw Confessional: How We Made the World's Most Notorious Horror Movie.* Chronicle, 2013.

Haraway, Donna. "Anthropocene, Capitalocene, Plantationocene, Chthulucene: Making Kin." *Environmental Humanities* 6.1 (2015): 159–65.

Harkin, Michael Eugene, and David Rich Lewis, eds. *Native Americans and the Environment: Perspectives on the Ecological Indian.* U of Nebraska P, 2007.

Harkins, Anthony. *Hillbilly: A Cultural History of an American Icon.* Oxford UP, 2005.

Harrington, Stephanie. "Who's Got the Last 'Hee Haw' Now?" *New York Times,* 4 January 1970, 97.

Hart, Henry. *James Dickey: The World as a Lie.* Picador, 2000.

Harvey, Daina Cheyenne. "Disasters as Hyper-Marginalization: Social Abandonment in the Lower Ninth Ward of New Orleans." In Carol Camp Yeakey, Anjanette Wells, and Vetta L. Sanders Thompson, eds., *Urban Ills: Twenty-first-Century Complexities of Urban Living in Global Contexts,* vol. 2. Lexington, 2013.

Havighurst, Craig. *Air Castle of the South: WSM and the Making of Music City.* U of Illinois P, 2007.

Hemphill, Paul. *The Nashville Sound: Bright Lights and Country Music.* U of Georgia P, 2015.

Herring, Scott. "'Hixploitation' Cinema, Regional Drive-ins, and the Cultural Emergence of a Queer New Right." GLQ 20.1–2: 95–113.

Hey, Donald L., and Nancy S. Philippi. *A Case for Wetland Restoration.* Wiley, 1999.

Hilburn, Robert. *Johnny Cash: The Life.* Little, 2013.

Hill, Jeremy. *Country Comes to Town: The Music Industry and the Transformation of Nashville.* U of Massachusetts P, 2016.

Hill, Shelley. "Cracker Barrel Faces Discrimination Lawsuit." *The Oklahoman,* 7 October 1999. oklahoman.com/article/2670219/cracker-barrel-faces-discrimination-lawsuit.

Hiraldo, Carlos. *Segregated Miscegenation: On the Treatment of Racial Hybridity in the US and Latin American Literary Traditions.* Routledge, 2003.

Hirsch, James S. *Riot and Remembrance: The Tulsa Race War and Its Legacy.* Houghton Mifflin, 2002.

Hobson, Fred. *Tell About the South: The Southern Rage to Explain.* Louisiana State UP, 1983.

Hochschild, Arlie Russell. *Strangers in Their Own Land: Anger and Mourning on the American Right.* New P, 2016.

hooks, bell. "No Love in the Wild." *NewBlackMan (in Exile): The Digital Home for Mark Anthony Neal,* 5 September 2012. www.newblackmaninexile.net/2012/09/bell-hooks-no-love-in-wild.html.

Hooper, Tobe, and Kim Henkel. *The Texas Chain Saw Massacre Revised Final Draft.* www.simplyscripts.com/scripts/texas_chainsaw.html.

Hopkins, Kate. *Sweet Tooth: The Bittersweet History of Candy.* St Martin's, 2012.

Horowitz, Gad. *Repression—Basic and Surplus Repression in Psychoanalytic Theory: Freud, Reich, and Marcuse.* U of Toronto P, 1977.

Hossfeld, Leslie, E. Brooke Kelly, and Julia Waity. *Food and Poverty: Food Insecurity and Food Sovereignty Among America's Poor.* Vanderbilt UP, 2018.

Howard, John. *Men Like That: A Southern Queer History.* U of Chicago P, 1999.

Hoyle, Brian. *The Cinema of John Boorman.* Scarecrow, 2012.

Huggins, Thomas, Sean Anderson, John Lambrinos, and Katie Brasted. "The English Turn Forests: Their Composition and Significance in Post-Katrina New Orleans." In Powelson, ed., *Hurricane Katrina and the Lessons of Disaster Relief.* 82–94.

Hughes, Charles L. *Country Soul: Making Music and Making Race in the American South.* U of North Carolina P, 2015.

Huie, William Bradford. "The Shocking Story of an Approved Killing in Mississippi." *Look,* 24 January 1956, 46–50.

Humphries, Reynold. *The American Horror Film: An Introduction.* Edinburgh UP, 2002.

Hurricane Katrina: Assessing the Present Environmental Status. Serial no. 109–77, 29 September 2005, 109–1. U.S. Congress, House Committee on Energy and Commerce, 2006.

Hutchings, Peter. *The Horror Film.* Taylor and Francis 2014, 2004.

Ignatieff, Michael. *American Exceptionalism and Human Rights.* Princeton UP, 2005.

Isenberg, Nancy. *White Trash: The 400-Year Untold History of Class in America.* Viking, 2016.

Jacobs, Will, and Gerard Jones, eds. *The Comic Book Heroes from the Silver Age to the Present.* Crown, 1985.

Jakle, John A., and Keith A. Sculle. *Fast Food: Roadside Restaurants in the Automobile Age.* Johns Hopkins UP, 2002, 1999.

Jameson, Fredric. "The Great American Hunter, or, Ideological Content in the Novel." *College English* 34.2 (November 1972): 180–97.

Jennings, Waylon. "Are You Sure Hank Done It This Way?" RCA Victor, 1975.

———. *Ladies Love Outlaws.* RCA, 1972.

———. "Luckenbach Texas," Bobby Emmons and Chips Moman, composers. RCA, 1977.

———, and Lenny Kaye. *Waylon: An Autobiography.* Grand Central, 1996.

Jensen, Joli. *The Nashville Sound: Authenticity, Commercialization, and Country Music.* Vanderbilt UP, 1998.

Jones, Anne Goodwyn, and Susan V. Donaldson, eds. *Haunted Bodies: Gender and Southern Texts.* U of Virginia P, 1997.

Jorgensen, Sven Erik. *Ecosystem Ecology.* Elsevier Science, 2009.

Kaufman, Michael, and Michael Kimmel. *The Guy's Guide to Feminism.* Basic, 2011.

Kemmerer, Lisa. "Multiculturalism, Indian Philosophy, and Conflicts Over Cuisine." In Luis Cordeiro-Rodrigues and Marko Simendic, eds., *Philosophies of Multiculturalism: Beyond Liberalism.* Routledge, 2016.

Keesy, Douglas. "James Dickey and the Macho Persona." In Kirschten, ed., *Critical Essays on James Dickey, 201–17.*

Kimmel, Michael S., and Michael Kaufman. "Weekend Warriors: The New Men's Movement." In Brod and Kaufman, eds., *Theorizing Masculinities,* 259–89.

King, Lovalerie. *Race, Theft, and Ethics: Property Matters in African American Literature.* Louisiana State UP, 2007.

Kirschten, Robert, ed. *Critical Essays on James Dickey.* U of Michigan P, 1994.

Kizer, Carolyn, and James Boatwright, eds. *James Dickey: the Expansive Imagination: A Collection of Critical Essays.* U of Michigan P, 1973.

Kosser, Michael. *How Nashville Became Music City, U.S.A.: 50 Years of Music Row.* Hal Leonard, 2006.

Kozlov, Mikhail, Elena Zvereva, and Vitali Zverev. *Impacts of Point Polluters on Terrestrial Biota: Comparative Analysis of 18 Contaminated Areas.* Springer, 2009.

Krech, Shepard. *The Ecological Indian: Myth and History.* Norton, 1999.

Kreyling, Michael. *Inventing Southern Literature.* UP of Mississippi, 1998.

Kristeva, Julia. *Powers of Horror: An Essay on Abjection.* Trans. Leon S. Roudiez. Columbia UP, 1982.

Krugler, David F. *1919, The Year of Racial Violence: How African Americans Fought Back.* Cambridge UP, 2014.

Kulka, Tomas. *Kitsch and Art.* Pennsylvania State UP, 2002, 1996.

La Chapelle, Peter. *Proud to Be an Okie: Cultural Politics, Country Music, and Migration to Southern California.* U of California P, 2007.

Laird, Tracey E. W. *Austin City Limits: A History.* Oxford UP, 2014.

———"Country Music and Television." In Travis D Stimeling, ed., *The Oxford Handbook of Country Music.* Oxford UP, 2017. 249–62.

Landry, Mark. *Bloodthirsty: One Nation Under Water.* Titan, 2016.

Lavelle, Kristen M. *Whitewashing the South: White Memories of Segregation and Civil Rights.* Rowman and Littlefield, 2014.

Lee, Christina. "Cool Breeze: A 'Dirty South' Champion." *RedBull Music Academy,* 26 March 2019. daily.redbullmusicacademy.com/2019/03/cool-breeze-dungeon-family-feature.

Lehman, Peter. *Masculinity: Bodies, Movies, Culture.* Taylor and Francis, 2001.

Lemire, Elise. *"Miscegenation": Making Race in America.* U of Pennsylvania P, 2002.

Levenstein, Harvey. *Paradox of Plenty: A Social History of Eating in Modern America.* U of California P, 2003, 1993.

Lewis, David Rich. "American Indian Environmental Relations." In Douglas Cazaux Sackman, ed., *A Companion to American Environmental History.* Wiley, 2010. 191–213.

Lidz, Franz. "How Benh Zeitlin Made *Beasts of the Southern Wild.*" *Smithsonian Magazine,* December 2012. www.smithsonianmag.com/arts-culture/how-benh-zeitlin-made-beasts-of-the-southern-wild-135132724/.

Lim, Clarissa-Jan. "There's A Lot Of Controversy." *Buzzfeed,* 22 January 2020. www.buzzfeednews.com/article/clarissajanlim/american-dirt-jeanine-cummins-controversy-explained.

Lincoln, Sarah L. "Dirty Ecology: African Women and the Ethics of Cultivation." In Moradewun Adejunmobi and Carli Coetzee, eds., *Routledge Handbook of African Literature.* Taylor and Francis, 2019.

Lindelof, Damon, creator. *Watchmen.* White Rabbit, Paramount Television, DC Entertainment, and Warner Bros. Television, 2019.

Lithwick, Dahlia. "The Creator of HBO's *Watchmen.*" *Slate,* 19 June 2019. slate.com/news-and-politics/2020/06/watchmen-trump-tulsa-masks-damon-lindelof-interview.html.

Lloyd, Christopher. *Corporeal Legacies in the US South: Memory and Embodiment in Contemporary Culture.* Springer International, 2018.

Long, Christian B. *The Imaginary Geography of Hollywood Cinema 1960–2000.* Intellect, 2017.

MacKenzie, Mairi. *Dream Suits: The Wonderful World of Nudie Cohn.* Antiques Collectors Club, 2011.

Malone, Bill C. *Don't Get Above Your Raisin': Country Music and the Southern Working Class.* U of Illinois P, 2002.

Manring, M. M. *Slave in a Box: The Strange Career of Aunt Jemima.* U of Virginia P, 1998.

Martinez-Alier, Juan. *The Environmentalism of the Poor: A Study of Ecological Conflicts and Valuation.* Edward Elgar, 2002.

———. and Tracey W. Laird. *Country Music, U.S.A.* U of Texas P, 1987.

Mason, Carol. *Reading Appalachia from Left to Right: Conservatives and the 1974 Kanawha County Textbook Controversy.* Cornell UP, 2009.

Max. "OutKast Winning Best New Rap Group at the Source Awards 1995." YouTube, 12 October 2014. www.youtube.com/watch?v=vwLG7aSYM3w.

Maxwell, Angie. "The South Beheld: The Influence of James Agee on James Dickey." *Southern Quarterly* 42.2 (Winter 2004)): 135–51.

McCandless, Peter. *Slavery, Disease, and Suffering in the Southern Lowcountry.* Cambridge UP, 2011.

McGehee, Larry T. "Vacant Kitchens for Sale." In John Egerton, ed., *The Best of Southern Food Writing.* Southern Foodways Alliance, 2002.

McGurty, Eileen Maura. *Transforming Environmentalism: Warren County, PCBs, and the Origins of Environmental Justice.* Rutgers UP, 2009.

McMillen, Neil R. *Remaking Dixie: The Impact of World War II on the American South.* UP of Mississippi, 1997.

McNeill, J. R. *Mosquito Empires: Ecology and War in the Greater Caribbean, 1620–1914.* Cambridge UP, 2010.

Melendez, Pilar. "Brunswick DA's Office Blocked Arrests." *Daily Beast,* 8 May 2020. www.thedailybeast.com/glynn-county-commissioners-say-brunswick-da-blocked-arrests-in-ahmaud-arbery-shooting.

Mencken, H. L. *Mencken Chrestomathy.* Knopf, 1949, 2012.

Mercer, Andrew, Claudia Deane, and Kyley McGeeney. "Why 2016 Election Polls Missed Their Mark." *Pew Research,* 9 November 2016. www.pewresearch.org/fact-tank/2016/11/09/why-2016-election-polls-missed-their-mark/.

Merritt, Naomi. "Cannibalistic Capitalism and Other American Delicacies: A Bataillean Taste of The Texas Chain Saw Massacre." *Film-Philosophy* 14.1: 202–31.

Metress, Christopher. "Sing Me a Song about Ramblin' Man: Visions and Revisions of Hank Williams in Country Music." In Cecelia Tichi, ed., *Reading Country Music: Steel Guitars, Opry Stars, and Honky-tonk Bars* Duke UP, 1998. 4–21.

Mickler, Ernest Matthew. *White Trash Cooking.* Ten Speed, 1986.

———. *White Trash Cooking II: Recipes for Gatherin's.* Ten Speed, 1996.

Mickler, Trisha. *More White Trash Cooking.* Ten Speed, 1998.

Miller, Adrian. *Soul Food: The Surprising Story of an American Cuisine, One Plate at a Time.* U of North Carolina P, 2013.

Miller, David. *Dark Eden: The Swamp in Nineteenth-Century American Culture.* Cambridge UP, 1989.

Miller, Edward H. Nut Country: Right-Wing Dallas and the Birth of the Southern Strategy. U of Chicago P, 2015.

Mitchell, Margaret. *Gone with the Wind.* Simon and Schuster, 1996, 1936.

Mitchell, Morris. *The Persistence of Sentiment: Display and Feeling in Popular Music of the 1970s.* U of California P, 2013.

Monk, Donald. "Colour Symbolism in James Dickey's *Deliverance.*" *Journal of American Studies* 11.2 (August 1977): 261–79.

Moore, Alan, Dave Gibbons, John Higgins. *Watchmen.* Titan, 1986, 2008.

———, Stephen Bissette, and John Totleben. *Saga of the Swamp Thing: Book One.* Vertigo, 2012.

Morris, Kendra Bailey. *White Trash Gatherings: From-Scratch Cooking for Down-Home Entertaining.* Ten Speed, 2006.

Murphy, Benjamin J. "Exceptional Infidelity: James Dickey's *Deliverance,* Film Adaptation, and the Postsouthern." *Mississippi Quarterly* 69.2 (Spring 2016): 205–25.

Murphy, Bernice M. *The Rural Gothic in American Popular Culture: Backwoods Horror and Terror in the Wilderness.* Palgrave, 2013.

Narine, Anil. "Global Trauma at Home: Technology, Modernity, Deliverance." *British Association for American Studies* 42.3 (December 2008): 449–70.

National Black Environmental Justice Network. "The National Black Environmental Justice Network's Health and Racial Justice Statement." nbejn.com/nbejn-health-statement.

Nel, Philip. *Was the Cat in the Hat Black? The Hidden Racism of Children's Literature, and the Need for Diverse Books.* Oxford UP, 2017.

Nelson, Willie. "Good Hearted Woman," RCA, 1972.

Nesper, Larry, and James H. Schlender, "The Politics of Cultural Revitalization and Intertribal Management: The Great Lakes Indian Fish and Wildlife Commission and the States of Wisconsin, Michigan, and Minnesota." In Harkin and Lewis, eds., *Native Americans and the Environment.* 277–303.

Neufeld, Josh. *A.D.: New Orleans After the Deluge.* Pantheon, 2009.

Newton, Michael. *White Robes and Burning Crosses: A History of the Ku Klux Klan from 1866.* McFarland, 2014.

"The 1995 Source Awards." *The Source.* United Paramount Network, 3 August 1995.

"Nixon Plays Piano on Wife's Birthday at Grand Ole Opry." *New York Times,* 17 March 1974, 1.

Nixon, Richard M. *Public Papers of the Presidents of the United States: Richard M. Nixon, 1971.* Best Books On, 1972.

Nudie, Jamie Lee, and Mary Lynn Cabrall. *Nudie: The Rodeo Tailor.* Gibbs Smith, 2004.

Oermann, Robert K. "Country on TV." *Billboard* 93.41 (17 October 1981).

Ortiz, Paul. *Emancipation Betrayed: The Hidden History of Black Organizing and White Violence in Florida from Reconstruction to the Bloody Election of 1920.* U of California P, 2005.

Otten, Terry. *After Innocence: Visions of the Fall in Modern Literature.* U of Pittsburgh P, 1982.

OutKast. "Southernplayalisticadillacmuzik." Organized Noize, 1994.

———. "Welcome to Atlanta." LaFace, 1994.

"Outlaw Country (Sirius XM)." *Sirius XM Wiki.* siriusxm.fandom.com/wiki/Outlaw_Country_(Sirius_XM).

Palast, Greg. *"Katrina Took Rap for New Orleans: The Real Culprit – Big Oil."* 12 July 2019. gregpalast.com/how-mother-nature-took-the-rap-for-destroying-new-orleans/.

Pascoe, Peggy. *What Comes Naturally: Miscegenation Law and the Making of Race in America.* Oxford UP, 2009.

Patrick, Richard. "Heroic Deliverance." *novel: A Forum on Fiction* 4.2 (Winter 1971): 190–92.

Peacock, Morgan. "Review of *The Southern Foodways Alliance Community Cookbook.*" *Southern Cookbooks Blog,* 2 November 2016. southerncookbooks.wordpress. com/2016/11/02/the-southern-foodways-alliance-community-cookbook/.

Pecknold, Diane. *Hidden in the Mix: The African American Presence in Country Music.* Duke UP, 2013.

———. *The Selling Sound: The Rise of the Country Music Industry.* Duke UP, 2007.

Peppiatt, Frank, and John Aylesworth, creators. *Hee Haw.* Yongestreet Productions and Gaylord Entertainment, 1969–97.

Perone, James E. *Music of the Counterculture Era.* Greenwood, 2004.

Petersheim, Steven, and Madison P. Jones IV, eds. *Writing the Environment in Nineteenth-Century American Literature: The Ecological Awareness of Early Scribes of Nature.* Lexington, 2015.

Phillips, Patrick. *Blood at the Root: A Racial Cleansing in America.* Norton, 2016.

Pitkethly, Clare. "Straddling a Boundary: The Superhero and the Incorporation of Difference." In Robin S. Rosenberg and Peter Coogan, eds., *What Is a Superhero?* Oxford UP, 2013. 25–29.

Plimpton, George. *Writers at Work: The Paris Review Interviews.* U of Michigan P, 2008.

Pollitzer, William S. *The Gullah People and Their African Heritage.* U of Georgia P, 2009.

Portelli, Alessandro. "Appalachia as Science Fiction." *Appalachian Journal* 16.1 (Fall 1988): 32–43.

Powelson, Michael, ed. *Hurricane Katrina and the Lessons of Disaster Relief.* Cambridge Scholars, 2017.

Public Papers of the Presidents, Richard Nixon. Vol. 1–6, 1969–74. U.S. Government Printing Office, 1974.

Purnell, Brian, and Jeanne Theoharis, with Komozi Woodard. *The Strange Careers of the Jim Crow North: Segregation and Struggle outside of the South.* New York UP, 2019.

Quittner, Jeremy. "Cracker Barrel Buckles." *The Advocate,* 4 February 2003, 24–25.

"Quoted: Paula Deen's Cook on the Dinner Bell Incident." *Reliable Source.* www.washingtonpost.com/news/reliable-source/wp/2013/07/25/quoted-paula-deens-cook-on-the-dinner-bell-incident/.

Ratledge, Ingela. "Anthony Bourdain's Celebrity Chef Smackdown!" *TV Guide,* 18 August 2011. www.tvguide.com/news/anthony-bourdains-celebrity-1036482/.

Rehagen, Tony. "Derivation of Dirty South: What Is the Origin of the Term?" *Atlanta Magazine,* 1 November 2012. www.atlantamagazine.com/culture/dirty-south/.

"Remarks by the President on the Ten Year Anniversary of Hurricane Katrina August 27, 2015." *The White House, President Barack Obama,* obamawhitehouse.archives. gov/the-press-office/2015/08/28/remarks-president-ten-year-anniversary-hurricane-katrina.

Reynolds, Leeann G. *Maintaining Segregation: Children and Racial Instruction in the South, 1920–1955.* Louisiana State UP, 2017.

Risen, Clay. *The Bill of the Century: The Epic Battle for the Civil Rights Act.* Bloomsbury, 2014.

Ritter, Tex. *Thank You, Mr. President.* Country Music Association Hall of Fame, 1973.

Ritz, David, and Robert Guillaume. *Guillaume: A Life.* U of Missouri P, 2002.

Rivlin, Gary. *Katrina: After the Flood.* Simon & Schuster, 2016.

Robinson, Sally. *Marked Men: White Masculinity in Crisis.* Columbia UP, 2000.

Rogers, Jimmie N. *Country Music Message.* U of Arkansas P, 1983.

Rogers, Katie. "Trump Says Jobs Report Made It a 'Great Day' for George Floyd." *New York Times.* 5 June 2020. www.nytimes.com/2020/06/05/us/politics/trump-jobs-report-george-floyd.html.

Romano, Aja. "S-Town, the controversial hit podcast, is being sued for exploitation." *Vox,* 17 July 2018. www.vox.com/2018/7/17/17581928/s-town-podcast-lawsuit-john-b-mclemore.

Romine, Scott. "God and the Moon Pie: Consumption, Disenchantment, and the Reliably Lost Cause." In Bone et al., eds., *Creating and Consuming the American South.* 49–71.

———. *The Narrative Forms of Southern Community.* Louisiana State UP, 1999.

———. *The Real South: Southern Narrative in the Age of Cultural Reproduction.* Louisiana State UP, 2008.

———, and Jennifer Rae Greeson, eds. *Keywords for Southern Studies.* U of Georgia P, 2016.

Rosenbaum, Walter A. *Environmental Politics and Policy.* CQ, 2002.

Rothman, Michael. "Paula Deen and Lisa Jackson Reach Settlement." *ABC News,* 23 August 2013. abcnews.go.com/Entertainment/paula-deen-lisa-jackson-reach-settlement/story?id=20051341.

Rubin, Rachel Lee. *Merle Haggard's Okie from Muskogee.* Bloomsbury Academic, 2018.

Saikku, Mikko, Barbara L. Allen, Megan Kate Nelson, Craig E. Colten, and Donald E. Davis, eds. *Southern United States: An Environmental History.* ABC CLIO, 2006.

Salkin, Allen. *From Scratch: The Uncensored History of the Food Network.* Penguin, 2013.

Samuel, S. "Big Boi Reflects on OutKast's Early Struggles." *SOHH,* 8 June 2009. www.sohh.com/big-boi-reflects-on-outkasts-early-struggles-hate-was-just-motivation-for-us/.

Satterwhite, Emily. *Dear Appalachia: Readers, Identity, and Popular Fiction Since 1878.* U of Kentucky P, 2011.

Saunders, Patrick. "Catching up with Cheryl Summerville." *Georgia Voice,* 6 June 2014. thegavoice.com/news/georgia/catching-cheryl-summerville-fired-cracker-barrel-gay/.

Savitt, Todd L., and James Harvey Young. *Disease and Distinctiveness in the American South.* U of Tennessee P, 1991, 1988.

Schechter, Harold. *Deviant: The Shocking True Story of Ed Gein, the Original Psycho.* Simon and Schuster, 2010.

Schmidt, Christopher W. *The Sit-Ins: Protest and Legal Change in the Civil Rights Era.* U of Chicago P, 2018.

Schmidt, Peter. *Sitting in Darkness: New South Fiction, Education, and the Rise of Jim Crow Colonialism, 1865–1920.* UP of Mississippi, 2008.

Schroeder, Daniel. "S-Town Was Great—Until It Forced a Messy Queer Experience into a Tidy Straight Frame." *Slate, 11* April 2017, slate.com/human-interest/2017/04/s-town-podcasts-treatment-of-queer-experience-hobbled-by-straight-biases.html.

Sepinwall, Alan. "'Watchmen' Writer on Trump in Tulsa, Bad Cops, and America's White Supremacy Problem." *Rolling Stone,* 17 June 2020. www.rollingstone.com/tv/tv-features/watchmen-writer-interview-police-brutality-white-supremacy-1014494/.

Severson, Kim. "A Powerful, and Provocative, Voice for Southern Food." *New York Times,* 9 May 2017. www.nytimes.com/2017/05/09/dining/southern-food-john-t-edge-profile.html.

Shabecoff, Philip. *A Fierce Green Fire: The American Environmental Movement.* Island, 1993.

Sharpless, Rebecca. *Cooking in Other Women's Kitchens: Domestic Workers in the South,1865–1960.* U of North Carolina P, 2010.

Shugart, Helene A. *Heavy: The Obesity Crisis in Cultural Context.* Oxford UP, 2016.

Sloane, Eric. *The Cracker Barrel.* Dover, 1967.

Smith, Dina. "Cultural Studies' Misfit: White Trash Studies." *Mississippi Quarterly* 57.3 (Summer 2004): 369–88.

Smith, Joel. *The Parish: An Americorps Story.* Beating Winward, 2015.

Smith, Jon. *Finding Purple America: The South and the Future of American Cultural Studies.* U of Georgia P, 2013.

Smith-Llera, Danielle. *Lunch Counter Sit-Ins: How Photographs Helped Foster Peaceful Civil Rights Protests.* Capstone, 2018.

Smothers, Ronald. "Company Ousts Gay Workers, Then Reconsiders." *New York Times,* 28 February 1991. www.nytimes.com/1991/02/28/us/company-ousts-gay-workers-then-reconsiders.html.

Sollors, Werner. *Neither Black Nor White Yet Both: Thematic Explorations of Interracial Literature.* Harvard UP, 1997.

Spears, Ellen Griffith. *Rethinking the American Environmental Movement Post-1945.* Taylor and Francis, 2019.

Stallybrass, Peter, and Allon White. *The Politics and Poetics of Transgression.* Ithaca: Cornell UP, 1986.

Stallings, L. H. *A Dirty South Manifesto: Sexual Resistance and Imagination in the New South.* U of California P, 2019.

Stanfield, Peter. *Horse Opera: The Strange History of the 1930s Singing Cowboy.* U of Illinois P, 2002.

Steinbock-Pratt, Sarah. *Educating the Empire: American Teachers and Contested Coloni-zation in the Philippines.* Cambridge UP, 2019.

Stephenson, William. "Deliverance from What?" *Georgia Review* 28.1 (Spring 1974): 114–20.

———. *Outlaw: Waylon, Willie, Kris, and the Renegades of Nashville.* HarperCollins, 2014.

Stokes, Ashli Quesinberry. *Consuming Identity: The Role of Food in Redefining the South.* UP of Mississippi, 2016.

Stoll, Steven. *Ramp Hollow: The Ordeal of Appalachia.* Farrar, Straus, and Giroux, 2017.

Strasser, Susan. *Waste and Want: A Social History of Trash.* Holt, 1999.

Streissguth, Michael. *Eddy Arnold: Pioneer of the Nashville Sound.* UP of Mississippi, 2010, 1997.

Strick, Philip. "Deliverance." [Review.] *Monthly Film Bulletin* 41.4 (1972): 228–29.

Struggle Jennings. "Outlaw Shit." Massbaum, 2013.

"A Letter from Our CEO." *Stuckey's.* stuckeys.com/letter-from-our-ceo/history/.

Styron, William. *The Confessions of Nat Turner.* Open Road, 1967, 2010.

Sutter, Paul. "Introduction: No More the Backward Region: Southern Environmental History Comes of Age," In Sutter and Manganiello, eds., *Environmental History and the American South.* 1–25.

———, and Christopher J. Manganiello, eds. *Environmental History and the American South: A Reader.* U of Georgia P, 2009.

Szczesiul, Anthony. *The Southern Hospitality Myth: Ethics, Politics, Race, and American Memory.* U of Georgia P, 2017.

Taylor, Dorceta E. *Toxic Communities: Environmental Racism, Industrial Pollution, and Residential Mobility.* New York UP, 2014.

Taylor, Heather. "Did a Real Man Inspire the Cracker Barrel Logo?" *Popicon,* 12 November 2018. popicon.life/did-a-real-man-inspire-the-cracker-barrel-logo/.

The Texas Chain Saw Massacre. Directed by Tobe Hooper. Vortex, 1974.

Tippen, Carrie Helms. *Inventing Authenticity: How Cookbook Writers Redefine Southern Identity.* U of Arkansas P, 2018.

Torres, Sasha. *Black, White, and in Color: Television and Black Civil Rights.* Princeton UP, 2003.

Trainer, David. "Cracker Barrel—Another Quality Restaurant to Fill Your Post COVID Portfolio." *Forbes,* 20 May 2020. www.forbes.com/sites/greatspeculations/2020/05/20/cracker-barrelanother-quality-restaurant-to-fill-your-post-covid-portfolio/#20aaa13c2daf.

Trump, Donald. ". . . have been greeted with the most vicious dogs." Twitter, 30 May 2020. twitter.com/realdonaldtrump/status/1266711223657205763.

———. "These THUGS." Twitter, 28 May 2020. twitter.com/realdonaldtrump/status/1266231100780744704.

Tschachler, Heinz. "'Un principe d'insuffisance': Dickey's Dialogue with Bataille." *Mosaic: An Interdisciplinary Critical Journal* 20.3 (Summer 1987): 81–93.

Turner, James Morton. *The Promise of Wilderness: American Environmental Politics since 1964.* U of Washington P, 2012.

Tuttle, William M. *Race Riot: Chicago in the Red Summer of 1919.* U of Illinois P, 1970.

12 Southerners. *I'll Take My Stand: The South and the Agrarian Tradition.* Louisiana State UP, 1930, 2006.

Twitty, Michael. "About Afroculinaria." *Afroculinaria.* afroculinaria.com/about/.

———. *The Cooking Gene: A Journey Through African American Culinary History in the Old South.* HarperCollins, 2018.

———. "Dear Disgruntled White Plantation Visitors, Sit Down." *Afroculinaria,* 9 August 2019. afroculinaria.com/2019/08/09/dear-disgruntled-white-plantation-visitors-sit-down/.

———. "Dear Sean, We Need to Talk." *Afroculinaria,* 23 March 2016. afroculinaria .com/2016/03/23/dear-sean-we-need-to-talk/.

———. "An Open Letter to Paula Deen." *Afroculinaria,* 25 June 2013. afroculinaria .com/2013/06/25/an-open-letter-to-paula-deen/.

Tyson, Timothy B. *The Blood of Emmett Till.* Simon and Schuster, 2017.

Van Ness, Gordon. *The One Voice of James Dickey: His Letters and Life, 1942–1969.* U of Missouri P, 2003.

Vance, J. D. *Hillbilly Elegy: A Memoir of a Family and Culture in Crisis.* Harper, 2016.

Vickery, John B. *The Prose Elegy: An Exploration of Modern American and British Fiction.* Louisiana State UP, 2009.

Visser, Steve. and Marcus K Garner. "Red Dog Disbanded." *Atlanta Journal-Constitution,* 11 August 2012. www.ajc.com/news/local/red-dog-disbanded/YX52PfLGA4pDORgnbcgJCK/.

Wallach, Jennifer Jensen. *Getting What We Need Ourselves: How Food Has Shaped African American Life.* Rowan and Littlefield, 2019.

Wasserman, David. "To Beat Trump, Democrats May Need to Break Out of the 'Whole Foods' Bubble." *New York Times,* 27 February 2020. www.nytimes.com/interactive/2020/02/27/upshot/democrats-may-need-to-break-out-of-the-whole-foods-bubble.html.

Watson, Harry L., and Jocelyn R. Neal, eds. *Southern Cultures: The Special Issue on Food* 18.2 (Summer 2012).

Wein, Len. *Swamp Thing: The Bronze Age,* vol. 1. DC Comics, 2018.

Wein, Len, and Bernie Wrightson. *Roots of the Swamp Thing.* DC Comics, 2009.

Weiner, Marli F., and Mayzie Hough, eds. *Sex, Sickness, and Slavery: Illness in the Antebellum South.* U of Illinois P, 2012.

When the Levees Broke. Directed by Spike Lee. 40 Acres and a Mule, 2006.

"Where Did Cracker Barrel Get Its Name?" *Southern Living.* www.southernliving.com/culture/where-did-cracker-barrel-get-its-name.

White, Caroline E. *Stand Your Ground: A History of America's Love Affair with Lethal Self-Defense.* Beacon, 2017.

White, Deborah Gray, Mia Bay, and Waldo Martin, eds. *Freedom on My Mind: A History of African Americans, with Documents.* Bedford/St. Martin's, 2012.

Whiteley, Sheila, and Jedediah Sklower. *Countercultures and Popular Music.* Routledge, 2014.

Whitted, Qiana J. "Of Slaves and Other Swamp Things: Black Southern History as Comic Book Horror." In Whitted and Costello, eds. *Comics and the U.S. South.* 187–214.

———, and Brannon Costello, eds. *Comics and the U.S. South,* UP of Mississippi, 2012.

"Whole Foods vs. Cracker Barrel Culture Gap Over Time." @Redistrict. Twitter, 9 November 2016. twitter.com/redistrict/status/796425689360637952?lang=en.

Williams, Kidada E. *They Left Great Marks on Me: African American Testimonies of Racial Violence from Emancipation to World War I.* New York UP, 2012.

Williams, Tony. *Hearths of Darkness: The Family in the American Horror Film.* U of Mississippi P, 2014, 1996.

Williamson, Jerry Wayne. *Hillbillyland: What the Movies Did to the Mountains and What the Mountains Did to the Movies.* U of North Carolina P, 1995.

"Willie Nelson: The 'Fresh Air' Interviews." *National Public Radio,* 5 July 2019. www.npr.org/2019/07/05/738490091/willie-nelson-the-fresh-air-interviews.

Willman, Chris. *Rednecks & Bluenecks: The Politics of Country Music.* New P, 2005.

Wilson, Anthony. *Shadow and Shelter: The Swamp in Southern Culture.* U of Mississippi P, 2009.

Wilson, Eric. "The Ballad of Ed and Lewis: Conflictual Mimesis and the Revocation of the Social Contract in James Dickey's *Deliverance.*" *Law and Humanities* 10.1 (2016): 115–60.

Wolanksi, Eric, John W. Day, Michael Elliott, and Ramesh Ramachandran. *Coasts and Estuaries: The Future.* Elsevier, 2019.

Wolfe, Charles K. *A Good-Natured Riot: The Birth of the Grand Ole Opry.* Vanderbilt UP, 2015.

Wolkowitz, Carol. "Linguistic Leakiness or Really Dirty? Dirt in Social Theory." In Campkin and Cox, eds. *Dirt,* 15–24.

Wood, Amy Louise. *Lynching and Spectacle: Witnessing Racial Violence in America, 1890–1940.* U of North Carolina P, 2009.

Wood, Robin. *Hollywood from Vietnam to Reagan . . . and Beyond.* Columbia UP, 1986.

Wray, Matt. *Not Quite White: White Trash and the Boundaries of Whiteness.* Duke UP, 2006.

———, and Annale Newitz, eds. *White Trash: Race and Class in America.* Routledge, 1997.

Wright, Richard. *Twelve Million Black Voices A Folk History of the Negro in the United States.* Echo Point, 2019, 1948.

Yaniz, Robert. "Jordan Peele Once Admitted the 'Emotional Discovery' Behind 'Get Out.'" *Showbiz Cheat Sheet,* 27 June 2021. cheatsheet.com/entertainment/jordan-peele-emotional-discovery-get-out.html/.

Yaeger, Patricia. "Beasts of the Southern Wild and Dirty Ecology." *Southern Spaces: A Journal About Real and Imagined Spaces and Places of the US South and Their Global Connections,* 13 February 2013. southernspaces.org/2013/beasts-southern-wild-and-dirty-ecology/.

———. *Dirt and Desire: Reconstructing Southern Women's Writing, 1930–1990.* U of Chicago P, 2000.

Zeitlin, Benh, director. *Beasts of the Southern Wild.* Fox Searchlights, 2012.

———, and Lucy Alibar. *Beasts of the Southern Wild: Final Draft Script.* Internet Movie Script Database (IMSDb), www.imsdb.com/scripts/Beasts-of-the-Southern-Wild.html.

Zinoman, Jason. *Shock Value: How a Few Eccentric Outsiders Gave Us Nightmares, Conquered Hollywood, and Invented Modern Horror.* Penguin, 2011.

Zvereva, Mikhail, et al., eds. *Impacts of Point Polluters on Terrestrial Biota: Comparative Analysis of 18 Contaminated Areas.* Springer, 2009.

INDEX

Goodman, Andrew, 43–44
Graham, Allison, 119–20
Grand Ole Opry, The, 52, 55, 58, 60–61, 64, 208n22
Guillaume, Robert, 43
guilt, 32–36, 202n11
Gullah culture, 189, 228n2

Haggard, Merle, 54, 58–59, 207n5, 208n20
Hall, Ruby Nell Bridges, 45
Hammons, David, 68
Hansen, Gunnar, 116, 131–32
Haraway, Donna, 223n8
Harkins, Anthony, 47, 204n27, 206n33
Hart, Henry, 87
Harvey, Daina Cheyenne, 227n34
Hatcher, Richard, 158
"Heap, The" (Air Fighters Comics), 225n21
Heart of Darkness (Conrad), 211n2
Hee Haw (TV), 49–56, 59, 64
Henkel, Kim, 134
Herring, Scott, 148
Hey, Donald, 162
Heyer, Heather, 14
Hilburn, Robert, 209n26
hillbillies: in *Deliverance* vs. *Texas Chain Saw Massacre,* 132; in Depression era, 206n32; *Hee Haw* and, 53–54; hillbilly exceptionalism, 98–99, 126–27; inbreeding and incest tropes, 126–27, 218n9; stereotype of, 46–47, 205n31; as term, 204n27. See also *Deliverance; Texas Chain Saw Massacre*
"Hillbilly Central," 72, 209n28, 210n35
Hillbilly Elegy (Vance), 85, 110–14
hillbilly vigilantism. *See* vigilantism
hip-hop, dirty South, 75–80
hixploitation films, 148
Hobson, Fred, 32–33, 37
Hochschild, Arlie, 114
hooks, bell, 177
Hooper, Tobe, 131–32, 134, 140–41, 142. See also *Texas Chain Saw Massacre*
horror films: disavowed or repressed anxieties in, 147–48; hand rising from the depths trope, 117–19; hixploitation films, 148;

Peele's *Get Out,* 148–52; place, operation of, 220n20; possession films, 148–49, 222n32; South as site of America's nightmares, 119–20; Universal monster icons and, 221n25; urbanoia, rape-revenge, and slasher films, 133, 220n19. See also *Deliverance; Texas Chain Saw Massacre*
Howard, John, 11
Huhndorf, Shari M., 16
Huie, William Bradford, 40
humanities, importance of, 22
Hurricane Katrina, 172–76, 226n30–227n32, 227nn34–35
hybridity and hybridization: Boorman's *Deliverance* and, 142; racial anxieties and, 29, 31–32; trash and, 25
hygiene discourses, 30–31

immigrants, 38–39
inbreeding trope, 126–27, 218n9
intimacy: in Boorman's *Deliverance,* 101, 121, 124–26, 129–30; in Dickey's *Deliverance,* 101; in Hooper's *Texas Chainsaw Massacre,* 139–40, 144–46; Reed's *S-Town* and, 8–9
I Spit on Your Grave (Zarchi), 220n19
Ivins, Molly, 33

Jacobs, Will, 167
Jameson, Fredric, 96
Jennings, Shooter, 74–75
Jennings, Struggle, 82–83
Jennings, Waylon, 49, 61–70, *63, 72*–76, 80–84
Johnson, Dion, 194
Johnson, Lyndon B., 85, 205n31, 222n1
Jones, George, 54
Jones, Gerard, 167
Just Above My Head (Baldwin), 149, 221n31
justice: dirty ethics and, 184–85; environmental, 160, 226n27; Floyd, Arbery, and, 194; hillbilly, in Dickey's *Deliverance,* 102–8, 113–14; in Vance's *Hillbilly Elegy,* 113–14. *See also* vigilantism

Keep America Beautiful, 155–56, 167, 222n5, 223n7

Streissguth, Michael, 209n28

Styron, William, 212n9

Summer of Deliverance (C. Dickey), 87, 116, 212n7

Sutter, Paul, 157–58, 162

Suzack, Cheryl, 16

Swamplandia! (Russell), 185

Swamp Thing (DC Comics), 153, 164–72, 178, 180, 183, 184

swampy ecology: dirty ecology, 160, 167–69, 171, 178–79, 224n11; dirty ethics, 156, 169, 177, 180–85; environmental movement, 153–55, 161–62, 224n14, 226n24; environmental racism and, 160, 180–81; Hurricane Katrina and, 172–76, 226n30–227n32, 227nn34–35; Keep America Beautiful "Crying Indian" spot, 155–56, 167; Landry's *Bloodthirsty: One Nation Under Water,* 153, 179–84, *182;* the South and ecological history, 156–61; "swamp" as contested term, 224n12; swamplands, eradication, and wetlands protection, 161–64; *Swamp Thing* (DC Comics), 153, 164–72, 178, 180, 183, 184; vigilante justice and, 184–85; Zeitlin's *Beasts of the Southern Wild,* 153, 175–79, 183, 184

Tate, Allen, 5

Taylor, Breonna, 194

Taylor, Dorceta E., 160

"terrible" places, 133–35, 141, 147

Texas Chain Saw Massacre (Hooper): about, 119, 131–32, 217n3; Boorman's *Deliverance* compared to, 132–33, 136–48, 221n30; hitchhiker scene, 136–40, *137;* as hixploitation movie, 148; Leatherface and dinner scene, 141–47, *143, 147;* as road movie, 134; setting and "terrible place," 133–35, 141, 147; as slasher film, 133; terrible people in, 135–36; Universal monster icons and, 221n25; witnessing in, 121, 142, 145

"The Dirty South: Contemporary Art, Material Culture, and the Sonic Impulse" (Crystal Bridges Museum of American Art), 186

Thoreau, Henry David, 224n12

Till, Emmett, 40–42, 102, 142, *143,* 194

Tometi, Opal, 3

trash: luminous, 47–48, 68–69; Strasser on sorting and value of, 23–24; trash bins and cycles of valuation, 186–87

Treme (TV), 185

Trump, Donald, 12–14, 38–39, 110, 114, 200n12, 216n27, 217n29

Tubb, Ernest, 71

Turner, James Morton, 154

Twitty, Conway, 54

Twitty, Michael, 186, 187–92, 196–97, 228n1

uncleanness: civil rights movement and South as space of, 34; in Hooper's *Texas Chain Saw Massacre,* 140; racial anxieties and, 30–31; removal of dirt to unclean spaces, 24; Southern ecological history and, 156

undeadness, 119

"Unite the Right" rally (Charlottesville, 2017), 14

urbanoia, 133, 220n19

value: in guilt and shame, 32–33; hillbilly, in Dickey's *Deliverance,* 92–96, 99, 107, 109, 112–13; outlaw country and, 67–69; of swamps, 162; trash and, 23–25, 186–87

Vance, James David, 85, 110–15, 217n29

van Heerden, Ivor, 174

Van Zandt, Steven, 74

Vickery, John B., 216n25

vigilantism: Arbery and Floyd murders, 193; assassinations, 205n30; Chaney, Goodman, and Schwerner murders, 43–44; in Dickey's *Deliverance,* 99–108, 215n22; El Paso shooting (2019), 39; Freedom Riders, attacks on, 42–43; Landry's *Bloodthirsty* and, 184–85; Martin murder, 2–6, 12–13; outlaw country and, 83–84; policing and, 193, 195; poor, rural, white southerner image and hillbilly stereotype, 45–47; Till murder, 40–42. *See also* justice

Wade, Rico, 75, 78–79

Wagner, Isadora, 223n8

Wagoner, Porter, 55–57, 65, 70, 207n14, 209n26